Man, Education, and Manpower

Grant Venn

Published by
The American Association
of School Administrators
1201 Sixteenth Street, N.W.
Washington, D.C. 20036

20223

Contents

Grant Venn

Preface

Man, Education, and Manpower was written to delineate the role of education in the development of manpower needs in a highly technological society.

The lack of manpower policies at the federal, state, and local levels has resulted in a hodgepodge of programs which have been neither comprehensive in meeting occupational demands nor effective in developing human resources—the only source of manpower. At a time when education is the basic link between the individual and his effectiveness as a citizen and worker we have failed to define the responsibility of our educational institutions in manpower development. During the sixties, federal financial support tended to bypass the schools and postsecondary institutions, institutions best able to develop new skilled and technical manpower. The emphasis was primarily on remedial and corrective programs rather than on programs to prevent human failure and to develop human resources. The net effect has been to end the decade of the sixties with a pool of unskilled and disadvantaged people nearly the same size as when we started. At the same time the nation faces its greatest shortage of skilled and technical manpower. We must take action to stop the flow of youth and technologically displaced adults into the pool.

This book attempts to suggest specific action that should be taken to support education in this urgent task and to identify the various agencies which should be involved in a comprehensive manpower program.

The philosophy of *Man, Education, and Manpower* is developed from a few premises based on the experience of the sixties.

First, any program to educate or train people outside or apart from the mainstream where the majority are educated will be seen as second-class by those enrolled, by those who employ the trainees, and by those who must pay the bill, the taxpayers.

7

Second, an overemphasis on remediation and correction rather than on development programs will not solve the problems of unemployment or manpower shortages, and the immediate and long-range costs will be greater.

Third, emphasis on entry job skills and employment are not enough to help those most in need. Every person aspires to career development with a future that has vertical and horizontal occupational mobility.

Fourth, whenever the labor market becomes tight, those without education or potential for learning new skills are the first to be fired.

I gratefully acknowledge the assistance of all those who helped in this endeavor, especially my wife, Olga. Thanks are also due to the first school board member whom I knew, my mother, Mrs. Vera Venn, who taught me that schools should make everyone successful rather than be concerned with a select few.

Grant Venn

Grant Venn received his undergraduate education and Ed.D. degree from Washington State University, Pullman. During his lengthy educational career, he has served as superintendent of schools in Wood County, West Virginia; Corning, New York; and Othello, Washington and as the director of field training and acting chief of the Division of Selection, the Peace Corps. He is also a past president of Western State College, Gunnison, Colorado.

Mr. Venn holds membership in many professional organizations, including the American Personnel and Guidance Association, the American Association of School Administrators, the National Society for the Study of Education, and the National Education Association.

In addition to numerous articles, he has published two books—*The Bellevue Story* (1951) and *Man, Education, and Work* (1964).

Mr. Venn is currently associate commissioner for adult, vocational, and library programs, Office of Education, U.S. Department of Health, Education, and Welfare.

Foreword

The decade of the sixties witnessed an awakening of the conscience of America. Those who lacked education, those who were unemployed, those who were caught up in poverty, despair, and discrimination became the primary targets for social reform.

During this same decade economists began to recognize that one of the major inputs to the economic growth of the nation and to its social upgrading was education. The first major effort for federal support to education was launched but never sailed; the "war on poverty" was started but hardly became a skirmish; and research became the great hope of America. All of these efforts were well intentioned and strongly supported with verbal statements and numerous conferences and position papers. Too often, however, these attempts at improving the nation's programs for people ended by identifying the problem and commissioning more studies.

In this book Grant Venn has suggested specific ways that the nation's schools, which serve everyone, can change to concentrate on the prevention of human failure and the development of human resources. He points out that educated and skilled manpower is the key to future progress and well-being. Our schools must keep the American dream a goal for all and the key to the security and development of all of our people.

This book was written by Dr. Grant Venn in his private capacity. No official support or endorsement by the Office of Education or by the U.S. Department of Health, Education, and Welfare was sought, is intended, or should be inferred.

The American Association of School Administrators is indeed pleased to publish this important statement on the past, present, and future of American occupational education— *Man, Education, and Manpower.*

Forrest E. Conner, *Executive Secretary, AASA*

9

Introduction

Has Success Spoiled the Schools?

Education has been too successful in doing what society has expected it to do. Two centuries of success tend to keep pressure on the schools to do more and better what they are presently doing. When weaknesses appear, the response is to increase the resources, change the methodology, or increase the effort. The generally accepted belief is that more of the same will result in continued success.

Unfortunately, the concept of what education is or what the school should do is the same for the most successful citizens as well as for the least successful. For example,

Most people believe that schools that are the most selective have the highest quality.

They believe that the percentage of graduates going on to college is a mark of a school's quality.

Most people prefer that the school their child attends contain mainly students that are like their own child.

They believe it is better that their child attend school without having to earn while he learns.

They want the schools to prepare their children for subsequent schooling.

Most people believe that schools that teach occupational skills are of low quality.

The fact is that our schools today do most of the things that people want them to do and do them quite well.

But the questions that become more pertinent everyday are: What must the schools be doing for the one-third of today's youth who are handicapped in finding employment and who encounter serious problems in making the transition from school to work? And what is the school's role in preparing the needed manpower in a society that by 1975 will find only 5 percent of the work force engaged in unskilled work?

11

The job the schools must do in a new society must be different than it has been in the past. Technology has created a new relationship between man, his education, and his work—a relationship that places education squarely between man and his work.

A New Concept of Quality

Historically, the schools of this nation have had an unstated assignment—to pick out those who should not continue formal schooling. This was once necessary because the labor force in the past was made up mainly of unskilled workers. Muscle power had salability at one time, and someone had to decide who picked the cotton, who mined the coal, or who worked in the factories.

The grading system and the curriculum of the elementary and secondary schools did this remarkably well. Today, this same grading system provides the manpower for the welfare and poverty pool through dropouts, but today there are few jobs for these partly prepared people on their entry into society. Yet the "quality" of educational institutions is still established by the selective process through which the student body is determined. Can we afford to continue this process?

Can a measure of quality be established based on how well the school helps those in greatest need of education—based on the practice of inclusion rather than exclusion?

Can we develop a method of financing the schools in terms of educational and manpower opportunities rather than according to where the wealth is or who has it?

Can accreditation of educational institutions be based on how well the school succeeds in reaching its goals rather than how much it is like another school?

Can educational quality be defined in terms of how well individual differences are developed rather than how well each student becomes like all the others?

Can quality be defined in terms of a student's behavior and contributions after he leaves school, rather than what he does while in school?

Can quality be defined other than through level of education or course content?

12

Can quality be defined in terms of individual achievements rather than group statistics?

The long-held definition of quality has forced the schools to ignore the lower third of the students in the normal curve. If there is no major and immediate breakthrough on this score, the alternatives appear to be:

1. The establishment of a federally funded system of education and training devoted to remediation and correction.

2. Acceptance of the belief that one-third of our citizens will remain essentially outside our system of equal opportunity and upward mobility.

3. A program which has as its base the manpower needs of the economy as the concept for developing the individual.

No National Manpower Policy

It is time to bring order and planning to the confusing, irrational, and contradictory manpower development efforts in our nation. Economists generally define manpower policy as that policy concerned with the development and use of human labor as an economic resource and with the way the individual provides himself and his family with income. This traditional concept is hardly adequate for a technological age in which more and more labor is provided by machines and in which individual welfare cannot be described in terms of goods and material things.

The traditional manpower goals have been:

1. Employment for all in jobs which provide adequate income and fulfill society's needs for goods and services (job creation).

2. Education and training to develop each individual's productive potential (trained manpower).

3. Matching men and jobs with maximum efficiency (placement).

A true manpower policy, however, must take into account much more than present needs and predictable demand in the economy. The fact that it is technologically possible to produce all the *things* we need requires us to assess manpower policy in terms of how well it develops the human potential.

The nation has really never had to look at this problem

13

in the past. First, we acquired a large share of our highly skilled and technical manpower through immigration. Second, until recently, it has been assumed that a growing economy would provide jobs for all. Most manpower efforts have been aimed at this goal. Third, every national effort has been aimed at eliminating unemployment (focusing on a symptom rather than a cause). Fourth, it has been assumed that more education, regardless of the kind, was a long-range solution. And fifth, the efficient allocation of national resources has never been considered a fundamental component of manpower policy until the last few years. Public expenditures for other than professional manpower needs—i.e., law, medicine, engineering, teaching—has never been considered a prime factor.

The technological explosion has changed all this. We now have "good times" and unemployment; high unemployment rates among youth and the elderly; depressed areas; decaying cities; severe labor shortages in skilled and technical areas; and many other problems related to the lack of people qualified to meet the manpower needs of the economy.

We must have a comprehensive manpower policy which spells out the role of the schools and which speaks to the professional, technical, and skilled manpower needs of the nation. This manpower policy must address itself immediately to the needs of the disadvantaged, the unemployed, and the underemployed. Such a policy should also increase the responsibilities of state and local governments. And, most importantly, it should operate in a manner that acknowledges that every individual is important—that organizations and institutions exist to serve individuals.

A manpower policy is a means, not an end. The end must be a society which serves the individual who in turn, through his contribution, develops the total structure of society and enjoys the fulfillment that comes with the best use of his talents.

Trends in Manpower Programs

The 1960's have seen a burgeoning number of responses to the problems of manpower development. Most of these responses have been directed at the problems of the unemployed and the disadvantaged and have come through federal legislation. Surprisingly, these efforts have been less and less related to the role of education or the schools. While multiple approaches are needed, there can be no doubt that in an increasingly technological society, education and skill development are the keys to a long-range solution—both for the individual and the society.

Can the solution to a national manpower policy be found if the federal government continues to invest four dollars in remedial programs for each dollar it invests in preventive programs at the subprofessional level? Will the solution lie in programs which require more and more educational inputs but which are unconnected with the schools? Will the solution be found if the financing is arranged so that no state or local resources are involved? Will the solution be found by relieving the schools of any responsibility for the students' success as adults? Can a national manpower policy be developed that is concerned only with remedial and corrective approaches? Or must it concern itself equally with prevention of human failure and the development of human resources? Will a solution be found which measures its success against the sole criterion of finding a job for everyone?

Flow and Pool Problems

In a technological society, especially in today's labor market, unemployment is more often the result of a lack of education and skill than of a shortage of job opportunities. Helping adults become employable is an essential national objective and will continue to be so in the 1970's. However, it is wasteful, unwise, and destructive to spend vast sums on these victims of our lack of a manpower policy without considering even more closely the causes of unemployability.

Unemployability and manpower shortages are both pool problems and flow problems. A review of the past ten years indicates that in spite of all our efforts, the pool of unemployed and disadvantaged has remained about the same size. It is likely to continue to be the same size unless we check the flow. We will make no progress, regardless of manpower policy or programs, until we do this. A national manpower policy which does not consider this side of the problem cannot be more than a stopgap measure.

15

The Role of Education

We have learned in the last ten years that simply providing a man with job skills is not enough. We must accept the belief that it is a responsibility of education to help young people find a meaningful role in society in which they can make increasing contributions and accept increasing responsibilities. Highest priority must go to a serious examination of the present and future role and status of adolescents and young adults in our society.

There may have been a time when our public educational system could have been on the sidelines in the development of manpower for this nation. It cannot today. No educator can be unconcerned with the problem of manpower development if he expects his school to be relevant to the students who attend.

John W. Gardner has said it well:

> We cannot speak of our values apart from the down-to-earth programs that are necessary to put them into effect. For example: if we believe in individual dignity and responsibility, then we must do the necessary, sometimes expensive, often complicated things that will make it possible for each person to have a decent job if he wants one. We must provide the kind of education that will enable him to hold a job, the kinds of work training necessary to prepare him for specific lines of work. If he has reached adulthood without learning to read and write, we must offer him basic literacy education.[1]

This country faces a choice. If we want an educational system less and less relevant to more and more students and taxpayers, all we need do is relax; we are drifting that way. If we want an educational system designed to serve each individual and to develop his creative potential in a self-directing way, then we have work to do and attitudes to change.

Children of Change

Despite all the other national issues we face, I doubt there is any more common topic within the family than that of the

[1] Gardner, John W. "What Kind of Society Do We Want? *Readers Digest,* September 1969.

16

youth movement in America.[2] There is not a family untouched by it. One senses that the stronger the denial of its effect, the more likely it is this phenomenon has either hardened present positions or truly brought about new public stances to be defended.

The causes of the youth movement lie in the disparity between a technological society and a system of public institutions established in a preindustrial age, a gap that must be obvious to everyone. The successes of these institutions, up to now, have been so great that they have allowed youth full time to devote their energies to moral and ethical problems rather than to economic ones. But there are few absolutes in the fields of morals and ethics—either in the past or present.

What "bugs" youth most is that adults are unaware of the gap between what they say and what they do. Consequently, most of the overt activity of youth is concerned with the condition of others: blacks, agricultural workers, the poor, and the handicapped. The most important learning inputs for our youth are from things that go on outside the classroom.

Young people have become irritating and revolutionary in spite of all our efforts to appease, to give them more, and to teach them. "Curiously, many college administrations in America [or school boards and administrators] do not seem to perceive they are all in this together. Like buffaloes being shot they look on with interest when another of their number goes down, without seriously thinking that they may be next." [3]

But out of all this seems to emerge certain strong suggestions on how schools might change. Broadly speaking, they can be defined as:

1. Involvement and participation of youth at an earlier age.
2. Youth volunteer activities as a part of schooling.
3. Involvement of the school and its students in the major issues of our time.
4. Provision of ways for individual students to participate in real-life action, not always just in preparation for living.
5. Giving youth responsibility as well as freedom.

Later chapters will point up ways this can be done.

[2] For a meaningful collection of essays on the youth movement, see "Children of Change." *Kaiser Aluminum News,* Vol. 27, May 1969. Kaiser Center 866, Oakland, Calif.

[3] *Ibid.*

17

National Issues and American Education

Regardless of the specific role of education in manpower development, the manpower developed must be able to help solve the major issues our country faces. Even more importantly, education must be recognized as being relevant to these issues, not separated from them. If education is truly the link between the individual and his role in society, than educational institutions must concern themselves with these national issues directly or they will not be relevant in the eyes of most Americans.

The goals of American education, in terms of dollars, program priorities, and personnel, must be spelled out in such a way that the American public can understand how these goals speak directly to the major issues of today:

Discrimination or unequal opportunity. This exists in housing, education, employment, recreation, health, and social mobility. We also must deal with unequal concepts of individual worth and the failure of many schools to be concerned about this problem.

The generation gap or lack of youth involvement. This is evidenced by the youth movement, riots in schools and colleges, drug abuse, dropping out of society, defiance of social institutions (including the home, parents, schools, and the economic system), the inability of youth to become involved in contributory activities related to society's problems, the economic liability of youth, the adult failure to share responsibility with youth, archaic child labor laws, the lack of a structure or process which would allow youth to move from adolescence to adulthood, and a lack of school responsiveness prior to the inevitable confrontation.

Unemployment and underemployment. We have the highest youth unemployment of any nation, concentrated pockets of almost total unemployment, city and rural depressed areas, lack of vertical or horizontal job mobility for many persons, manpower shortages in skilled and technical areas, the rapid decline of unskilled work, and the lack of relevance of much education in terms of a work role.

Lack of quality and relevance in education. Nearly one million youths leave high school before graduating, and 60 percent of those who enter college fail to graduate. Many youths are unable to read, write, or compute. There is no system for transition from school to work for the 80 percent who do not graduate from college, lack of concern with career planning, isolation of school from other societal institutions, the growing assumption of responsibility by the federal government for those who fail in school, new federally supported educational programs (i.e., Neighborhood Youth Corps, Manpower Development and Training, and others) which emphasize the failure of the schools while allowing them to avoid facing the problem of educating everyone.

Decay of cities and regions in the nation. This shows up in welfare costs, health and housing problems, hunger, loss of tax income, one-half the cities and counties losing population, lack of jobs where people live, industry shifts, pollution, traffic, crime, isolation of ethnic groups, nonresponsible citizen involvement, political extremism, and a manpower drain from areas most in need of leadership and talent.

Disrespect for law and order. The result is violence, high crime rates, riots, low public opinion of courts and police, greater use of National Guard for law enforcement, draft evasion, family breakdown, the youth movement, and a lack of belief that the law protects those most in need of protection.

Lack of hope for many adults. Symptoms are 23 million adults with less than an eighth-grade education, the signing away of job seniority rights because of education level, technological displacement from work, people in depressed areas afraid to move where jobs are, age discrimination in hiring, rising taxes for retired people, inflation, rising costs of health care, fear of youth, political retreat to the past, backlash response to pressures for change, nonparticipation in society, early retirement, loss of self-dignity, belief that there is no place for the aged.

Conserving national resources. Examples are air and water pollution, inadequate recreation facilities, use of leisure time, spray and chemical pollution, sewage and trash disposal, wildlife and natural resource depletion, human congestion, lack of time and programs for self-renewal, disappearance of craftsmen and artisans, the failure to reward artistic and humanistic efforts, the population explosion, the lack of a role for youth and the elderly, the potential use of the bomb.

19

Public financing of social programs. Evidence of this includes rising costs of welfare, the space program, research on social problems, educational inequalities, the role of private enterprise in solving social issues, the tax revolt, the push for guaranteed annual incomes, inequality of taxes, cost of national defense, the growth of industrial conglomerates, cost of health care, money for remediation but not prevention, establishing national priorities in spending, the role of state, local, and federal governments.

The structure and organization of education. Examples of this can be found in the rigidity of elementary, secondary, and higher education, the church-state issue, state-local-federal responsibilities, citizen involvement or local control, certification and licensing, lack of youth involvement, cost effectiveness of education, accountability for results, institutional versus professional loyalties, size of education units versus efficiency, overlapping tax jurisdictions, federal control, effective planning, unequal educational opportunities, disparity between needs and funds, the establishment and the critics.

This statement of issues is neither definitive nor discrete, but it highlights what the general public, and thus the legislators (who decide on programs through legislation and priorities through appropriations at all three levels of government), are concerned about. Education's goals, programs, and efforts must be stated in reference to these issues or they will not be seen as relevant.

Rightly or wrongly, this nation hit upon education as the major social institution to provide solutions to its problems. We must look at the goals of education and at the activities of the school not just in terms of what is ideal but in terms of the environment in which education functions, the attitudes of people, and the role of the other financial, political, and social agencies in our society.

1. The Manpower Revolution

Man, Education, and Work

Technological change has, rather suddenly, thrown up a dramatic challenge to this nation's political, economic, social, and educational institutions. Though the full scope of this challenge may not be comprehended for years to come, its dimensions are now clear enough to call for a massive response on the part of American education. All levels of education must quickly move to assume greater responsibilities for preparing men and women for entry into the changed and changing world of technological work. Unless far more and far better education on the semiprofessional, technical, and skilled levels is soon made available to greater numbers of citizens, the national economy and social structure will suffer irreparable damage.[2]

There can be no doubt that damage has been done to the social order, especially in terms of the disenchantment of youth with the relevance of their education. This is true both for those who are attending college and for those who terminated their education much earlier. Student strikes, riots, and actions against the educational structure continue to grow at an exponential rate, reaching now even into the junior high school.

[1] The bulk of this chapter originally appeared in *Man, Education, and Work* by Grant Venn, published by the American Council on Education, Washington, D.C., 1964.
[2] Venn, Grant. *Man, Education, and Work*. Washington, D.C.: American Council on Education, 1964.

Technology has created a new relationship between man, his education, and his work, in which education is placed squarely between man and his work. Although this relationship has traditionally held for "some" men and "some" work (on the professional level, for example), modern technology has advanced to the point where the relationship may now be said to exist for all men and for all work. Yet, though technology today in effect dictates the role that education must play in preparing man for work, no level of American education has fully recognized this fact of life. Tragically, the nation's educational system, when viewed as a whole, is in what Edward Chase describes as a gross imbalance, its attention concentrated on the 20 percent of students who go through college.[3] Thus, when Sputnik, one symbol of technological advance, flashed before the world's eyes, the U.S. response was predictable: Congress passed the National Defense Education Act, designed primarily to bolster science, language, mathematics, and engineering opportunities for the academically talented, degree-seeking student.

But what about the other 80 percent who will not graduate from college? Unfortunately, the "pursuit of excellence" has left most of them behind. At the junior high school, high school, and junior college levels, most students, whatever their abilities, aptitudes, and interests, study those subjects that form the high road to the baccalaureate degree. More than a few of them have difficulty appreciating the logic of this course. Despite propaganda about the importance of staying in school, they drift out of educational institutions in droves: the system loses 35 percent of its enrollees during high school, 45 percent of its high school graduates, and 40 percent of its college entrants.[4] Some of this attrition is unavoidable, of course, but large numbers of these dropouts are simply early leavers who are capable of considerably more education than they received. "Lack of interest" is by far the most frequent

[3] Chase, Edward. "Learning To Be Unemployable." *Harper's Magazine,* April 1963. p. 33.

[4] U.S. Department of Health, Education, and Welfare, Office of Education. *Digest of Educational Statistics.* Washington, D.C.: Government Printing Office, 1967-68.

24

reason they give for leaving, because they do not fit into the present college-track plan of education.

And what happens to them when they leave? Turned out of an educational system oriented toward someone else's college degree rather than their own work needs, and entering a labor market whose jobs require constantly higher levels of education and skill development, their prospects are bleak.[5] The youth unemployment rate, higher than it was during the depression, reaches higher levels month after month. Those who do find work end up in low-skill, low-pay jobs, jobs without security and without a future, jobs frustratingly below their occupational potential. Industry has little to offer the young worker without a skill; the armed forces have fewer and fewer opportunities for him. At the same time, with two or three years of occupationally oriented education at the high school or junior college level, a great many of these same people could qualify for meaningful jobs on the skilled, technical, and semiprofessional levels, where there are acute manpower shortages. That so many of today's youth did not receive adequate occupational education points up a serious shortcoming of the educational system.[6]

The case for greater occupational orientation can be made in terms of a particular number of trained persons needed in certain technical occupations or of employment opportunities needed for the million or more youth not in school and not at work. Important as manpower and jobs are, however, they represent only the opening wedge of the economic and social dislocations the new technology is forcing upon us. To understand the problem more fully, we must look behind these symptoms and examine the new technology and the nature of the changes it has wrought in the relationship between man, his education, and his work.

[5] The unemployment rate for all workers over sixteen in 1968 was 3.6 percent; for the sixteen- to nineteen-year-olds it was 12.6 percent. Nonwhite youth unemployment was 24.9 percent in 1968.

[6] Total enrollments in vocational education have risen 52 percent since the passage of the 1963 Vocational Education Act, but this still represents a very small percentage of the youth that need skill training. Unpublished statistics, U.S. Department of Health, Education, and Welfare, Office of Education, Division of Vocational–Technical Education.

25

The New Technology

No one has yet given an adequate definition of the new technology. The term is used here to describe the changes now besetting the social and economic institutions of the industrial nations of the world. The emergence of a youth unemployment problem in this country is but one phenomenon indicating the impact of this new technology, an impact which Chase promises will be "impersonal, nonideological, relentless, and possibly overwhelming." [7]

The most significant aspect of the new technology is described by the word *change*. It is not simply a case of new sets of social and economic relationships replacing older ones, but of the new ones themselves being replaced at a faster and faster rate, with only those adapted to change surviving. This concept of change is not new; what is new is the *change in the rate of change*. This has come as a result of the tremendous increase in the rate of scientific activity; significantly, the rate of that increase is not constant, but exponential.

One illustration is the federal expenditure for research and development. It took nine years to double the 1944 expenditure, six years to double the 1953 expenditure, and three to double the 1959 expenditure; in 1963 the federal government alone spent $14 billion on research and development, ten times the amount spent for that purpose twelve years before. This money is fed to a growing army of scientific, engineering, and technical personnel, who have, according to a Stanford Research Institute Report to the U.S. Senate, "invented the art of systematic invention." The traditional tools of the "art" have been vastly augmented by the development of data processing, linear programming, systems analysis, and simulation. The decision theorists of the new technology now seek, in the words of economist Daniel Bell, "the compass of rationality itself."

Many theorists of the new technology have contemplated whether all this represents a revolution comparable to the industrial revolution begun two centuries ago. Perhaps it is too early to answer that question; as John Diebold put it,

[7] Chase, Edward. "Politics and Technology." *Yale Review*. March 1968. p. 321.

this is "an extremely complex subject—we are long on conjecture and short on all but the most basic facts."[8] But by considering the changes already brought about by the new technology, its potential for change, and the rate at which change is occurring, it is possible to accept Donald Michael's thesis that the new technology is something "so different in degree as to be a profound difference in kind."[9]

The landmark of technological developments has been the introduction of automation and computers into industry and commerce. Automation encompasses a class of devices that automatically perform both the sensing and motor tasks formerly performed by human labor. Thus, automated machines can mine coal, pick cotton, cast and finish engine blocks, sort bank checks, roll aluminum, grade oranges, and weave cloth. Computers are devices which rapidly perform traditional human tasks involving experience, memory, analysis, logic, and decision making. Such devices now can diagnose symptoms for the physician, research a case for the lawyer, read envelopes for the postman, design a plant for the architect, prepare war and defense plans for the military, screen volunteers for the Peace Corps, and keep inventory for the merchant. These machines are being "taught" to translate languages, compose music, play chess, transcribe speech, and "see" objects; already they correct their mistakes and identify trouble spots in their mechanisms.

The impact of these devices on the labor market has been profound. Automatic elevators have displaced 40,000 elevator operators in New York City alone. New equipment in the Census Bureau enabled fifty statisticians in 1960 to do the work that required 4,000 people in 1950. The check-writing staff in the Treasury Department has been reduced from 400 people to four. The airline flight engineer and the railroad fireman may soon disappear completely. In the last four years ponderous mechanical cotton pickers have reduced farm jobs in lush Tulare County, California, from 25,000 to

[8] Diebold, John. Governor's Conference on Automation. New York, June 1-3, 1960.
[9] Michael, Donald. *Cybernation: The Silent Conquest.* Santa Barbara, Calif.: Center for the Study of Democratic Institutions, 1962. p. 5.

17,000. Thirty thousand packinghouse workers have been "automated out" of their jobs in the past few years. Enormous machines have helped reduce employment in the coal fields from 415,000 in 1950 to 136,000 in 1962. While construction work has leaped 32 percent since 1956, construction jobs have shown a 24 percent decline. Comparable statistics exist for the chemical, aircraft, communications, metals, transportation, and other industries. In many additional cases where automation and computers have been introduced, the effect has not been to fire or lay off, but rather to put a freeze on new hiring.

Assuredly this is only the beginning; a steady increase in job dislocation can be predicted as the nation accelerates into what Daniel Bell labels a "postindustrial society." Domestic and international competition compel greater reliance on the speed and precision possible only with automated devices. In turn, these devices are being designed to do larger and larger portions of the tasks now performed by human labor while at the same time they are becoming less expensive in relation to the costs of human labor. It seems only a matter of time until a substantial part of the present national employment succumbs to technological advance; many of the present tasks of farm workers, laborers, semiskilled operatives, service workers, craftsmen, and middle management administrators have a high likelihood of technological elimination.

The full impact of the new technology has been slow to register on the American consciousness. To date, the instances of "technological unemployment" are like the cap of an iceberg: the difficulty of appreciating what is below lures many into believing we can sail blithely ahead without changing course. Indeed, the nation has been assured for years that for every job destroyed by automation two new ones are created, and this notion has been slow to die. Because automation and computers have been introduced selectively, their impact has often been limited to the individual or a local community. Thus, many educators and other public leaders have not discerned that the forces of technology are *immediate* in importance and *national* in scope, and that they carry serious consequences for the economic and social life of the entire country.

The nation's task is to make certain that the human promise of America is not lost to the economic promise of technology.

In this decade young people are entering a technological world of work unequipped with the tools they need for survival. More than a million of them are now out of school and out of work and, given the circumstances, this figure will continue to rise. The alternatives before the country are clear:

We can try to hold young people in school and off the labor market for a longer period of time, by simply expanding the educational system.

We can let them remain idle.

We can put them to work "raking leaves from the public lawn."

We can equip them in school and in college with the skills they need to become competitive in a technological work world. But as of now, James B. Conant warns us, "unemployment of youth is literally nobody's affair."

The nation actually has provided a series of new programs and institutions of special assistance to the poor, the unemployed, and the uneducated. However, the suggestion to prepare youth in schools and colleges for employment in a technological world has not been seriously considered by the federal government. The enormous increase in the number of children and youth in school has made it difficult for the states or the local school districts to take on the task, simply because of the nature of the tax structure.

. At this point in time, a total of 248 million dollars of federal money has been allocated to vocational-technical education in the schools and colleges of the nation. This amount is the federal government's share of construction, equipment, instruction, teacher training, curriculum development, vocational guidance, administration, and all necessary auxiliary services. The funds are to be used for secondary, postsecondary, and adult levels throughout the United States and territories.

It seems that youth unemployment is still nobody's affair—until the young man or woman drops out of school or graduates with little or no assistance in getting a job. There are now programs such as the Job Corps (recently downgraded), Neighborhood Youth Corps, and Manpower Development and Training, which will assist youth to train for and get a job—*if he can prove he is a failure in the school system!* But there is still no major effort aimed at providing a positive program of skill training for employment in many of the schools of the nation.

As Rupert Evans has said:

American education is designed for one basic purpose—to prepare the student for subsequent schooling. Actual practice in elementary schools, secondary schools, junior colleges, and baccalaureate programs show far too little recognition of the role of the school in preparing students for citizenship and for employment. Only at the graduate school level are employability skills given careful attention by the majority of instructors, and anyone who drops out of the educational stream prior to graduate school is regarded as a failure.

Intelligence tests are designed to predict success in only one undertaking—schooling. Guidance counseling is limited almost entirely to helping the student choose and prepare for a higher level of schooling. Teachers and curricula alike are judged on the proportion of students who succeed at the next higher level of schooling.[10]

Man and Work

The changing nature of the work force continues in directions started twenty years ago. A recent study by Seymour Wolfbein predicts the following:

1. By 1975 one and one-half million jobs will be needed each year to absorb the rise in the labor supply.

2. There will be one million fewer people aged thirty-five to forty-four in the labor force in 1975 than in 1965.

3. There will be eight and three-fourths million more people aged twenty-five to thirty-four in 1975 than in 1965.

4. There will be an increase of more than 50 percent in the number of nonwhites in the early twenties age group.

5. Those in the professional and technical fields will exceed skilled craftsmen by 1975.

6. *The unskilled will fall below the 5 percent level.*[11]

[10] Evans, Rupert N. "School for Schooling's Sake: The Current Role of the Secondary School in Occupational Preparation." *The Transition from School to Work*. Report based on the Princeton Manpower Symposium, Princeton, N.J., May 9-10, 1968.

[11] Wolfbein, Seymour. *Manpower Problems of the 1970's.* Washington, D.C.: U.S. Chamber of Commerce, 1969.

The past few decades have seen many changes in the American work world. Child labor has disappeared; the arrival of the forty-hour (or less) workweek means that people do less work; the use of machines (and of machines to control machines) means that work is physically less demanding. But these obvious changes obscure more fundamental alterations in the world of work.

Work becomes more cognitive. The industrial revolution greatly affected the way in which people worked. As animal and human muscle power was replaced by steam and electric power, the blue-collar operative and the skilled tradesman became the dominant figures in an economy based on industrial production. Now, the advent of the new technology has led us into a stage of work activity in which the emphasis has shifted from the manipulative powers to the cognitive powers. Lee A. DuBridge has described how technology has changed the industrial production processes in terms of—

> The multiplicity of electronic devices now used to control industrial processes—to monitor the quality of the product and adjust the machine to correct for deviations, to compute in advance the rate at which materials and parts of particular types should be fed into a complex assembly line, and to continue the process of taking over more and more of the repetitious processes formerly done by hand —and performing them with a delicacy, precision, and speed that human hands could never match.[12]

Automation, then, supplants human manipulation and control of machines with electronic control devices, replacing machine operators with a supervisor of the automatically controlled operating system. In the automated office, high-speed computers and data-processing equipment have necessitated revamping the procedures and the job descriptions for such processes as auditing, bookkeeping, account-keeping, payroll, and inventory. Employers in both plant and office look for people with higher levels of education and more sophisticated skills to perform the more cognitive work functions involved.[13]

[12] DuBridge, Lee A. "Educational and Social Consequences." *Automation and Technological Change.* (Edited by John T. Dunlop.) Englewood Cliffs, N.J.: Prentice-Hall, 1962. p. 30.
[13] Yale economist Neil Chamberlain, in a paper on "Automation and

TABLE 1. Major Occupational Groups as a Percentage of Total Labor Force

Occupational Group	1900 *	1947 **	1960 **	1975 ***
White-collar workers	17.6	34.9	43.1	48.5
Professional and technical	4.3	6.6	11.2	14.8
Managers and proprietors	5.8	10.0	10.6	10.4
Clerical workers	3.0	12.4	14.7	16.9
Sales personnel	4.5	5.9	6.6	6.4
Blue-collar workers	35.8	40.7	36.3	34.0
Craftsmen and foremen	10.5	13.4	12.8	13.0
Semiskilled operatives	12.8	21.2	18.0	16.9
Laborers (exclusive of farm and mine)	12.5	6.1	5.5	4.1
Service workers	9.0	10.4	12.5	13.8
Farm workers	37.6	14.0	8.1	3.2

* Computed from U.S. Department of Commerce, Bureau of the Census. *Historical Statistics of the United States, Colonial Times to 1957.* Washington, D.C.: Government Printing Office, 1960. pp. 75-78.

** *Manpower Report of the President,* including *A Report on Manpower Requirements, Resources, Utilization, and Training* by the U.S. Department of Labor, transmitted to Congress, March 1963. Washington, D.C.: Government Printing Office, 1963. pp. 100, 143.

*** *Manpower Report of the President,* including *A Report on Manpower Requirements, Resources, Utilization, and Training* by the U.S. Department of Labor, transmitted to Congress, January 1969. Washington, D.C.: Government Printing Office, 1969. p. 235.

The shift from manual to cognitive work is reflected in the long-term changes in the occupational distribution of the labor force, shown in Table 1. In 1900 the number of white-collar jobs was less than half the number of blue-collar jobs; by 1975 it is projected to be more than 44 percent greater. Equally important, semiskilled operatives, traditionally the

Labor Relations" delivered at Reed College, November 17, 1961, cited a Bureau of Labor Statistics study of the effect of electronic data-processing equipment installations on office personnel. "In offices where the new equipment was introduced, 17 percent of the original work force had not completed high school. After the new equipment had been installed, among those retained, the number of high school non-graduates decreased to 5 percent. Among new hirees for positions in these installations, there are only 1 percent who have not reached this educational level. In the same operation only 7 percent of the original group of employees had completed four years or more of college, as against 42 percent of those retained for the new installation, and 78 percent of those newly hired."

backbone of the industrial (and manual) work force, have reached their highest proportion and have begun to decline. Within the blue-collar and white-collar groups similar trends are apparent. Within the blue-collar ranks, only the skilled and highly skilled craftsmen are expected to maintain their proportion in the labor market, and in recent years the biggest employment gains within the white-collar area have been made by the most highly educated and skilled group (professional and technical workers). These shifts indicate that white-collar jobs will continue to encroach into all sectors of the labor force and that, with the exception of service workers, the occupations that will grow the most are those demanding higher levels of education and skill development.

In the past, increases in white-collar employment came from the expansion of jobs in teaching, banking, government, insurance, and the like. But in recent years a considerable portion of the increase has come from within industry. Between 1948 and 1960, for example, the number of blue-collar production workers *declined* by nearly half a million while non-production white-collar workers rose 1.5 million. In large corporations such as General Motors, U.S. Steel, DuPont, and Standard Oil, 35 percent of all employees are now white-collar. The magnitude of this shift, essentially from manual to mental work, can be seen in Table 2.

Data for 1967 indicates a continual reduction of production versus nonproduction workers. The figures for total private

TABLE 2. Ratio of Nonproduction Worker Employment to Total Employment, Selected Industries

Industry Group	1947 *	1962 *	1967 **
Ordinance	18.5	54.0	48.6
Instruments	20.2	36.3	37.1
Petroleum	23.1	35.7	37.4
Transportation equipment	18.5	31.8	26.4
Machinery	20.9	30.4	30.4
Total private payrolls	12.1	16.5	17.0

*Manpower Report of the President, including A Report on Manpower Requirements, Resources, Utilization, and Training, March 1963. p. 165. "Nonproduction workers" include people in personnel, administration, marketing, research, and the like.

** Manpower Report of the President . . . , April 1968. p. 274.

payrolls show a shift of 0.5 of 1 percent between 1962 and 1967 in favor of the nonproduction employees. The reversal of this trend in ordinance and transportation may be indicative of the impact of the Vietnam War on the production of military equipment and ordinance. Yet the inevitable trend is the replacement of men with machines in operative production jobs.

Industries in the so-called primary sector of the economy, largely agriculture and mining, which in the past have employed large numbers of unskilled workers, have undergone drastic job reductions in recent years: counting only production workers, mining and agricultural employment has decreased about 40 percent in the last fifteen years.

In industry, the secondary sector, production and overall employment have gained, but employment of laborers and semiskilled operatives has shown no increase at all. Employment opportunities in the lower reaches of the spectrum—the jobs that require lesser amounts of education and skill development—have become severely limited. Yet these jobs have been the traditional entry point for most young workers. The contemporary technological economy has little to offer the untrained, undereducated, would-be worker. There is no room at the bottom.

Occupation and status. As technology changes the world of work, it inevitably affects the relationship between man and his work. The crucial factor is the importance of the job itself to the individual in American society. Without an occupational status, "the individual has few other statuses which are capable of offering him a respected position in the community." [14]

This was not always so. Before the Civil War, for example, the national economy was centered on the primary industries—agriculture, mining, forestry, fishing, construction, transportation, and the like. The function of work in that economy was the production of goods, such as food, clothing, shelter, and raw materials. The prime instruments of production were human and animal strength, and the very inefficiency of these instruments meant that production could never be much above

[14] Brookover and Nosow, "A Sociological Analysis of Vocational Education in the United States."

34

subsistence levels; it took four families on the farm to feed one in the city. Economists label this condition "scarcity."

In such a setting work was defined in terms of physical effort. A man's status was determined, not by the job he held, but by the amount of work he could do, by the amount of goods he could produce through physical effort. Americans heard the same message from the pulpit: the Puritan work ethic taught that hard work was necessary to salvation. The lone exception was the "gentleman"; whatever his occupation, what he did was not classified as work.

Today the forces of industrialism and technology have altered the meaning of the word *work* and man's relation to the world of work. The displacement of muscle power by the automated machine makes possible the production of vast surpluses of goods; abundance has replaced scarcity.

The blue-collar to white-collar shift in the employment force signifies that the primary function of work today is to secure the distribution of goods, not the production of goods. In 1900, for example, 70 percent of the nation's labor force was engaged in production, compared with less than 40 percent today. And only a very small percentage of the present labor force is engaged in what earlier centuries would call "hard work."

This situation leads to the problem at hand. As Gerard Piel points out, any hard work that a machine can do (and that includes virtually all such work) is better done by a machine; "hard" these days means mostly boring and repetitive, whether in the factory or the office. But the instinct for workmanship, the need to feel needed, the will to achieve are deeply felt in every human heart. "They are not," says Piel, "universally fulfilled by the kind of employment most people find." [15] Indeed, with the enactment of social legislation such as workman's compensation and unemployment relief and with the steady downgrading of manual occupations, work itself is no longer an absolute necessity for subsistence or a means of gaining status. *In the place of work we have substituted "the job."* A man's occupation in American society is now his single, most significant, status-conferring role. Whether

[15] Piel, Gerard. *Consumers of Abundance.* Santa Barbara, Calif.: Center for the Study of Democratic Institutions, 1961. p. 9.

it be high or low, a job status allows the individual to form some stable conception of himself and his position in the community.[16]

The social and psychological effects of joblessness are painfully apparent in America today. They can be seen in the faces of those standing in line for relief checks; none of them may be starving, and there may be work around the home that could keep them busy, but without a job they are lost. Tens of thousands of jobless youths cast about at loose ends, with 80 to 90 percent of the juvenile cases in the courts coming from their ranks. Job discrimination creates a hard knot of frustration in the Negro, frustration that explodes in bitter racial conflict. Also included in this group is the middle-aged woman whose children are grown and who now wishes to get a job. There still may be plenty of work around the home and the family may not need the money, but she feels a need for new identifications found only in holding a job. This crucial importance of the job to the individual in American society must be borne in mind in any discussion of man, his work, and his education. Statistical compilations of the effect of technology on the labor market can be compelling, but for millions of Americans the problem of joblessness is real and personal.

Youth without jobs. Important as a job may be to adults, it is no less important to the young person leaving school. For him it is initiation into the adult world. Here again things have changed, for although the psychological and social significance of initiating youth into adulthood has been recognized by every society, it seldom has involved getting a job. In primitive societies initiation often took the form of a prolonged, formal test of physical endurance. Knighting and the sacrament of confirmation performed a similar function in medieval society. In more recent times, American youngsters looked upon shoes or their first pair of long pants as a symbol of adulthood. Some girls had a formal coming-out to mark their adulthood; for most, marriage was the turning point. But *not* work. Work was something they experienced long before adulthood, whether in the form of helping on the farm or being put into a factory at the age of ten. A child's capac-

[16] Brookover and Nosow, *op. cit.,* p. 26.

36

ities were not left idle when the family subsistence depended upon these resources.

But modern society increasingly denies opportunities for work during youth. There are no fires to build, wood to chop, or cows to milk for most young boys and girls. A boy may mow the lawn or wax the car, a girl may vacuum the rugs or wash dishes, but little formal work awaits them until they get a job. Since the modern economy hires only mature workers, and since adults themselves measure status in terms of jobs, a job becomes the symbol of acceptance into the adult world. Neither religious ceremonies (which come too early), nor marriage (which for many comes too late), nor school graduation ceremonies (a good excuse for new clothes and a round of parties) rank even close to a job as an initiation symbol.

This is not to suggest that something is wrong with the value system of American youth. These are simply the values of the adult world, and every young person has always looked forward to becoming an adult and doing things adults do. Today, this means getting a job, the assumption of an occupational status. The big difficulty is that when young men and women leave school, they find there are no jobs for them.

There are now more than one million young men and women under twenty-two who have left school and are not working. At any given time 30 percent of the high school dropouts will be unemployed; even high school graduates average 15 percent unemployed. The figure for college dropouts is considerably lower, but they share the same problem as those who have dropped out of the system earlier: there is little room in the labor market for the undereducated, unskilled young worker. Instead of initiation they find rejection.

The consequences are enormous. The alarmingly high incidence of delinquency and crime among jobless youth is well documented: less widely appreciated is the tremendous reservoir of idleness, frustration, resentment, and defeat that lies within their burgeoning numbers. Lacking jobs, "their badge of belonging," these young men and women represent "tomorrow's castoff and chronic dependents, those who will live in

37

poverty of body and mind, and who will bring up their children in their own image." [17]

A series of government reports and studies have documented over and over again the consistent relationship between one's self-image and one's job. The President's Commission on Law Enforcement and Administration of Justice made specific recommendations on the school's role in securing jobs for youth.

The general mandate of the schools should be broadened to include responsibility not only for preparing youth for productive, responsible and satisfying adulthood—but for guiding them into adult positions. This would have a number of implications, including at the most general level, the fact that the schools would have the responsibility for the welfare and development of youth up to some specific age such as 19—whether or not they are in school. According to this view, then, if a student dropped out at 16, he would still be the school's charge.

Another implication is that the school would be primarily responsible for occupational placement and for subsequent guidance among work-bound youth. Moreover, part of the school's accountability should be its record in sending non-college bound youth into labor markets.

One means by which this broadened mandate can be implemented is the creation of an Occupational Placement and Follow-Up Office in each school, whose responsibility would be not just occupational placement but continuing guidance, training, and re-employment assistance—and reporting its record of performance to administrators and the public. We suggest that such an office could eliminate much of the randomness that now characterizes entry into occupational careers. If effective, it would increase the rationality of job preparation and placement and thereby increase the sense among students that there is more operating for them than fate alone. . . .

Unless there is a "pay-off" for kids who stay in school, dropout and delinquency problems will not be solved. This

[17] President's Committee on Youth Unemployment. *The Challenge of Jobless Youth.* Washington, D.C.: Government Printing Office, 1963. p. iv.

"pay-off" must be either opportunity for further education, training, or experience leading to jobs, or immediate
placement in jobs in the community—a placement which
offers opportunity for training and advancement.

Peace Corps and Vista are two types of experiences
available for youth. However, these "volunteer" activities will provide opportunities only to those who can
afford one or two years of "financial irresponsibility"
and will consequently attract mainly those youth who are
economically secure. Job Corps will meet the needs of
a very small number of those with whom we are concerned. Neighborhood Youth Corps offers larger-scale
possibilities, but its eligibility requirements are too often
high, and many of its job offerings have been largely
"make-work" with no future. Both these programs,
however, have offered models which may well help to
provide answers to the problems of locked-out youth.
*The combination of work-for-pay, skill development and
education if it can lead to job placement with career-
ladder possibilities, seems to offer the most promising
solution to the needs of this growing number of youth
for which the traditional system offers small promise.*

Jobs, however, are hard to come by for youth from
ghetto areas, areas which are producing the greatest numbers of dropouts and delinquents. *This existing and projected lack of meaningful employment opportunities for
large numbers of youth growing into adulthood is perhaps
the major domestic problem in America today.*

The school must share the responsibility not only for
training for jobs, but also for *job development* and *job
placement.* Local educational agencies can and must
participate in cooperative and comprehensive job development efforts . . . with industry, labor, community action, employment services, and other community groups.
(Italics mine.) [18]

Youth with jobs. Public discussion of the problems of youth
and work has generally focused on the plight of the high

[18] President's Commission on Law Enforcement and Administration
of Justice. *Task Force Report: Juvenile Delinquency and Youth Crime.*

school dropout who cannot find a job. Of equal concern should be the youth who is underemployed.

A job is vital to a young person, and it is also vital that the job provide an outlet for his abilities, that it be compatible with his aspirations. These conditions are seldom met by the entry jobs now available to young men and women with limited education and skills. The high school dropout may find a job washing dishes or parking cars; if he has graduated from high school or attended college awhile, he may clerk in a store or become a route salesman. These are dead-end jobs, and he knows it. He becomes frustrated; initiation for him has become a personal defeat. Chances are he will soon quit his job and seek another; job turnover among people under twenty-two is far higher than among older workers and is more happenstance than planned. At the Los Angeles Trade-Technical College the average student (now in his twenties) has gone through approximately ten jobs before coming to Trade-Tech. "They have been defeated," says Dean of Instruction Franklin R. Johnson. "You can see defeat in their eyes." [19]

Some people believe that the solution to the problem of youth and work is simply to keep all students in school at least through high school. Many college administrators, who watch 40 percent of their entering freshmen drop out along the way, act as though the whole problem were far removed from their province, as though any time spent in college is good. Their assumption seems to be that the best and only necessary preparation for a job today is the longest possible immersion in academic and professional subjects.

This assumption fails to heed the factor of youth unemployment and misapprehends the relevance of general education. Academic studies do enhance the long-range civic and occupational competence of a person; they do not, at least below the baccalaureate degree level as a rule, qualify young people for meaningful job entry. The technological work world is one of specialization and sophisticated skills, and being a

Report on Juvenile Justice and Consultants' Papers. Washington, D.C.: Government Printing Office, 1967. pp. 270, 282.

[19] Quoted by Leonard, George B. "Are We Cheating Twenty Million Students?" *Look,* June 4, 1963. p. 38.

"bright young man" cuts relatively little ice with employers looking for someone with skills to do a specific kind of work. A review of the "help wanted" section of any newspaper confirms this. Norman C. Harris says:

> The fact is that although business and industry would like to have employees with a higher level of general education and a concomitant higher potential for subsequent promotion, for entry jobs in the American economy today competence and skill of a rather high order, in some facet of the world of work are absolutely essential.[20]

When the dropouts from four-year colleges and graduates of junior college academic programs do not find meaningful entry jobs, they experience underemployment rather than unemployment, and their underemployment heightens unemployment among those with no college work. The young man with a year or two of college working in a supermarket may well have the ability to be a highly skilled craftsman or technician. By taking a job at the supermarket, he creates a double loss in our manpower pool: the job at the higher ability level remains vacant while he displaces the lower ability person who could function well in his position.

Job selection in the technological work world has become a desperate affair, often subject to wildest chance and unrelated to the young job seeker's aptitudes and abilities. Many young people are unaware of the range of occupations and have had little opportunity to observe work in its setting. A century ago the young boy or girl participated in the work of the family and had a good idea of what the other men and women of the community did. Today young people may know what the home repairman, policeman, shopkeeper, and truck-driver do, but they know little about the work of the chemist, the electrician, the lathe operator, or the construction worker. Thus intelligent transition into the world of work becomes

[20] Harris, Norman C. "Meeting the Post-High School Educational Needs of the Vast 'Middle Group' of High School Graduates." Presentation to the North Central Association of Colleges and Secondary Schools, Committee on Articulation of Schools and Colleges, Chicago, March 19, 1963. p. 3.

all the more difficult and vocational guidance all the more essential.

Work and Education

The institutions of the technological society are intellectual, and the use of cognitive facilities has become paramount in work, as it has always been in education. Over a wide range of occupations in the new technology, job entry and upgrading have become increasingly a matter of education, and what is basic to successful performance in today's occupations can best be taught within formal educational frameworks.

Occupation linked to education. The relationship between educational achievement and occupational entry and upgrading is demonstrated by the median years of schooling of workers within the major occupational groups shown in Table 3. The educational level of persons within these different occupations is shown in Table 4.

The tables do not tell the full story of the educational requirements for young people entering an occupation today. A high school diploma is a minimum prerequisite for most production workers, and a bachelor's degree, often in engineer-

TABLE 3. Median Years of School Completed as of October 1952, March 1962, 1967 by Major Occupational Group *

| | Median Years of Schooling | | |
Occupational Group	1952	1962	1967
White-collar workers			
Professional and technical	16+	16.2	16.3
Managers and proprietors	12.2	12.5	12.7
Clerical workers	12.5	12.5	12.5
Sales personnel	12.3	12.5	12.5
Blue-collar workers			
Craftsmen and foremen	10.1	11.2	12.0
Semiskilled operatives	9.1	10.1	10.8
Laborers (exclusive of farm and mine)	8.3	8.9	9.5
Other			
Service workers	8.8	10.2	11.0
Farm workers	7.5	8.5	8.6

* *Manpower Report of the President,* including *A Report on Manpower Requirements, Resources, Utilization, and Training,* April 1968. p. 262.

TABLE 4. Levels of Educational Attainment Within Major
Occupational Groups, by Percentage *

	Percent With		
Occupational Group	Less Than High School Diploma	High School Diploma Only	Some College Education
Professional and technical	6	19	75
Proprietors and managers	38	33	29
Clerical and sales workers	25	53	22
Skilled workers	59	33	8
Semiskilled workers	70	26	4
Service workers	69	25	4
Unskilled workers	80	17	3
Farmers and farm managers	76	19	5

* U.S. Department of Labor. *Manpower, Challenge of the 1960's.* Washington,
D.C.: Government Printing Office, 1961. p. 17.

ing, may be a prerequisite for a foreman or supervisor. A college education is the only ticket for entry into the professions, with graduate study often a necessity for advancement. The technical, skilled, and semiprofessional occupations all demand substantial amounts of postsecondary education for entrance. In the accelerating job-upgrading process of technology there is a steady increase of higher education and skills needed for entry and retention. Education has become the crucial ladder to the rewarding positions in society.

Of the undereducated and untrained, Willard Wirtz says:

The reason for the increasing concentration of unemployment among unskilled workers is that machines are taking over the unskilled jobs. These are the jobs which have, up to this time, absorbed the casualties of the educational system: Those who for one reason or another have left school without having added to the strength which is in their arms and backs the skill it takes to do something more than "common labor." This wasn't too bad when there were enough common labor jobs around. Now there aren't.

Today, unskilled workers make up 5 percent of the work force, but almost 15 percent of all the unemployed are in this group. Unemployment is over twice as high

43

among the young worker groups and among non-white workers—the two groups in which there are the largest percentages of unskilled workers—than it is in the work force as a whole.[21]

The relationship between education and work, in terms of occupational entry and upgrading, is fixed and firm.

Broadening the relationship. The link between education and work at the highest occupational levels is well recognized. In the research and development field, for example, the line between education and work is very thin. Both university and industry take on cost-plus contracts in the same field, and interchange of personnel between the two is frequent. Many of the space research companies are direct university offshoots; overall, the great bulk of research and development is concentrated geographically around the top universities. It has long been agreed that the professions are a proper subject of academic attention, and preparation for them should take place within a formal educational framework.

Today, technology has advanced many occupations on the technical, skilled, and semiprofessional levels to a point where they require higher levels of specialization and related knowledge that are best learned and taught within educational frameworks. Manifestations of this upward push are to be found, for example, in engineering, where the two-year engineering technology curriculums of today compare in rigor and breadth with the four-year engineering curriculums of twenty-five years ago. As engineering continues to become more complex and specialization is delayed, graduate study will become a must for the engineer; by the same token, it is probable that within the present decade the bachelor's degree will become a must for many technical occupations. Similarly, the skilled crafts are now making their appearance on the junior college level.

Inevitably, in the same way that pupilage and apprenticeship gave way to professional education in law and medicine, on-the-job training and apprenticeship are giving way to occupational education within the educational system. The time

[21] Statement of W. Willard Wirtz before the Senate Committee on Labor and Public Welfare, Subcommittee on Education, on S. 580, "National Education Improvement Act of 1963," April 30, 1963. p. 2.

has come for schools and colleges to recognize that the new occupations of technology must be taught where they are best able to be learned.

Man and Education

At a time when the demand for education, especially higher education, has never been greater, is it necessary that vocational and technical occupations be taught within the educational system? In the past, perhaps no; now, however, yes, because technology is demanding workers with a degree of training and related education that can best be offered in a system of education. To ignore the demand is to accept social and economic dislocations that will vitally affect the American economy and the personal well-being of our citizens.

The impact of technology. The labor market will be the focal point of these dislocations: as a technological economy expands, the largest increase in jobs will occur in occupations that require the most education and training (see Table 5).

These dislocations have already begun to appear. The most obvious, already cited, is the heavy concentration of unemployment among the poorly educated and the unskilled, where despite the current liveliness in the economy, some 4 percent of American workers cannot find work, including 18 percent of our out-of-school youth. The concentration of this unemployment in certain areas of our country, i.e., the large

TABLE 5. Percentage Change in Employment, by Major Occupational Groups, 1965-75 *

Occupational Group	Percentage Increase, 1965 to Projected 1975
Professional and technical	45.2
Managers and proprietors	23.3
Clerical workers	32.5
Service workers	34.4
Sales workers	25.0
Skilled workers	23.1
Semiskilled operatives	10.5
Laborers (exclusive of farm and mine)	− 2.4
Farm workers	− 21.6

* *Manpower Report of the President,* including *A Report on Manpower Requirements, Resources, Utilization, and Training,* January 1969. p. 235.

45

cities and depressed rural areas, has brought our nation to the brink of social anarchy.

There are some forecasts that the coming years will be characterized by great economic growth in this country; equally reputable forecasters, however, tell us bluntly that our unemployment rate can be expected to continue its long-term upward climb. Columbia philosopher Charles Frankel has pointed out that as technology continues to loosen the spirit of invention and innovation, not only will we have technological unemployment, "but we can count on it as a *normal feature* and sign that our system is doing well." Although all the consequences of technological innovation cannot be foreseen, we do know that its social and economic effects are dislocating. Therefore, adds Frankel, we should not panic, treating the dislocations as an "accident," as "something that shouldn't happen." What we must do, he concludes, is deliberately *establish permanent preventive institutions* carefully designed to cope with such dislocations as we can anticipate.[22]

In an attempt to solve these problems the Departments of Housing and Urban Development and Transportation have been created, and numerous federal laws and programs enacted. But we have yet to see a substantial diminution of the pool of poor and disadvantaged, and we have yet to make a major effort at changing our educational programs so as to reduce the flow of people into the pool of unemployed. We have also yet to experience the difficulties that could occur from an economy which would create a soft labor market.

Impact on employment. Unemployment—a dislocation we can anticipate—is in part caused by the technological means of economizing the use of labor outrunning the pace at which new uses for that labor are found. Estimates of the number of workers displaced each year by automation now run in the order of one and one-half million. These people become difficult to absorb in a labor market already burdened with unemployment and an increasing number of job-seeking youth.

At the same time that technological unemployment grows, there are, by various rough estimates, millions of unfilled jobs in the country today. Technology, as it destroys jobs, also

[22] Remarks at 1961 National Conference on Social Welfare, quoted in Chase, "Politics and Technology," p. 329.

creates new ones; for example, while elevator operators are losing their jobs to automatic elevators, new jobs have been created in the design, building, sale, installation, and servicing of the new equipment. But the newly created jobs are not likely to be filled by the displaced workers unless they have the educational potential and training opportunities to meet the requirements. The problem, then, is one of distribution of the labor force, of matching job requirements and the potential of people to meet them.

If holding a job is as important to the individual as this report has indicated, then full employment must be a national goal. And in the words of Willard Wirtz, "full employment in this country depends on full education." [23]

At one time there existed a general consensus that the problem of persistent unemployment could be solved simply by stepping up the rate of national growth. Now, however, it is clear that no *attainable* rate of growth can in and of itself solve this nation's employment problems. This is a remarkable shift in contemporary economic thought. The unemployed are the undereducated and underskilled; in the years ahead, economic growth, increasingly a creature of technological advance, will not substantially increase the number of jobs for such people. Preventive measures to meet the dislocations of technological displacement must include the development of new occupational competencies for a major part of the labor force. This task will essentially be an educational one. Wirtz summarizes this point as follows:

> What this means in terms of educational needs is obvious. We simply cannot any longer afford to let boys and girls leave the educational system unprepared to use their minds as well as their muscles. We must, in one way or another, see to it that they have what today's—and tomorrow's—labor market requires. The margin for educational error or failure, which is what the unskilled jobs in the old work force constituted, has been taken up by the machine. [24]

[23] Wirtz, testimony on S. 580, *op. cit.*, p. 1.
[24] *Ibid.*, p. 2.

47

Economic growth. A second technological dislocation pointing to the necessity for more and better occupational education is economic in nature and involves the increasing shortage of personnel in many skilled, professional, and technical occupations. It will be the personnel in these fields who will be most involved in the work that engenders further technological advance. In this age of the art of systematic invention and innovation, the *rate* of invention and innovation—or more broadly of technological advance—depends to a large extent on the number of technical "artists" available for the tasks at hand. In the decades ahead the rate of economic growth will be increasingly dependent upon the rate of technological development. And since the rate of technological advance depends on the availability of technical personnel, the education of people in the professional, technical, and skilled occupations becomes a prime factor in increasing the growth rate of the national enterprise.[25]

Recent indications are that we may be getting close to saturation in the professional fields, with certain exceptions such as medicine and other health-related occupations. The long and continual support of and assistance to higher education and professional manpower seem to have been effective. The status of higher education and the faith long-held by our society in the returns from this level of education seem to have been successful in producing manpower commensurate with demand.

The need for technical personnel, however, is not so clearly understood and deserves greater attention immediately. Industry is learning that it not only is faced with shortages of scientists and engineers but that it often is not making full use of those it has. Various studies show that many of the routine functions of the scientist and engineer could be performed

[25] Walter W. Heller, former chairman of the President's Council of Economic Advisers, noted recently that "a series of studies for the United States shows that about half of the increase in output over the last fifty years must be attributed to factors other than the increase in the stock of tangible capital and man-hours worked," with "technology and brainpower" inputs accounting for the rest of the growth. Interestingly, most of these "intangible inputs," says Heller, "originate in education and training" ("Men, Money, and Materials." *Educational Record,* January 1963. pp. 13-14).

by people with more limited, specialized training. Thus, in the years ahead we will need many more technicians than scientists and engineers; for example, while the most desirable ratio of technicians to scientists and engineers is between 2 to 1 and 4 to 1, recent inventories showing existing ratios of from 0.5 to 1 to 0.9 to 1.[26] This gross misuse of professional manpower can be corrected only through a greatly stepped-up program of technical education, geared to an output of approximately 130,000 graduating technicians a year.[27]

A similar situation prevails in the skilled occupations. An estimated 5.2 million jobs will open up in this area during this decade, all requiring people with highly developed skills and considerable related knowledge. Many of these occupations are in the apprenticeable trades; however, apprenticeship completions will probably number no more than 300,000 to 400,000 during this ten-year period, as this traditional but increasingly unsuitable source of skilled workers continues to decline. This leaves an annual shortage in this area of nearly one-half million skilled craftsmen, a shortage that will make itself acutely felt in the years ahead. The ability of education to meet the need for skilled workers has been amply demonstrated over the years by the better vocational trades and industry programs on the high school and post-high-school level in several states, and more recently by the ambitious programs of many of the California community colleges. The need for a sustained educational effort in this area is great.

Impact of increase in population. During the 1950's the number of young workers entering the labor force each year was relatively stable; in 1959 there were only one-half million more of them in the labor force than in 1950. During the

---

[26] Emerson, Lynn A. "Technical Training in the United States." *Education for a Changing World of Work: Report of the Panel of Consultants on Vocational Education.* Washington, D.C.: Government Printing Office, 1963. Appendix I, p. 36. Department of Labor, Bureau of Labor Statistics. *The Long-Range Demand for Scientific and Technical Personnel.* Prepared for the National Science Foundation. Washington, D.C.: Government Printing Office, 1961. p. 44.

[27] Estimated annual need in 1978 by the Department of Labor, Bureau of Labor Statistics, "Technician Manpower: Requirements, Resources, and Training Needs," BLS No. 1512.

present decade, however, the number of young workers seeking to enter the labor force will increase by six million. The flood of World War II babies, now completing their education, is about to surge into the labor market; for every three young entrants into the world of work during 1963, there will be five in the years beyond 1965. It is clear what is happening: the number of youths seeking job entry is rapidly increasing, the number of traditional entry jobs is not, and the youth employment problem, with all its attendant social and psychological problems, is going from bad to worse. Obviously, this situation could develop into one of the most serious social problems this nation has ever encountered.

A significant part of the answer lies in providing more and better occupational education within the educational system. More young people must be prepared to enter the world of work at the higher occupational levels where there is room for them and where they are urgently needed.

Student potential. The magnitude of student potential is illustrated by the large numbers of students leaving school each year and seeking labor market entry, including nearly one million high school dropouts, more than one million non-college-bound high school graduates, and several hundred thousand college dropouts. As a group these represent 75 to 80 percent of all our youth, and the educational preparation and occupational well-being of this group will in large measure determine the course of this nation in the years ahead. As they leave school, they are ambitious and idealistic. In the world of work, however, they are likely to be underemployed, if they find employment at all.

At all educational levels, these unprepared school-leavers entering the work world represent a waste of vital talent. Consider the high school dropout. He is pictured as a dull, rebellious young person. Yet study after study has shown no substantial difference in intelligence between the dropout and his age group as a whole; a recently completed study showed, for example, that two-thirds of all dropouts were in the IQ range of 90 to 109.[28] These are *average* young men and

[28] Department of Labor, Bureau of Labor Statistics. *From School to Work: The Early Employment Experiences in Seven Communities, 1952-1957.* Washington, D.C.: Government Printing Office, 1961. The sample involved 22,000 students.

women, with considerable potential for occupational development within the schools. They are rebellious only in the sense that for most of them the subjects they studied in school were of little interest. Professor Harris declares that "without a doubt the biggest task facing the American high school today is to make its curriculum meaningful to students. For hundreds of thousands of boys and girls this meaning must be found in subject and curriculums related to the world of work." [29]

Much of the same is true of the high school graduates who do not go on to college. This group, more than a million strong, represents a high-potential force for post-high-school occupational education. As things stand now, they are having many of the same difficulties in the work world encountered by their classmates who left school before graduation. Fifteen percent of these graduates are now unemployed, and undoubtedly a high percentage of those who do have jobs are underemployed. Fifty to 60 percent of the people in this group must eventually find employment as middle-level manpower in the technical, semiprofessional, and skilled occupations for which a one- or two-year college-level program of semiprofessional, technical, or vocational education would provide the ideal preparation.

Higher education also contains a considerable student potential for occupational education of less than the baccalaureate level. In many states high school graduates can enter college more readily than they can get a job. For most students going on to college this means further academic study leading to the bachelor's degree. There are many students in academic programs of higher education who would find a fuller realization of their abilities and interests in a shorter term, specialized occupational program beyond the high school. How much a student profits from his educational experience is more important than the number of years he spends in school.

In this category are a large proportion of the C students in higher education, some of whom drop out, but many of whom drift through four years of college without either finding themselves or quite appreciating what college is all about. Also included are many college dropouts (40 percent of all

[29] Harris, *op. cit.*, p. 4.

entrants) whose experience in higher education would have been more successful had they enrolled in an occupationally oriented program. Similarly, many junior college students enrolled in a college transfer program might be better off in a career occupational program; in point of fact, only half of the transfer students actually continue their education.

At the tenth-grade, twelfth-grade, and fourteenth-grade levels the problem is essentially the same. The educational system strives to give each student every opportunity to develop his talents to the highest possible level. But the highest possible level is always defined as the highest possible level of academic or formal education. The A, B, or C student in high school whose real aptitude and ability potential is such that he would find it fully expressed as an engineering technician is nonetheless guided into engineering; when he becomes an engineering dropout holding some low-level job, it is considered a shame but somehow not the responsibility of higher education. Education pays lip service to the importance of providing an educational response for the wide range of student aptitudes, abilities, and interests but largely limits that response to general or academic studies of varying degrees of rigor. There are many young people to whom such studies offer little relevance or challenge, but whose motivations toward educational achievement could be renewed in a more practical program of occupational development suited to their real abilities, aptitudes, and interests. The large number of students with average and above average IQ's found in the attrition between the tenth and fourteenth grades (those who most frequently list "lack of interest" as their reason for leaving school) and the significant number of students with promising IQ's who languish in secondary and higher education with mediocre academic records are testimony that we are providing inadequate and inappropriate responses to the educational needs of many young men and women. The value of rigorous liberal studies for the academically talented and of a sound general education for all should not lead to the conclusion that these are the only worthy educational endeavors or that this is where the responsibility of education ends.

52

Occupational education provides the diversity and practicality that the educational system now lacks. Indeed, it is no accident that the city with the most extensive program of secondary vocational education (Milwaukee) is the one city that graduates 94 percent of its students from high school, and that the state with the greatest occupational education opportunities beyond the high school (California) has been able to induce so many of its high school graduates to continue their education.

Continuing education. The nature and rate of technological change militate against the concept of terminal education. As technology upgrades the skill and knowledge requirements of jobs, education can no longer be confined to the traditional twelve, fourteen, or sixteen years of formal schooling. The Department of Labor projects that the average youth of today will probably shift occupations some five times over the next forty years. A life of continuing occupational adjustment will mean a life of continuing education to meet changed or additional educational requirements.

Here, flexibility becomes a factor in the school's response to the world of work. For example, subjects might be taught for one week or ten weeks, one year or three years, day or evening, in courses not necessarily coinciding with the academic term or taught by a person with three published articles to students working for degree credit. Robert Weber, pointing to the upgrading of skills with each change of occupation, says that "education must become more modular (less dependent on academic time and status) and that man must go through life with the educational umbilical cord uncut." [30]

Education of women. The education of women for the world of work poses special problems for the years ahead. The need in this area is not the same as that of older workers or youth: one does not find substantial numbers of women on the unemployment lists, the social and psychological implications of a woman not working are not so grave, and the shortages of personnel in most of the subprofessional fields in which women traditionally work are not so acute. On the

[30] Weber, Robert. "Man and His Environment—1980." Background paper prepared for the annual meeting of the Board of Trustees of the Educational Testing Service, May 7-8, 1963. p. 27.

other hand, the movement of middle-aged women from the home to outside employment can be expected to continue; projections indicate, for example, that the number of women over forty-five in the labor force will increase by 30 percent during this decade.[31]

Women have traditionally found employment in the clerical, sales, light manufacturing, and service occupations. But in light manufacturing, employment opportunities will be fewer; the long rows of women soldering circuits on the electronics assembly line will be replaced by automated circuit-printing machines. Many of the jobs in the service fields are too low-level for the better-educated women now seeking reemployment; many other service functions are increasingly subject to automation. A similar situation exists in the clerical and sales fields: these jobs too frequently fall below the ability and aspiration levels of women entering the labor force, and, despite government figures predicting many new job opportunities in these occupations, the matter is increasingly one of doubt.[32] In short, the future of women in the world of work may increasingly be subject to the dislocations already apparent among other working groups.

Therefore, serious attention must be given to the education and employment of women. A significant breakthrough in this regard is certainly called for in the professions, many of which remain male preserves; similarly, the woman college graduate often finds her education is of little avail unless she possesses clerical skills. These employment barriers (plus other factors) continue to keep high-ability women working at low- and middle-level jobs, jobs that could be filled by women with less education and fewer skills. At the same time greater educational and employment opportunities for women must be made available in the technical occupations, many of which are eminently suited to the particular abilities of women.

Cutting across occupational considerations is the need for educational updating, training, and retraining opportunities

[31] The Bureau of Labor Statistics projects that 34 percent of the labor force in 1980 will be women. *Manpower Report of the President,* April 1968. p. 301.

[32] See, for example, Michael, *Cybernation: The Silent Conquest.* pp. 14-17.

for women. Given opportunities, many women, who have already had considerable education, could find job entry on the technical level or could become greatly needed aides in teaching, health, recreation, and the social services.

Education of Negroes. Almost any of the problems already discussed could be multiplied by a factor of three to arrive at a fair picture of the size of the problems of the Negro worker. The U.S. Department of Labor reports that during 1962 about one out of four nonwhite teen-agers in the labor force was unemployed, compared with about one out of eight white teen-agers. Since 1955, the jobless rate among Negro youth has risen twice as fast as among white. Nonwhite girls have a much higher unemployment rate than any other group in the entire labor force. Only about one-fifth of the young Negro workers with a high school diploma have white-collar jobs; more than one-half of the young white workers have such jobs.[33]

These national averages obscure much uglier situations in many of our large cities. Although a near-total neglect of this problem makes statistical analysis difficult, the pioneering *Unemployed Out-of-School Youth Survey* highlights how tragic a situation may exist.[34] This survey of 1,200 youths (aged sixteen to twenty-two, and involving more than 9,000 separate household contacts) in a Negro district revealed that 63 percent of the out-of-school youths were unemployed, a situation undoubtedly duplicated in other ghetto sections of large cities in the United States.

The Negro population holds an extraordinary disproportion of lower-class jobs. Comparing only nonfarm workers, one out of three white workers is classified as unskilled or semi-skilled, but three out of four Negro workers are in this category. With jobs at this level shrinking, the employment gap between whites and nonwhites is bound to become even more pronounced.

Other figures emphasize the gravity of the Negro employment problem and underscore the point that the Negro is

[33] U.S. Department of Labor, Office of Manpower, Automation and Training. *Young Workers: Their Special Training Needs.* Washington, D.C.: Government Printing Office. pp. 9-11.
[34] Cleveland Public Schools. *Unemployed Out-of-School Youth Survey.* Cleveland, Ohio: the Schools. pp. 8, 12.

losing ground in the occupational area. Bell, in discussing the postindustrial society of the future, says that, with education now the chief means of social mobility, we can sketch a rough picture of the nation thirty years hence by charting the kind and level of education each group is receiving and matching it against future labor force skill requirements: class lines in the United States will be predominantly color lines.[35]

No one can deny the fact that the greatest threat to our nation at the present time is the division between blacks and whites. Leaders of the early sixties in the black communities have been replaced by more militant leadership. Black leaders today demand cash reparations, a guaranteed percentage of blacks in all occupational fields, and job guarantees for their people. Again and again the color lines have been drawn mainly on the basis of jobs.

Unfortunately, the educational and skill level of blacks continues below that of whites. Until the quality of education and vocational training is available where needed most, this could continue to be our greatest national tragedy.

The present situation demands that much greater efforts be devoted to Negro education and employment. Equal employment opportunities must be made available. The high incidence of school dropout among Negro youth must be cut. Equally important is the necessity of providing opportunities for occupational education through the schools and colleges.

The federal-state cooperative program. Since 1917 the principal vehicle of subprofessional occupational education has been a federal-state cooperative program of vocational and technical education. It was originally a high school program until amendments channeled some federal money to the two-year college level.

Between 1950 and 1960 secondary school attendance in this country increased some 50 percent. During this same period enrollments in the federal vocational-technical program rose 10.7 percent. On the high school level, only 6 or 7 percent of all students were enrolled in full-time preemployment courses supported by the federal program. Only some 5 per-

[35] Bell, Daniel. "The Post-Industrial Society." *The Impact of Technological and Social Change.* Boston: Liberty Mutual Insurance Co., June 14, 1962. (Multilithed.)

cent of all junior college students were enrolled in the federally supported technical education program. *Only 2 percent of the 12 million full-time high school students in this country were enrolled in the program's vocational trades and industry division.*

Since 1960 there has been a shift toward a larger enrollment in vocational education. Total enrollment in secondary schools has increased over 40 percent between 1960 and 1969. Vocational enrollment during this same period has nearly doubled. Postsecondary enrollment has increased nearly 500 percent and today includes almost one-half million students. This growth represents a major shift, yet the total vocational enrollments, excluding home economics and agriculture, is less than 15 percent of the total high school and postsecondary enrollment.

Money available. Over the past decade the national expenditure for education increased by about 170 percent. The increase in federal, state, and local expenditures for vocational and technical education was 87 percent. Thus, this form of education, never well financed, has been getting a diminishing portion of the national expenditure on education.

In 1960 the federal expenditure for vocational education was $45 million; in 1966 it had risen to $234 million. The Vocational Education Amendments of 1968 authorized expenditures of over $900 million, and the House of Representatives passed an appropriation of $488 million for vocational education. The budget for 1969 was $248 million, and for 1970 it is $279 million with support for regular vocational programs at the 1969 level.

It is fair to say that federal policy has consistently been to reject vocational education as a viable way to solve national problems. This policy has continued in spite of two presidentially appointed task forces during the 1960's which studied the problem and recommended major action to expand this program many times over. The response to the need for vocational education has come mainly from large increases at the state and local levels.

The vocational track. Vocational education has a dual purpose: to provide the people it serves with an education *and* to train skilled workers for the labor force. The fact that the program often does *neither* of these things well has made its acceptance by industry and education all too often lukewarm.

Although the major effort in vocational education is conducted within the public education system, its place within that system has never been clearly defined. Administrative regulations tie it to education's standards and practices, but practical considerations force it to look to industry for its curriculum and teachers. Achievement in vocational subjects may be dependent on achievement in academic subjects, but the two are usually taught without reference to each other. In a great many school systems only those students who appear to have no hope at all of getting into college or who are independently determined to study vocational subjects are guided to the vocational school, which is likely to be labeled "of lower quality," partly because of the students it receives and partly because of a perverted definition of *quality.*

Finally, though the learning process is by no means reserved to the academic subjects, learning outside these subjects, and especially that obtained in vocational subjects, often finds little recognition. Once a student elects a vocational curriculum, he may be foreclosed from continuing his education in another field; credit for his learning in the vocational area will not be given. His alternatives then are to go back to school for a year or two and take the approved courses or leave school. In many states, vocational schools have found that the only way to avoid this dilemma is to burden their students with one or two hours of extra class work each day, so that the students obtain the full load of academic subjects required by the state for graduation and by the colleges for admission. Needless to say, the lengthened school day does not bring students flocking to the doors of the vocational school, particularly when it may mean their giving up after-school jobs or extracurricular activities.

The election of a vocational program, since it is not the approved form of preparation for further liberal or professional studies, will often severely limit the student's chances of getting into college. For many students a vocational program in high school represents a closed-end track: since this form of education occupies an ambiguous, peripheral position on all educational levels, there is no clear and acknowledged path to specific occupational goals running up through the secondary and collegiate levels. Vocational subjects may be elected at any stage from the tenth grade on, but there is no logical progression leading to a post-high-school or collegiate degree or potential further study.

It is only in the past few years that voices are beginning to be heard regarding the basic problem of learning versus education. The 1968 Amendments to the Vocational Education Act of 1963, the voice of youth, and the obvious failure of our three-hundred-year-old curriculum to function today are all creating a new understanding. Most of all, the possibility of the creation of a dual school system because our present one has not changed to serve all people and the new needs of society brings about serious thought—even action.

Stanley Ruttenberg, former assistant secretary for manpower in the Department of Labor, said it well:

> I believe it is time that we ended the artifical cleavage between vocational education and so-called academic education. All of our citizens require education to function effectively as citizens and to realize their potentials as human beings. Moreover, we know that literacy and the basic skills which should be developed in any educational process are also necessary for people to learn work skills properly and to advance in their jobs.
>
> We also regard it as nonsense to have an imaginary line separate the individual's academic education and his participation in his life's career. Academic education would be enhanced, not compromised, if vocational preparation were introduced into our general school system. Moreover, an increase in vocational education might help to end the false hierarchy of values which educators have consciously or unconsciously introduced through their treatment of vocational education, the notion that preparation for a life career is a second-class activity for second-class citizens.[36]

First-job preoccupation. It is an open question whether present forms of vocational and technical education are equal

[36] Ruttenberg, Stanley. "Manpower Training—The Seeds of a Dilemma." *Manpower,* January 1969. p. 13.

to the demands of a changing world of work. As mentioned earlier, swiftly changing job patterns mean that the subprofessional person must look forward to five or six occupational shifts over the next forty years, so that continuing education will increase in importance. In addition, the more cognitive work functions to be performed will demand higher levels of related knowledge and general education, and the anticipated shorter workweek means that more attention will need to be paid to the use of leisure time and to the potential for greater civic participation.

The high degree of specialization found in many vocational and technical curriculums appears to be misguided. High school students in the federally supported vocational trades and industry program, for example, must spend a minimum of 50 percent of their time in shop work alone. In many technical curriculums only 10 percent or less of the school time is allotted to general education subjects. Indeed, the difficulty of placing young people in jobs today, with the premium going to the person who can step into the job with the least amount of company instructional time, seems to act as an inducement to vocational and technical schools to concentrate on the expertise needed for nearby job openings. These schools pride themselves on how closely their shop facilities duplicate real job conditions, and many of them do have excellent first-job placement records for their graduates. But this does not necessarily mean that the school has given the graduate the education he may really need. What is called for is more and better occupational education, to be sure, but occupational education on a more general basis—devoting more time to the development of broader technical understanding, of communication and computational abilities, and of appreciation of civic, cultural, and leisure activities.

This is more easily said than done. The preoccupation of many vocational and technical education programs with first-job placement is in part the result of inadequate understanding between education and industry. Many schools offering these programs simply do not have the academic resources to give their students the related knowledge and general education background they need, nor do teachers and administrators in related and general disciplines have the interest or inclination to help vocational and technical educators design the special courses that may be needed. At the same time that the vocational and technical school perceives that its program must develop broader occupational and civic understanding in its students, the personnel officer at the local plant is asking graduates of the program, "What job can you do?" and the foreman complains, "This kid fouled up my machines!" on his first day on the job. This points to the need for occupationally oriented schools and business and commercial interests to maintain close and continuing relationships.

An appropriate division of labor is called for between education and industry, with education doing what it can do best (educate more broadly for a life of work and citizenship) and industry doing what it can do best (train for a specific job). Such a relationship already exists in engineering: educators in the various disciplines have paid considerable attention to the improvement of the liberal and related knowledge content of the engineering curriculum, and industry has accepted the necessity of spending a longer time breaking in the recent graduate. This relationship must be extended to other occupational fields, particularly the technical and semiprofessional. But only with new status and acceptance within both education and industry will this be possible.

The 1968 Vocational Education Amendments take full cognizance of this problem. The former requirements for expenditure of funds in certain specific occupational areas have been abolished. Special funds have been authorized to expand cooperative education which allows contracting by local educational institutions for specific on-the-job training and instruction by employers.

The term "vocational education" means vocational or technical training or retraining which is given in schools or classes . . . and such term includes vocational guidance and counseling (individually or through group instruction) in connection with such training or for the purpose of facilitating occupation choices; instruction related to the occupation or occupations for which the students are in training or instruction necessary for students to benefit from such training; job placement; the

61

training of persons engaged as, or preparing to become, teachers in a vocational education program or preparing such teachers to meet special education needs of handicapped students; teachers, supervisors, or directors of such teachers while in such a training program; travel of students and vocational education personnel while engaged in a training program; and the acquisition, maintenance, and repair of instructional supplies, teaching aides [sic], and equipment . . . .[37]

National versus local needs. Vexing problems arise in attempts to gear vocational and technical programs to the present and future world of work. On the one hand, the choice among occupational offerings is in the hands of local boards and administrators, who are under pressure to tailor the program to the more immediate manpower needs of local (taxpaying) industry. On the other hand, the industrial complex of the nation is being made and remade so swiftly and plant and worker mobility are so high that narrow, local training may have short relevance for the new worker. This again points to the importance of a more broadly based vocational-technical education, one consonant with long-term regional and national manpower demands.

Lag. The lag between what is taught in the school and what is actually practiced in industry constitutes a related problem. The school that invests heavily in shop and laboratory equipment in an attempt to duplicate industrial conditions soon learns it cannot afford the constant replacement that industry finds necessary. This constant falling behind—due to become even more pronounced in succeeding years—invites institutionalization of obsolescence. Elimination of such instructional facilities would probably make vocational and technical programs too academic or theoretical for the tastes and aptitudes of many of the students they serve. There are no easy answers to this problem. Certainly much new thinking must be devoted to vocational and technical pedagogy, a realm visited by very few educators for a great many years. Perhaps the time has come for the educational community (with its overall experience in matters of teaching and learning) and

[37] The 1968 Amendments to the Vocational Education Act of 1963.

industry (which has many of the facilities to do the job) to reexamine their long-standing antipathy toward involvement in such questions.

Prestige. The problems in vocational and technical education are compounded by the present program's low prestige. Its students too often are the dropouts or castoffs of the academic curriculum. Its teachers, often less academically oriented, enjoy relatively low status within the teaching profession in many states. Its buildings are often the oldest, its facilities the poorest, its extracurricular programs the weakest. Its subject matter suffers from the general debasement of manual and blue-collar occupations in contemporary social values.

The low repute of a program is harmful in many ways: good students shy away, teachers are difficult to recruit, industry remains standoffish, other educators show little interest, and money is difficult to come by. Vocational and technical educators, faced with the dangers of indifference to or suspicion of the program, often devote more time to self-protection than to self-improvement. It is pointless to argue who is to blame. A step forward would be national recognition of the real importance of this field within the scope of the total educational effort needed for the years ahead.

Again the 1968 Vocational Education Amendments truly speak to this question not only in terms of money authorized but in broadened programs. Yet, the problem of prestige will remain until the educational community, at all levels, makes preparation for a work role a real purpose of education; evaluates its success in term of placement in a job which matches the student's potential for earning and learning; and provides the necessary time, money, and personnel. Prestige and status come from what people do, especially important people in the order of society. This problem has been spelled out by the National Advisory Council on Vocational Education:

> At the very heart of our problem is a national attitude that says vocational education is designed for somebody else's children. This attitude is shared by businessmen, labor leaders, administrators, teachers, parents, students. . . .

63

The attitude infects the Federal government, which invests $14 in the Nation's universities for every $1 it invests in the Nation's vocational education programs. It infects State governments, which invest far more in universities and colleges than they do for support of skill training for those whose initial preparation for the world of work precedes high school graduation. It infects school districts, which concentrate on college preparatory and general programs in reckless disregard of the fact that for 60 percent of our young people high school is still the only transition to the world of work. It infects students, who make inappropriate choices because they are victims of the national yearning for educational prestige.

The attitude must change. The number of jobs which the unskilled can fill is declining rapidly. The number requiring a liberal arts college education, while growing, is increasing far less rapidly than the number demanding a technical skill. In the 1980s it will still be true that fewer than 20 percent of our job opportunities will require a four-year college degree. In America every child must be educated to his highest potential, and the height of the potential is not measured by the color of the collar. Plumbers, carpenters and electricians make more than many school superintendents and college presidents; only the arrogant will allow themselves to feel that one is more worthy than the other.

We recommend that the Federal government immediately exercise its leadership and allocate more of its funds to cure our country of our national sin of intellectual snobbery.[38]

Teachers. The recruitment of competent teachers is especially difficult in vocational and technical education. Teachers in this area, particularly with the program's present emphasis on shop instruction and job expertise, must have a high level

[38] U.S. Department of Health, Education, and Welfare, Office of Education. "First Annual Report of the National Advisory Council on Vocational Education." Vocational Education Amendments of 1968, Public Law 90-576, July 15, 1969.

of job knowledge and experience. But the good skilled craftsman or technician can earn far more in industry than he can within the present salary scale of a public school teacher.

Only within vocational agriculture and home economics do the colleges graduate a good number of people each year who are qualified to teach these subjects. In other vocational and technical areas the problem is acute. The most common "solution" has been to take the willing craftsman or technician (often an older worker whose earning power in industry has become limited), run him through three or six credits of education courses (for teaching techniques), and put him in front of a class.

This creates some difficulties: the new instructor's subject matter knowledge tends to be circumscribed by his job experience. That experience may include little acquaintance with the related skills and knowledge that should be taught. The instructor may not have had much formal or informal education in mathematics, English, speech, industrial relations, or civic and cultural matters. Then, too, he may not be abreast of newer thinking in his field. By the same token, once he settles into the teaching routine, he tends to be isolated from newer developments in industry, for he will find few opportunities or publications to update his knowledge.

The assumption has been that it is better to convert a journeyman into a teacher than to have a teacher acquire the necessary job skills and related knowledge. Perhaps within the present situation this assumption is warranted, at least to the degree that shop-oriented instruction does require shop-oriented instructors, and that such instructors may have greater empathy with their students than the person who has never worked in a production job. However, the future role of shop- and lab-oriented instruction and the potentialities of a work-study program of teacher preparation suggest that, cooperatively, higher education and industry could bring about important breakthroughs in vocational and technical teaching. This is particularly true of teaching on the technical and semi-professional level, where content and level of instruction lessen the experience and empathy factors.

No final answers are available, but the expansion and improvement of vocational and technical education are heavily dependent on some resolution of the teacher-training question. This cannot and will not happen through the efforts of people already in the field; higher education in particular must assume leadership in the preparation of vocational and technical teachers.[39]

Guidance. The present inadequacy of guidance activities is illustrated by the fact that close to half of the states receiving federal funds for their programs spend less than 1 percent of that money on occupational guidance and counseling. The problem begins in college-oriented high school guidance departments, which too often are staffed by people who have neither the knowledge to help students select an occupation nor the inclination to direct them toward the appropriate vocational or technical education opportunities. It continues in the vocational or technical school; although no other segment of education has recognized the importance of vocational guidance to the extent that these schools have, lack of funds, reliable testing materials, and appropriately trained vocational guidance counselors limits what the vocational and technical school is able to do.

As indicated earlier, the occupational life of the young person will be largely determined by the kind and level of education he receives. Student decisions are therefore crucial ones. They will, in effect, determine whether vital manpower needs will be met, whether human resources will be equal to economic potential. Further, the student's decision about his education will to a large extent define his future occupational role. But student knowledge of the world of work is today quite circumscribed, inasmuch as most work situations are unseen by and unknown to young people. Only proper guidance within the educational system can direct the necessary numbers of qualified people into them.

It is also important that once the student is placed, the bond between the school and the worker be maintained; the

[39] Title II—Vocational Education Leadership and Professional Development Amendment of Higher Education Act of 1965 of the 1968 Vocational Education Amendments speaks to this problem. It provides for leadership development awards; exchange programs, institutes, and in-service education for vocational education teachers, supervisors, coordinators, and administrators; and for familiarizing teachers with new curricular materials. It has yet to be funded.

66

school must alert him to opportunities for continuing education and updating and must be prepared to reeducate and re-enter him into the work world as technology makes this necessary. Such a continuing relationship between the institution, the graduate, and his work career already exists in many of the better professional schools within higher education. It must be extended to a broader range of occupations.

Loss in human dignity. This nation can no longer tolerate the loss in human dignity and the financial burden of thousands of persons unemployed because they lack the academic and vocational skills required for employment. Underemployment of thousands of workers in the labor force remains a serious problem. These workers must be upgraded through education and training to raise the quality of the country's manpower as well as to meet manpower demands. Changes in our educational system that place more emphasis on the concept of learning for earning are a must. With a plan and with support, vocational education can lead the way.

2. Education and a Technological Society

Man's knowledge or lack of it, his view of what is and what should be, as well as his fears, his basic assumptions about life, the past and the future all become the framework within which he structures his social institutions. As knowledge increases, as unknowns become known, as the future becomes the present, and as new knowledge is applied in the service of man, things change.

Yet man's social institutions tend to persist, in fact, even to resist change, mainly because it is much easier for people to hope that things will get better than to do things that will make them better. Social institutions are formed because of people's needs and "stay on" because people don't know what future needs will be or because they still serve some, if not all, of the people. Formal education is structured in social institutions—schools.

The next three decades, or less, will determine if our educational system will change enough to serve all of the people and the manpower needs of a nation which has little use for the uneducated and unskilled. Or will another social system or institution replace the schools as the instrument of education for many of our citizens? Can the schools change fast enough to serve those persons in our society whom they do not now serve?

Scarcity

One hundred years ago our educational system was pretty well established. The decision had been made that education was a responsibility of the states when the U.S. Constitution was adopted. The most basic situation that man faced was a scarcity of food, shelter, warmth, and protection from the elements. It was understood that some people would always be poor and hungry since scarcity was a condition man had always known and his social institutions had accepted. The Bible said that the "poor will always be with us." Starvation, plagues, disease, and early death seemed to be conditions over which man had little control. Causes were often attributed to the supernatural, to man's failure to observe proper mores, or to his inability to prevent these disasters by himself.

Most of the people in the United States were engaged in securing food and preserving, preparing, and storing it for times when it would be scarce. Most families produced, stored, and prepared their own food. This is still true in most parts of the world.

The work force of the nation was engaged in the production and processing of food, shelter, clothing, and heat-producing materials. Food and fiber were the object of most of man's work. The man who didn't work or couldn't work efficiently was not likely to share in the amount available.

Even with all these efforts, many people got a much smaller share of the necessities than did others. The basic assumption by society was that there was not enough for everyone. Man had always known and would always live with a condition of scarcity. The major social question then was, "What is each man's fair share?" The greatest problem society faced was how to divide among everyone an amount that would never be enough for all.

Some of the more common beliefs or assumptions of the time were these:

1. Success was primarily measured in terms of the amount of material things a man could accumulate—money, property, slaves, buffalo hides, crops, animals, buildings, or mineral claims.

2. The man with a large family would most likely be successful because his sons and daughters could provide the manpower to produce and fabricate foodstuffs or fibers or work to provide income to support the family, including grandparents, in-laws, and dependent or handicapped relatives.

3. The best security a man could leave to his family was property or money.

4. Everyone would do well to look out for himself and his own first.

5. Folk heroes, such as Paul Bunyan and John Henry, were developing. They produced more than other men through muscle power.

6. Work was a condition of man—six days a week, ten hours a day. If a man wanted a larger share, he worked longer or put his children to work at ten, twelve, or fourteen years of age.

7. Muscle power was the prime producer of goods, food, and shelter.

All these beliefs were concerned with obtaining a fair share of the necessities of life. Laws protecting property were generally passed early and enforced strongly. Horse thieves were hanged. Thieves had their hands cut off. Men were shot for stealing irrigation water. Material resources were protected better than human resources since there was a limited amount to go around.

It was during these times that our schools and other major social institutions were structured and formed. Political units were established—states, cities, counties, school districts. Economic institutions were begun—taxes on land and personal property, permanent title to property, and financial institutions like banks and savings and loan groups. The condition of scarcity dominated man's consideration of social organization and structure, including his educational system.

Stability

The other condition which dominated society one hundred years ago was stability. Basically, change was yet to become a factor in man's life. People were still talking about one person being able to read all that had been written; much of the world was still little known; man's efforts were still used almost entirely to secure the necessities of life.

Man's experience led him to believe that things would be the same for his children as they had been for him and for his grandparents. Food and fiber were still produced, harvested, and processed as they always had been. Transportation, in terms of the speed with which man could travel, was essentially the same. The same diseases, the same remedies, and the

71

same treatments were in effect. The same sources of power and energy were used, namely, animals and men, and the same methods of communication were in use—the spoken and written word. Man had the same goals his ancestors had—freedom from want, from fear, and freedom of thought. The same kinds of work were carried on as had been for centuries. The separation of nations and of people from people were the same. All of man's history and experience tended to verify the constancy of his environment.

There was a constant search for the right way—the right system of education, the right system of politics, the right religion, the right system of economics. All men sought the absolute, because if it were found, it would be good forever. There was also a search for the man who knew—for the individual who had the answer and the system that would work. It was in this environment and under these conditions that our educational system was established.

The greatest breakthrough, insofar as education was concerned, was the Constitution and the Bill of Rights, which proclaimed that the power to govern rests with those who are governed. Educated citizens, people who could read, write, and compute, were needed in order that they might govern themselves wisely and select the best men (those with the right answers) to govern. It was not assumed, at the time our system of education was formed, that everyone should be educated. Education was restricted to those who had the power to govern, and this was defined by selected voting privileges. How this affected the structure of education and its role today will be discussed later. The seeds of revolution were planted, though, when our nation determined that free public education had a role in the welfare of the country.

Abundance

Abundance occurs when an increase in production of material goods creates a problem while at the same time reaching one of our historical goals of a greater share of goods for every man. Abundance raises other issues. Each man, especially the poor and undereducated, develops rising expectations. Differences between those who have and those who have not become more evident. Poverty becomes relative. Abundance

72

portends a "good life" for all members of society. The conditions that man has lived with "forever" have changed.

In our society we know we can produce, if we so will it, the necessary food, clothing, and shelter for everyone's needs. The question has changed. It is no longer, "What is each man's fair share?" The question is, "How does each man get what he needs?"

Our abundance is illustrated by the following examples:

1. Payments of public funds are made to farmers to reduce their production of food.

2. Steel production is kept below capacity, because it cannot all be used.

3. Production of automobiles is stopped each year, because of unsold inventories.

4. Stores and shops are filled with food and clothing that people can't purchase.

5. Vacations are longer and the workweek has been reduced.

6. A growing percentage of individual income is spent on nonessential things.

7. The poor finally have a stake in the production of goods, the organization of society, and the distribution of its abundance.

8. More knowledge has developed in the last ten years than man had developed in all his previous history.

All these conditions of abundance which are so new to man are not easily understood when we reflect that until the past few decades man has lived with scarcity. His methods of solving society's problems have been different. As someone has said, "We still have the answers; somebody has changed the questions."

Change

The other condition which raises new questions is that of change. Change itself is certain from now on, but it may be slow when applied to people. Computer programs can be changed overnight, but it takes time to change a farm boy into a computer programmer, to change a Congressman elected in the 1920's, to change a school board, a teacher, a superintendent of schools born in the early 1900's. It will take even

73

more time to change our social institutions, which were started two hundred years ago, or our financial, economic, and political units, formed over a century ago.

What are the characteristics of our society within this new dimension of change?

1. The majority of work once done by muscle is now done by machines.

2. Food, fiber, and basic production account for a small portion of the total labor force.

3. The majority of workers are engaged in distribution and services.

4. Over one-half the population of the nation is under the age of twenty-five.

5. Crime rates are rising.

6. Pollution of air, water, and cities is creating social and economic problems.

7. People who a few years ago were economic assets are today economic liabilities. Their sense of self-worth is gone.

8. There is a growing sense of fear of "other kinds" of people.

9. Opportunity gaps between the uneducated and educated are getting larger.

10. Essentially there is a growing clash between nineteenth-century thought, which formed today's technology, and societal institutions which are the products of a largely rural, agricultural society of the seventeenth and eighteenth centuries.

11. Most institutions seem to be fighting change.

The rapid progression of development and the increasing application of technology and automation are illustrated by the accelerating rate of change in several common areas. This nation and Western civilization in general (including Japan) have changed so much and so fast in the last decade or two that the result cannot properly be looked at as a change of degree, but as an entirely new factor—a change of kind. The application of science and technology to the agricultural, industrial, and commercial institutions of our society has been so great as to create a revolution in the social, economic, and cultural activities of the country.

This has been essentially a revolution of manpower—a revolution in which the individual plays a role as a necessary and functional part in meeting his needs, improving his life, and being an essential person, a necessary part of mankind. In effect, a revolution of man and his power!

If this concept of change were plotted on a graph, the lower coordinate would represent time—the lower left corner being the beginning of man's history about 10,000 years ago and the lower right corner being the present. The vertical coordinate would be change, represented by a number of factors —the speed with which man moves over the face of the earth, the amount of knowledge he has accumulated, the amount of material goods available, the increased availability of energy, actual change in the nature of work or the population of the world.

We could then see the dimension of change in relation to time and in relation to the last twenty years. The curve would run almost flat along the whole distance of the horizontal axis for about a mile, to a point in time around 1900. It would then swerve upward at an exponential rate for nearly the entire vertical distance to the present, but that seventy years would be represented by 2.5 inches of the line as compared to the previous one mile.

Historically, man has based his educational system and preparation for a work role or an adult role in society on a concept of stability. Changes which occurred took place over a period of generations. Our present adult population was educated with this concept in mind and grew up under those conditions. But the present generation of young people find themselves engulfed in extreme change. We are, in effect, the first generation charged with helping to educate young people to these new conditions of abundance and change.

Historically, man has always seen work as a fundamental part of his life—and he still does. In the past, work was a necessity for nearly everyone, since the major source of energy was man. Eventually animals were added to the power source, yet scarcity still existed for nearly everyone. This kind of work was so distasteful and painful in many ways that it is even today used as a form of punishment in parts of the world and in some states in our country.

Work in the past, in nearly every culture, was the activity that every man had to do if he was to live. Basically, nearly everyone did the same kind of work. Differentiation into kinds of activity, or jobs, was really developed when mechanization began. A person then had a job and traded his specialized efforts for goods and services which someone else produced. Work became institutionalized as part of the ethics and morality of Western civilization. Failure to work became a moral factor as well as an economic one.

The relationship between education and work was very tenuous. The majority of youth received a minimum of schooling and then apprenticed themselves to a profession or often were indentured to a person for a number of years to learn a trade. It was not too long ago that many fathers said, "Son, I hope you get an education so you won't have to work like I do."

The concern of the schools for what kind of work the student did as an adult was not evident in their curriculum or activities. The nature of work in the past was mainly manual, learned on the job, or acquired in many informal ways not related to formal education. In addition, there was generally more work to be done than people to do it. Anyone able and willing to work could find something to do, however meager the return, if he wished to.

Work Today

What one does today is more the badge of his position in society and his future place than at any other time in history. The kinds of work that were done by most people in the past are undesirable from a status point of view. *Farming* has become a term for anti-intellectual work; an unskilled job is not the first rung on the employment ladder, but rather a dead-end. The amount of physical work that a man could do was once a mark of a man, but more often today it is seen as a mark of ignorance and stupidity.

Work is more mental than physical; by 1975, the labor force will contain less than 5 percent unskilled people. At the same time many jobs which require manual skills and physical activity have come to pay better incomes than some white-collar and professional work. Plumbing, electrical work, or some operative jobs pay more than clerical or teaching jobs.

Most parents and public agencies urge young people to stay in school so they can get a job. A recent study showed that in the Boston metropolitan area there were more than four hundred private schools devoted to teaching specific job skills.

These schools ranged from hair dressing, body and fender repair, auto mechanics, typing, and clerical work to computer programming and laboratory technology. The nature of work has changed so drastically that a father today is more likely to say, "Son, I hope you get a good education so you can work."

We have now reached a point where the work force, which acted as a second school system for the majority of our youth, has closed down for all practical purposes. The teacher can no longer advise the young man or woman who isn't interested in school to quit and go to work. Youths without at least a high school diploma or some work experience are not likely to be employed; if they are, it will be in dead-end jobs that are likely to retard their future upward mobility. The profits that used to be made by muscle power are now made by machines which don't tire, don't make mistakes, and produce much faster.

Today, machinery and technology do not lessen the demand for labor, but they demand a new kind of laborer. We must develop a manpower policy that enables people to get and hold these new jobs and gives them the education and skills to move upward and horizontally in the changing world of work. Man versus machines—this hard contest is the nub of the question of manpower policy and educational change today.

Work Tomorrow

In 1940 the typical male worker had 8.7 years of schooling; in 1952, 10.4 years; in 1962, 12.1 years; in 1967, 12.3 years.[1] The U.S. Department of Labor predicts that in 1975 all laborers under the age of twenty-five will have an educational attainment of 12.4 years; those twenty-five to forty-four, an educational attainment of 12.6 years.[2]

[1] U.S. Department of Commerce, Bureau of the Census. *1940 Census of Population.* Occupation Characteristics, Table 4; and U.S. Department of Labor, Bureau of Labor Statistics. *Educational Attainment of Workers.* Special Labor Force Report No. 30, March 1962. p. 509. *Manpower Report of the President,* including *A Report on Manpower Requirements, Resources, Utilization, and Training,* U.S. Department of Labor, transmitted to Congress, April 1968, p. 259.

[2] *Manpower Report of the President,* April 1968, p. 305.

There can be no question that the future will see even larger increases in the kinds of work that require mental skills and education. Walter Heller has said:

It is unquestionably true, we believe, that greatly re-inforced education is needed to press the attack on pockets of long-term structural unemployment that have plagued the economy for a long time . . . . The clearly indicated rise in the requirements for teachers, scientists, physicians, engineers, technicians, and nurses poses obvi-ous demands on education in general and higher education in particular. And increased demands for many special skills create needs for expanded programs of vocational education and for more persons with basic high school education.[3]

Highly developed technology permits no compromise with ignorance. The preparation of workers in a technological society must be of the highest quality. More and more, our lives depend on the performance of informed, skilled techni-cians and other occupational specialists. In hospitals, patients are dependent upon scientific accuracy and upon a competent understanding of techniques by the technicians and nurses. The use of aircraft and automobiles places travelers' lives in the hands of the people who designed and built the machines and those who maintain, repair, and operate them. The water and food we use must be guarded from chemical or biological contamination by highly informed scientists, technicians, and skilled workers. The general well-being and attitudes of our population are becoming increasingly dependent upon teachers, social scientists, and even upon the specialized knowledge of merchandising and distribution—which touch the lives of us all.

Increased application of technology in a society thus auto-matically sets a mandate for an educational requirement. More and more specialized education must be provided for larger numbers of people. Many of the special skills and competencies which must be learned require organized study of basic sciences plus actual work in a learning situation. Examples are the

[3] Heller, Walter W. "Employment and Manpower." *Men Without Work, The Economics of Unemployment.* (Edited by Stanley Lebergott.) Englewood Cliffs, N.J.: Prentice-Hall, 1964. p. 29.

clinical practices for nurses and internships for doctors. Basically, these are cooperative work experience arrangements. Since mistakes caused by ignorance or carelessness can be so serious in these situations, much of the specialized education must be acquired after the individual has become an adult, with mature capabilities for judgment and attitudes of stability, consistency, and responsibility.

Much of the specialized education for nonprofessional, but highly skilled workers must also be provided. This education must be equivalent to a college learning experience and more and more is being described and recognized as nonbaccalaureate specialized occupational collegiate education.

There is overwhelming evidence that our population is sufficiently educable to meet the challenge of the complications of today's world of work. One indication of the general ability of our population is evident from the tests given to all who enter the armed forces. The Army general classification test has been given to hundreds of thousands. Those tested show wide variations in the amount of formal education, but more than half scored higher than many college graduates and even higher than some who held doctoral degrees. More than two-thirds of the high school graduates had scores that were higher than many college graduates.

The increasingly critical shortage of specialized technical and supportive workers, on the one hand, and the evident supply of educable persons, on the other—those who have left high school or who have graduated from high school but who are not pursuing organized programs of education to prepare themselves for careers in a technological society—represents an unprecedented challenge to junior and community colleges. Our traditional Horatio Alger concept of self-determination and our singular emphasis on liberal education requiring a baccalaureate degree or more have been major factors in the failure to provide educational programs for the nonbaccalaureate technician—the specialized occupational person unique to this society.

In 1964, Heller stated several channels of attack on the problem of structural unemployment:

> improved labor market information; improved guidance and placement services; improved programs of ap-

79

prenticeship; strengthened programs to reduce discriminatory hiring and employment practices by race, sex, or national origin; expanded and more effective programs of vocational education, general adult education, and retraining; basic improvements in the quality of our educational system at all levels; measures to enlarge educational opportunities for children of low-income families and minority groups; programs to assist geographical movement of workers; expanded policies to strengthen the economic base and to speed the economic growth of distressed communities and regions.[4]

It is rather disappointing to see how little has been done in our schools to respond to these basic approaches. While some attempts have been made, they have been in the form of technological "gimmicks" which simply try to change the methodology of what is already being done. Few federal programs have really been aimed at a basic change in the purpose or goals of the schools. To put it another way, few changes have been made that would involve new basic concepts of motivation, success, reward, or relevancy to each student's aspirations. In regard to work experience as a learning technique and the nature of what schools must do in the future, President John F. Kennedy made some pertinent remarks:

> The great enemy of the truth is very often not the lie—deliberate, contrived and dishonest but the myth—persistent, persuasive and unrealistic. Too often we hold fast to the clichés of our forebears. We subject all facts to a prefabricated set of interpretations. We enjoy the comfort of opinion without the discomfort of thought.[5]

In the future the nature of work will become more and more the basis for man's place in society, a way to determine his self-worth and dignity, the way in which he contributes to society, and the way in which his unique talents contribute to the total pool of manpower skills that advance society and the general welfare. Work will continue to become less and

[4] *Ibid.*, p. 91.
[5] Commencement address at Yale University, June 11, 1962.

less a process of producing goods, less and less a necessity in order to live, less and less a repetitive application of energy.

The old concept of work as the curse of mankind will be replaced by a concept of work as the way in which the individual can become most creative and contributory. Individuals will be able to choose work suited to their talents, interests, and desires. If this is true, then work as a part of education, and education as a part of man's work success, points to an early and developing marriage of convenience and choice between the two—not a union of force demanded by the economics of the times.

3. Schools Yesterday

This nation was born through revolution. It was begun by a group of different, dissident, unhappy, and generally poor people because society failed to hear their pleas to speak freely and to live the way they wanted. The final break came when the old society refused to allow these people to participate in the operation of that society.

This group of outcasts then proceeded to frame a Constitution and a Bill of Rights which they hoped would prevent government from taking away "self-evident truths" and "inalienable rights" from anyone. Their purpose was to provide guarantees by which those governed could govern themselves —a new concept in societal operation and individual responsibility.

There was long and serious debate about who should be allowed to participate. As we know, the idea was so new that it did not include women, slaves, people who did not hold property, those too poor to pay the poll tax, and others in the society who were "incapable" of being trusted with this much authority. Still, it was a great step forward.

There was considerable debate about the inclusion of education in the Constitution. Those like Jefferson wanted to guarantee this right, but the times and the old federal-state argument prevailed. The fear of government control of the education of the young and the fear of knowledge itself becoming too generally available was widespread. For example, in 1670, Governor Berkeley of Virginia expressed popular feeling by saying: "I thank God there are no free schools and I hope we shall not have them for one hundred years; for learning has brought disobedience and heresy and sects into the world." One hundred years later this fear was still so pervasive that the constitutional convention did not include education even though the major author of this masterpiece of human thought was strongly in support of including it. To this day our Constitution does not speak of federal responsibility for education. It does speak of the general welfare and national defense, however, and in 1958 the national defense was still the best constitutional peg on which to hang federal support for education in science, mathematics, and foreign languages in the form of the National Defense Education Act.

The understanding that those who govern themselves have to be educated and the religious precepts of the young nation—that the Bible was the true source of religious doctrine rather than the church—resulted in a rapidly expanded program of education, as compared to the rest of the world. The goal of the schools was to teach the basic skills of reading, writing, and arithmetic. Slowly science, the study of government, and other social sciences were added. From the beginning Greek and Latin were taught because they were needed in later religious training and in professions such as medicine. The so-called frills and electives which now make up a large part of the curriculum today, i.e., music, art, social studies, and vocational education, were practically unknown in the elementary or high schools prior to the turn of the century.

Surprisingly, in 1910 only 16.2 percent of the population over twenty-five years of age had high school diplomas and 23.8 percent of the population had not completed the fifth grade. In 1930, only 23 percent of those over twenty-five had completed high school; by 1960, about 50 percent of the adults over twenty-five had completed high school.

In 1900, the average number of days attended per pupil was 99; in 1966, this had risen to 164. But educational attainments still vary in the United States; in 1960, the median in Kentucky and South Carolina for those over twenty-five years of age was 8.7 years of school completed, while in Utah it was 12.2 and in Washington, Alaska, California, Colorado, Nevada, and Wyoming it was 12.1.[1] These data are pre-

---

[1] Data taken from U.S. Department of Health, Education, and Welfare, Office of Education. *Digest of Educational Statistics*. Washington, D.C.: Government Printing Office, 1968; and U.S. Department

sented to point up the wide gap in educational opportunity which still prevails in the United States, especially as this relates to adults and their ability to use their education as a path to employment.

Society and the Schools

First, in the past, the great majority of the people spent most of their lives doing mean, manual work, often for more than ten hours a day, six or more days a week. Even children were involved in full-time manual work. The average man had little, if any, use for education; in fact, he had little time or energy even for reading. What reading was done was mainly in connection with the church and the religious activities of the family.

Second, there was little reading material available, and what was available was too expensive for most people. Even libraries were primarily started as resources for the educated and as recreation for the general public.

Third, the relationship between education and work was not even a concept for argument. Education was for those who did not work, for those in law, religion, education, philosophy, logic, and so on. This concept is so much a part of our ethic that in 1962 while I was with the Selection Division of the Peace Corps I had an experience which should be related here. One question on a form to be filled out by all volunteers was, "What kind of work does your father do?" One young man responded by writing, "My father no longer works; he is now a minister, but he used to work as a carpenter."

Fourth, the majority of the work force in the nineteenth century was engaged in the basic industries—agriculture, forestry, mining, and the processing and fabrication of raw materials. Thus, educational pursuits and schooling had to be scheduled to allow people to spend their time in these activities when they could.

Fifth, the population was not mobile or highly concentrated; thus, the structure and organization of education had to be fitted to the lack of transportation and to where people lived.

of Commerce, Bureau of the Census. *Statistical Abstract of the United States.* Washington, D.C.: Government Printing Office, 1969.

Sixth, the chances are that the environmental gap between the uneducated and the educated was greater in terms of aspiration and motivation than it is today. Education was not considered necessary, except for some, and even basic learning was needed by only a portion of society. The homes of the frontier family, the slave in the South, and the miner in Appalachia must have been vastly different from the homes of the doctor, professor, and affluent businessman in the emerging cities.

Seventh, and not least, was that the basic Protestant ethic of work, frugality, and revolt from the "establishment" of the day taught that one could do anything if he tried hard enough.

It was in this climate of thought, conflict of interests, and fears, in an agrarian society with revolutionary ideas, that our schools were begun.

The following principles caused our schools to be formed the way they were and are why they are operating in the same way today.

Education took place when the necessities of the environment allowed it. Therefore, school was held when the children did not have to help plant, tend, and harvest the crops. When the weather prevented adults and children from working, it was time to hold school. This is the primary basis for the school year as it is at present. As industry and business developed, they followed this pattern in terms of employee vacations, meetings, and employee in-service training.

In a democracy almost everyone needed basic education to be a citizen. Therefore, the basic curriculum was reading, writing, and arithmetic, plus certain other fundamentals which were added as times changed and the amount of education needed increased.

Education was essentially the accumulation of knowledge and facts. The best way to achieve this was to have a teacher —a person who knew. Knowledge was then stored only in written form—books.

Most people would spend their lives doing manual labor. Therefore, too much education would be dangerous for some. This situation built into the schools of yesterday the need to "select out." The development of the normal curve as applied in intelligence testing and academic achievement provided an "objective" basis for this function of the school. This principle also emerged in the form of grading systems, examinations for the next level, prerequisite courses, and scholarships.

If too much public money was spent on education, it would reduce the true wealth of the nation. This concept persisted until this past decade and accounts for some of the lag in public investment in some kinds of education, i.e., greater personal costs for high school, college, and adult education rather than greater public expenditures.

A democracy requires equal opportunity for all; therefore the basic curriculum should be the same for everyone. This aided in the adoption of a standard curriculum through high school and led to the problems of status ways to learn and rigidity of programs.

Education was not related to most people's work. Eventually the three R's were recognized as fundamental to most people's work, and there was a goal of elementary education for all. Today the goal is for everyone to complete high school. This concept precluded occupational preparation in the schools, except in the professions.

Work was primarily learned on the job. This was essentially true in the last century, and the development of internships and apprenticeships grew from this basic understanding. There even evolved at this early age the belief that education that was too practical or too oriented toward problem solving was inferior.

Education beyond a basic level was primarily a privilege of the powerful and idle rich. The fear that schools would become egalitarian was the cause for the early funding of higher education with private money rather than public.

The strength of some of these basic concepts can be illustrated by several recent events. When Congress launched its attack on poverty and unemployment, it did not turn to the educational community for help, but instead created new social institutions, such as the Office of Economic Opportunity and the Manpower Development and Training Act, with great emphasis on the use of private industry and on-the-job training. When Sputnik frightened the nation into recognizing the need for scientists, mathematicians, foreign language specialists, and technicians, Congress turned in the other direction—toward the schools—and passed the National Defense Education Act of 1958.

Another example of these principles in action was the New York State Regents Examinations, which were mandatory until the early 1950's. Every high school in the state was required to give these exams to all high school students on the same day at the same time. The results of this exam determined if the student graduated from high school. At the same time, they were given to the junior high school students in the basic courses. This program was changed to make these exams optional, and a student can graduate with either a Regents or a non-Regents diploma.

The net effect of this program was to force a large number of junior high school students not to go on to high school, to force others to drop out of high school before taking these tests, and generally to make the schools highly selective, factual in content (facts can be easily tested), and rigid in curriculum. Another interesting fact is that New York State spends a smaller percentage of state funds than most states on public higher education, although this is changing rapidly.

State examinations were in use in most states until the late twenties and thirties. Generally, these were given at the end of the eighth grade. One who did poorly didn't have to be too smart to see that it would not be wise to continue in school. The European system, which was based on this concept entirely, is now being drastically changed in Britain and in the Scandinavian countries. Other nations also are questioning its value.

Throughout the history of the schools, we see constant pressures to eliminate students, based solely on their ability to do school work and to proceed up the single educational ladder. Teachers were rewarded on the basis of how many students were going on to higher education. It was cheaper to offer an academic and general curriculum, and it required less space and equipment. In general, the entire population did not believe that education for all, to the limits of each person's potential, was a sound public investment. Some people—generally in the academic world—believed that our future really rested on the maximum education of the gifted. If this were accomplished, they believed, it would solve all our problems.

The schools of yesterday were essentially narrow, selective, and rigid because man's society and environment were narrow, selective, and rigid. Today we need schools that are comprehensive, inclusive, and diverse to meet the needs of our diverse human resources and changing environment.

There was a time when merely sending a child to school for a given number of years was enough to prepare him for a future role. Now we know that it is not enough.

There was a time when a young person could drop out of school, get a job, and enjoy a reasonably secure future. Now we know this is not true.

Once we considered education a public expense. We know now that it is a public investment.

Once we thought everyone could have a job if the economy flourished. We know now that education is the only route to employment.

The American dream of each person developing fully, without restrictions and barriers, cannot be accomplished with the schools we designed and built yesterday. The gap between ideals and realities is the problem. The schools helped bridge this gap in the past. They cannot do it today with the same methods used in the past.

The essence of the schools of yesterday was contained in the concept that the order of things was stable, that God or nature prescribed the woes of the world and they were unchangeable. Neither that concept nor the schools that were designed to support it will work today.

4. Schools Today

Success

The success of the American school system cannot be questioned in terms of statistics—the number of students completing high school, the average income of high school or college graduates, the literacy level of the United States, or the number of Nobel prizes won by Americans. In fact, these successes are so well known that most Americans, abetted by the college professors, assume that the highest function of the public schools is to prepare youngsters for college. God help the school administrator who cannot issue a good press release or present a speech on how well his schools are doing this job.

When historians come to write of the great contributions of American civilization, they will surely give prime attention to our amazing public education system. This truly great accomplishment of the United States, not yet fully achieved, is the marvel of present civilization. It is now recognized as the basis for our economic growth, our technological superiority, and our sometimes uncomfortable political leadership role in the world. But the major question today is, can our educational structure adapt and change to fit the future?

In 1787, the Continental Congress passed the Northwest Ordinance, which stated, "schools and the means of education shall forever be encouraged." We as a nation are stronger today because we have honored that commitment. In this nation today—

1. Over 40 percent of all high school graduates go on to higher education.

2. Close to 80 percent of all children in the fifth grade graduate from high school.

3. Nine hundred and seventy-six of every one thousand pupils in the fifth grade complete the eighth grade.

4. Sixty percent of all Americans between the ages of five and thirty-four are in school.

5. More people in this country go on to graduate-level education than in any other nation.

This is only a short list of the successes of American schools. But today, more than ever before, the improvement of education is urgent. Today, for every individual, education is an unfinished task.

Failure

Today, nearly eight million adult Americans have not finished five years of school, more than twenty million have not completed the eighth grade, and close to sixty million have not completed high school. One student out of every four will drop out before completing high school. He will become the last hired and the first fired in today's labor market. Almost a million young people a year will quit school. The major reason they give is that the schools do not interest them, that education is not relevant.

A large percentage of our most able high school graduates will not go on to higher education, and many others will drop out before they receive a degree. The process of going to college in this country is still more closely related to family income than it is to ability. Many dropouts complain that college is not relevant today.

Unemployment of youths with an eighth-grade education or less is four times the national average. Jobs filled by high school graduates increased by over 40 percent in the last decade. Jobs for those with less schooling decreased by 10 percent.

There is an even darker side. In the school year 1967-68, we spent $623 a year per child in our public schools. But it cost $2,400 a year to keep a delinquent youth in a detention home; $3,400 a year for a family on relief; and $4,800 a year for a convict in a state prison. Total criminal offenses against persons per 100,000 population rose from 285 in 1960 to 589 in 1968; offenses against property per 100,000 inhabitants rose from 964 in 1960 to 1,940 in 1968.

On February 14, 1965, Secretary of Labor Wirtz released a report on the nation's first Neighborhood Youth Corps Project in Newark, New Jersey. He indicated that the project cost was $520,000 for 240 enrollees or over $2,000 per enrollee, but the important things are the conclusions which the Secretary said were warranted as a result of the Newark project:

1. The Neighborhood Youth Corps can provide the kind of special, interested attention that schools often cannot provide.
2. Work with the Neighborhood Youth Corps does stimulate a desire to return to school. . . .
3. Neighborhood Youth Corps enrollees perform in their jobs with interest and effectiveness.

All these data are like the tip of an iceberg; we can only see the obvious problems. The big hidden agenda is not seen. The following questions must be asked:

What about the thousands who do not become statistics of failure? Are they involved in work which is challenging? Are they living up to their potential? Have we developed procedures in our schools to measure our effectiveness in helping young people reach their greatest potential?

What about the fact that early childhood education may be the greatest factor in future success, but only one-half of the states have kindergarten, and most compulsory attendance laws begin at seven or eight years of age?

What about the fact that expenditures for education in this nation were 4.1 percent of the gross national product in 1933 and 6.9 percent in 1967, yet the enrollment in public education at all levels more than doubled, especially at the upper levels where actual costs were much greater?

What about the fact that many things youth learned as part of the home, community, and work experience are not now part of his life, yet there is no program to teach these things in our schools?

What about the fact that we spend most of our time and effort in the schools on programs and equipment for those

93

who learn best and give much less time to those who come to school behind the main group?

What about the fact that in the 1967-68 school year, expenditures per pupil in elementary and secondary schools ranged from $314 in Puerto Rico, $413 in Mississippi, and $486 in South Carolina to $1,125 in New York, $943 in New Jersey, and $921 in Maryland?

What about the fact that the curriculum, methods of teaching, individual assistance and tutoring, and special courses are about the same as they were thirty years ago, regardless of the individual student's background, needs for special help, motivation, parental interests, home environment, or level of learning when he starts school?

What about the fact that the school buildings and facilities are used less than one-half the days of the school year and only five hours a day?

What about the fact that the best buildings, newest equipment, best paid teachers, most money for research, and longest school term are for students who also have the most private support for summer camps, learning in the home, best food and health care, as well as parental help?

What about the lag between what we know should be done in the schools and what is actually being done?

Research and Change

Recently, a friend of mine in the field of biological research said that the mistakes of research are not too important when compared to the mistakes of teaching. Mistakes in research only waste money and the results can be thrown away, but mistakes in teaching last a lifetime and even longer.

The amount of money invested in this country for research in education as compared to other kinds of research indicates that not many people believe my friend. The research and development that is done in education certainly does not have much effect on teaching in this country. No doubt most research that is done is expected to create change in the school. Yet little of it has been successful because research by itself does not bring about change. People and institutions change because of new pressures which create a desire to change. Pressure can be either negative or positive. There may be pressure to avoid a situation because it is uncomfortable or unsuccessful, or there may be pressure to achieve new rewards or to develop more pleasant situations. Most educational research has created neither kind of pressure, in terms of quantity or quality. Too often research projects, demonstrations, and experiments are conducted under conditions so unlike the typical school situation that the results don't appear to be transferable to the practitioner. The researcher too often looks for the university, the school district, or the private contractor with the most know-how, the best financial situation, the most research-oriented staff, and the least day-to-day operational problems.

These conditions make it easier to carry out research, but they are not likely to produce relevant results for the school board in West Virginia or Mississippi. Scarsdale, New York; Harvard University; Stanford; the General Learning Corporation; and Litton Industries are not comparable to the school district in Rocky Ford, Colorado, or the elementary school in Harlem.

Most research in education is aimed at doing better what is already being done in the schools. A lot of parents and students feel the schools should be doing something different. What if we do learn to teach math twice as fast as we do now; what will we do about the student who doesn't want to learn math at all?

Perhaps what research needs to look for is a school district that needs to change; one that has little money; one that has high dropout rates; one that has the least chance of writing a good research proposal or knowing how to evaluate the results statistically; but one that says it will put its own money in the program when it has been shown to work.

To encourage change in education we had better invest more research and development money where there is a state and local commitment to change. We can buy the technical know-how to help do the job, but we can't buy commitment from schools that need to change.

More innovative money should be put into the kinds of activities the schools are not doing and have never done, activities which are now being handled by other social agencies as direct benefits to the child.

Perhaps if we learned how to allow all our young people to participate in school activities in such a way that they could see success, they would be motivated to learn. Perhaps if we learned how to help every youth make the transition to a successful adult role, school would become more relevant. Perhaps if we provided volunteer programs where all of our young people had a chance to participate and to give, they would learn more. Perhaps if the school taught some of the skills, habits, and attitudes previously learned in the home and community, it would be relevant.

In the final analysis, there are some things we do know:

1. Individuals learn best when they are successful, when there are immediate rewards, and when the activities are relevant to their short-term and long-term goals.

2. People and institutions change, not because they should, but because they have to.

3. Change occurs when the rewards are obvious to those who run the institutions. In the case of schools, these people are in the local communities, and most of them have been treated well by the schools.

Excellence—What Is It?

When most of us speak of excellence in education, certain things come to mind: Harvard, Yale, hard grading, high tuition, valedictorians and salutatorians, John Gardner, James B. Conant, John F. Kennedy, etc. When others think of excellence in education, their thoughts may be more along this line: new shoes for school, F in reading, unsatisfactory deportment, late bills, the finance company, George Wallace, Stokely Carmichael, Adam Clayton Powell, etc.

Today, the concept of excellence in education, in spite of our great progress, is seen as a hurdle. Excellence may mean doing more of the same, only doing it better. School is too often the social institution which adds burdens to the family and child rather than providing solutions to problems.

Is it not a paradox that today for a youth to receive health care, money to stay in school, work to earn his own way, special educational tutoring, a student loan for college or transportation money, he must prove that he has been failed by the school system or that his parents are failures?

The Sputnik Phenomenon

In 1958 when Russia launched the first space vehicle, the response in this country was frantic. The emphasis in education immediately shifted to the gifted child. Special federal financing of mathematics, science, foreign languages, and technical education was started. Summer programs for the gifted, special classes and courses for the college-bound, and advanced placement programs were begun. There was not a principal, superintendent, or college administrator who did not have a speech ready on new programs for the academically talented.

College entrance requirements were increased; more students failed in college; the national administration proposed that no federal dollars be spent on vocational education, which was considered virtually useless. The nation was so fearful that educators immediately retreated to their former safe position of quality in selectivity.

We may now be rushing in the other direction. Ever-increasing expenditures for job skills, separate and apart from broader education, and occupational flexibility may lead us toward an equally short-range solution to improving the situation for all our citizens.

We have gone through a phase of over-concern for the gifted, followed by a swing to concern for the less academic student. The situation today demands the maximum development of every individual. The mark of excellence for the schools is how well this is accomplished.

College Will Get You to Heaven

Probably the greatest problem we have in education today is the belief that a college degree or even a few months in college will automatically be better than any other possible experience. This simply isn't true for everyone. In fact, many of our most able and academically talented are asking if it is true even for them. The program in the high schools is slanted too much toward college and, what is worse, is based on the concept that college is still another "fact-packaging factory."

Many of the most exciting options available in this age of technology are in areas where talents other than those needed for college are most applicable. The great need for technolo-

97

gists in the health, social services, education, conservation, recreation, and human service fields permits not only a quick entry into an adult role from high school, or after one or two years of postsecondary education, but also allows for future advanced education if desired. Jobs in the engineering and science fields, which require seven technologists for every one professional, offer great challenge and greater options. Income from these new kinds of work is often greater in the early years of employment than it is from many baccalaureate fields. Unfortunately, few of the parents and too few of the counselors in our schools are aware of these careers.

College is no guarantee of a happy career, a successful life, or even a mark of achievement. No student should be counseled to go to college unless his studies will lead to a goal set by that student. It does not have to be a career goal, but it must be one personal and relevant to the student, not to his parent or teacher.

Our intellectual snobbishness regarding college has damaged many young people and is crippling our public school system. We must not continue to delay adolescence for our young people. They must discover a purpose in life earlier if learning of any kind is to have meaning and relevance for them.

Changes in Structure and Organization

If the goal of the schools remains to push as many young people as possible up the next step in the educational structure, there is no need to change, and the statistics prove it. However, to accomplish the goal of educating everyone to their true potential, several new approaches will be required.

The first would be full-time operation of the schools—all year long and much longer during the school day. This would allow students to spend part of their time in other activities, such as work, volunteer activities, and individual study.

The second would be a change in the systems of accreditation of schools and certification of instructional staff to allow schools to plan programs geared to students' needs and goals in terms of individual progress rather than by grade levels. We need to bring into the schools, on a part-time basis, people from the "outside" world—people whose skill and knowledge

98

cannot be provided by the regular teachers. The teachers would become professionals, with technicians as assistants to carry out those specific duties which the teacher does not have the time—or the know-how—to do.

The third new approach would be career educational planning and study. This would require a much closer relationship among parent, student, and school and planned orientation and exploration of career roles for students by adults in the community who could advise and counsel them on options and opportunities.

The fourth would be special services to help the child learn; these would include medical care, dental care, glasses, hearing aids, special tutoring, money to stay in school, and transportation funds for special school attendance. These services must be provided when they are needed, not as remedial or corrective measures which may come too late.

The fifth would involve children in early childhood education as part of the school's services. Where it is necessary to involve parents in adult basic education or special counseling and guidance, such services should be part of the operational structure and organization of the schools. This does not necessarily mean that they would have to be part of the structure of the school itself, but they should be purchased and delivered by the school.

The sixth new approach would be residential education for those youths who may need full-time supervision and care to learn effectively. This may also be desirable in certain areas of the nation where special kinds of education cannot be provided because of sparsity of population.

The seventh would be mandatory involvement of the community in planning, evaluating, and participating in school programs. The specific roles of school personnel and citizens must be defined, discussed, and thoroughly understood prior to this involvement if jurisdictional arguments and conflicts are to be minimized.

Finally, the current concept that all students must be in school full-time during their school career and must not become involved in any other activity, regardless of its learning value, is indefensible. What we must aim for is a great deal more interaction between youth and the rest of society and between the school and other agencies in society. The structure of the school and its organization must be basically changed so that it becomes an institution to serve rather than the sole evaluator of youth.

Emerging Ideas

Because of the problems faced during the sixties, new ideas have developed which will have a major impact on schools today.

In a technological society *every person must obtain occupational preparation during his educational career.* For most, this will occur in high school or in one or two years of post-secondary education; for others, in college; and for some, in professional or postgraduate education.

It would be highly desirable for *all students in high school to have some work experience prior to graduation.* The work experience should be aimed at orientation, exploration, or acquisition of occupational skills, and it should be related to career and educational goals. For some students this experience may take the form of volunteer activities concerned with the civic and social service needs of the community. Present work-study and Neighborhood Youth Corps programs, primarily aimed at providing money to stay in school, should be integrated with the schools and with the learning process. This idea should not be misunderstood. It plans to use work and other activities of the community as a laboratory in which youth can find real problems and situations that require learning and which may motivate them and sharpen their interest in education. It is not on-the-job training.

One of the most popular images of our schools and young people today is that both are on an island—separated from the major problems, realities, and responsibilities of life. The *transition from adolescence to adulthood is one of the most difficult journeys today;* in fact, many youngsters never complete it. The schools today do not help to bridge this gap; they widen it. The year-round school idea is not proposed just to save money in education, but to make all of education more relevant to youth. The year-round school would allow time to develop a closer active relationship between the school and the community. One of the side benefits of this system is the adult-adolescent one-to-one relationship in an individual work or volunteer role which many youngsters no longer get at home or in any other way. It will be necessary to redesign the school in order to utilize it effectively. Yet, this appears to be one of the most hopeful new concepts.

This proposed variety of learning and experiences for youth in a changing society means that all adults will have to add to their education also. Continuing education, or even a more narrow concept of adult education, means that the schools will have to expand greatly their role in upgrading, retraining, and broadening the education of adults in the community. While the colleges and universities now do this for their graduates in the professional fields, the high schools and community colleges will have to become fully available to and be used by the community to expand the knowledge and skills of any adult wishing to learn. The basic new idea is that education ought to be available to any adult who needs it. It is a public investment that would pay off in terms of worker productivity, personal income, and taxes returned to the government.

The nature of work today is so different from work in the past that schools can no longer limit their efforts to traditional education content nor can they provide substitutes for real-life involvement. *Schools today must establish working relationships with business, industry, and other employers in the community.* Not only will this provide laboratories for student work experience, but it will also provide transitions from school to work for many youths. The costs to the employer for expenses beyond the input of the student worker is a legitimate cost of education.

As the demand for more education and specific occupational skills increases, *the development of a new institution, the community college, seems to be a promising idea.* Many argue that we should now have such institutions within commuting distance of everyone. The changing manpower pattern evolves most rapidly in the technical and highly skilled areas, which usually require one to two years of education beyond high school. If these institutions can recognize their true role and contribution to society, that of furnishing a unique kind of education, rather than trying to become four-year colleges, they will serve the people and the nation well.

101

Time spent in school is not any guarantee of knowledge or competence. The range of people and the variety of institutions, resources, and criteria for educational credit is such that many thinkers feel that educational credit should be made available on the basis of tests or demonstrated skills rather than on time served. This idea, if accepted by employers, could revolutionize the educational credit monopoly enjoyed by schools and colleges. It is well known that most employers use educational courses and diplomas as criteria for employment, often with little correlation to the demands of jobs. Time in the armed forces, self-learning, reading, and work experience might all become educationally acceptable if a program for measuring what one has learned, regardless of how or where, could be developed.

Accountability for educational results is probably one of the most difficult areas from the standpoint of measurement. Yet, today, this new idea seems to be interesting many school people, as well as taxpayers. As the demands for more education and the costs of education increase, *the schools will have to find better ways of accounting for the public's dollar.*

Greater federal aid to the states and local education units seems necessary. *The idea of distributing these dollars in a way that will equalize educational opportunity may be the toughest problem before Congress.* The variety of proposals is staggering, but the necessity of accomplishing the job is critical. If a solution cannot be worked out between the legislators and the educators, then it will have to be done through some vehicle other than public education.

The need to lower the age at which youngsters may become involved in certain kinds of work experience is as important as the need for child labor laws. *What may be needed even more is a kind of earner-learner classification so the young person does not have to be either an employee or a student.* Some countries have already created this new kind of classification to facilitate learning both in and out of school.

The Education Gap

Perhaps education's biggest hidden problem is the widening gap between the educated and the uneducated. More people

102

are getting more education, but those who are uneducated find themselves locked out of society in many ways.

There is a gap between the older adult, who finds himself displaced because of technology, and the availability of new work that he can do.

There are gaps between the educational opportunities of the suburbs and the inner cities.

There are gaps between the poor states and the wealthy ones.

There are widening gaps between racial groups, which have more to do with education than with skin color.

There are generation gaps often caused by the differences between the education adults received and that of their children.

There are gaps between the college graduate and the high school graduate which are showing up in terms of attitudes about race, politics, and the future.

There are educational gaps between the academic disciplines.

There are gaps between the practitioner, the administrator, the manager, the planner, the evaluator, and the programmer.

How do we close these gaps? How do we make education truly comprehensive, truly relevant, highly technical, and more specialized all at the same time? The answer comes back to the individual and to his potential, his needs, and his aspirations. There can be no other way.

5. Schools Tomorrow

The new frontier, the future, is in the mind, in the minds of this nation's more than 200 million citizens, and most specifically in the minds of over half the population which is under the age of twenty-five. No exploration of the West, of the ocean bottom, or of the moon can be nearly as complicated or as important as this partially explored asset of man. We still know very little about how a person learns, how memory functions, or how new knowledge is created.

We are constantly amazed, even frightened, by the complexity of our computers, our automated production processes, our space program, our heart transplants, our new inventions, but none of these is as complicated, as delicate, or has as much potential as the mind of a child.

Today all economists, politicians, scientists, businessmen, and educators know that human resources are the nation's greatest asset. In fact, failure to develop the full potential of any single person results in a loss to society, the nation, the state, and the local community. Everyone loses, even you and I.

The only social institution in the United States unique in structure, organization, and management when compared with other countries of the world is our educational system. It is really not a single system, but rather a number of systems held together by the belief in the worth of the individual. It contains a variety of institutions, a variety of approaches and methodologies, and a variety of financing arrangements. Yet it is this conglomerate of systems that is the tool for exploring this new frontier, the future. It is from the minds of the children now in school that will come the solutions to the problems of the future.

105

Francis Keppel, former U.S. Commissioner of Education, said:

The first revolution in American education was a revolution in *quantity*. Everyone was to be provided the chance for an education of some sort. That revolution is almost won in the schools and is on its way in higher education. The second revolution is *equality* of opportunity. That revolution is underway. The next turn of the wheel must be a revolution in *quality*.[1]

The debate continues over the question of equality, which is really far from being achieved, and certainly the debate has really yet to begin on the definition of quality. Quality is the issue around which the schools of tomorrow must be discussed.

The question of quality revolves around the concept that education must prepare students for the kind of world in which they will be living as adults. If education does not do this, it will fail in its purpose, no matter how "well educated" our citizens become, no matter what level of educational attainment is reached.

In the world which is already upon us, the goal of education must be to develop individuals who are open to change, who are flexible and adaptive, who have learned how to learn, and are thus able to learn continuously. Only such persons can constructively meet the perplexities of a world in which problems spawn much faster than their answers. The goal of education must be to develop a society in which people can live more comfortably with *change* than with *rigidity*. In the coming world the capacity to face the new appropriately is more important than the ability to know and repeat the old.[2]

Perhaps one answer to how to teach people to adjust to change and to continue learning would be to have youth participate earlier in the processes of our society rather than exclude them from the real activities of our culture until after they have completed school. It has been said that many of our youth continue to be adolescent until they have completed

[1] Keppel, Francis. *The Necessary Revolution in American Education.*
[2] Rogers, Carl R., as quoted in "On Education," *Kaiser Aluminum News,* No. 1, 1967. p. 22.

their postdoctoral work. After thirty years of preparation, dependent on someone else all this time for food, clothing, and the necessities of life, they are suddenly to become adults.

Has our society created a situation in which our young people are prevented from assuming adult roles, responsibilities, and rewards for such a long period that they are ready to reject our total system? College youth on one end of the scale and disadvantaged youth in the cities on the other end are both asking the same questions: How do we get a piece of the action? Why can't we participate in the decisions, policies, and directions of our society?

One group suffers from an overabundance of education and asks the question, "for what?" The other wants to get some of the rewards of the technological age and are unable to find jobs which will give them real futures. It is interesting that Harvard University and Eastern High School in Washington, D.C., are both centers of student revolts, sit-ins, and riots. Certainly the student bodies are dissimilar in background and wealth as well as options for the future.

Career-Oriented Education

For nearly one hundred years the curriculum in our schools forced students into one of three programs: general, college preparatory, or vocational. In nearly every high school, most students have been urged to select the status road of "college prep," often despite the student's aptitudes, interests, or gifts. Those who did not drop out or were able to put up with mediocrity were assigned to the general curriculum. A few hardy souls, with parents who either didn't care about school for schooling's sake or were wiser than the teachers, chose the vocational program (which was often in such low esteem in the school that its quality was lower than any other program).

In the new technological society of the future, all instruction will have value for occupational purposes. The changed nature of work and the career role that work will play in the future, as contrasted to a job solely for income purposes, could become a basis for study much earlier in the educational experience. The fact that a career in the future will mean several changes in specific jobs or occupations during a lifetime miti-

107

gates against the old concept of vocational skills as sufficient for specific jobs that will last a lifetime.

One of the great American tragedies of the past two decades has been the almost total isolation of young people from effective roles in society. In many ways, public schools have functioned as a mechanism for keeping students disengaged from the major social issues of the age and from the major social activities of the individual—work, responsibility, decision making, and problem solving.

Recent years have witnessed the results of this alienation of youth. Youngsters by the millions have been dropping out of school, and often out of society, as early as the seventh and eighth grades—if not dropping out physically, then mentally and emotionally. One of the most vivid symptoms of this problem is coming to the surface in nearly every community today: rebellion for a greater piece of the action. Youth wants in, and schools and society must find ways to let them in.

This may mean making it possible for one boy to earn enough money while in school to buy a secondhand car. Or it may mean making it possible for another youngster to get deeply involved in helping a handicapped child in the local hospital. Whatever the particulars, it is clear that young people are asking adults to give them opportunities to make direct contributions to society. It is up to the schools to meet this demand.

The schools must design a new approach to the curriculum which will provide a means for the student to render a service worthwhile enough to receive pay or educational credit, a service regarded as necessary by the community, the nation, or mankind. When students are serving, life is no longer meaningless. They no longer feel useless or excluded. They feel responsible and necessary.

Surely in this new, amazing society, we can find a way to relate learning to a contributory role having worth and dignity. It is hard for a young person to gain any sense of participation from the invisible processes of the future. Responsibility comes most quickly when one can see the consequences of one's actions. This implies participation in a vital daily activity.

The most vital daily activity of all adults is work necessary to the functioning of society. To exclude our youth from this activity is to exclude them from the most basic part of society. For these reasons, the school of tomorrow must develop a concept and a program which will make education relevant to the adult role. The most specific relevant activities for many young people will be those in which they work and prepare directly for more mature and advanced work roles.

My argument is for a career-oriented curriculum. Most young people have little knowledge of the kinds of work that will be done when they become adults. The time when youngsters knew about work by casual acquaintance with it in the community is gone. Schools must begin career discussions and orientation at the elementary school level. At the junior high school level, exploration into broad occupational areas should be available to all students.

For example, the health field includes work from the relatively low-skill levels of nurse's aides and orderlies through the increasing skill levels of laboratory technicians, nurses, and doctors. In the future, the number of new jobs can be expected to expand rapidly as new equipment, new diagnostic procedures, new kinds of therapy, geriatric care, nursing homes, and preventive medicine develop new kinds of work. Exploration of educational requirements, relationships between various courses to the career skills needed, helpful training and work experience, and entry-level jobs, as well as ways one can continue his education in order to move up the career ladder, would be most meaningful. There are enough jobs to allow almost any student to choose the health care field as a career. An exploration of the broad fields of social services, electronics, electromechanics, sales and distribution, agriculture, science, humanities, and public service would provide additional bases for educational and career planning. In addition to reading and discussion, visits to plants, businesses, and institutions would be ways of providing understanding and motivation for staying in school.

At the high school level, students should continue investigation into careers, with emphasis on group vocational guidance coupled with work experience for school credit and wages. Volunteer activities related to career choices—such as service in hospitals, schools, government offices, and private organizations—should offer a chance to gain not only information but actual job skills. Everyone needs the opportunity to learn employability skills, such as responsibility, cooperation, taking instructions, being on time, and remaining on the job. More people lose jobs because of the lack of these skills than for any other reason.

Selection of courses and curriculum would be related to the career interests, goals, and aspirations of the student. Courses would still lead to college, vocational programs, postsecondary technical programs, or directly to work, but the reasons for the course work would be related to the individual's goals. (The fact that most students electing the college prep course have no career plans—or, worse, have made no study of career options—tends to make their school experience nonrelevant to their own goals.)

The basic purpose of the career-oriented approach is not to force students to make an early selection of a specific career, but rather to make all young people aware of the options available to them. The school then becomes the vehicle for achieving their goals rather than a prestructured institution to which they must adapt. This approach will be discussed further in a later chapter.

The basic concept is that education for the world of work means fundamentals, adaptability, and skill flexibility. This is what every student needs. We also know that people learn best when they have success, the rewards for their efforts are immediate, and their efforts are relevant to their immediate and long-range goals.

The idea that a general education will suffice in the future is eighteenth-century logic; it does not fit with what we know about the nature of our present environment. In the future everyone must receive occupational preparation and training; the only question is when it should take place. For some it should be in high school; for some, in one- and two-year postsecondary schools; for some, in baccalaureate programs; for some, in professional schools; and for some, at the graduate and postgraduate level.

The dichotomy between academic and vocational education is out of date. All education, to be acceptable, must be relevant. Adaptability to change is as important as initial preparation. The needs and goals of individuals must be the basic foundation of education instead of the present needs of the labor market.

The Year-Round School

As mentioned earlier, the school year was designed for an agrarian society with little mobility and few resources for family vacations. Industry, over the years, has adapted its employee vacation schedule to the operational pattern of the schools. During the past several years, the year-round school has been tried in several places, mainly as a device to lower the cost of education. Generally, it has failed, because it simply extended the period of time in which to carry out more of the same programs. The school of the future needs an entirely different set of criteria. These criteria rest on conclusions which need some explanation.

The nation has lost its physical frontiers, which in the past offered unlimited opportunity to adults and young people. These frontiers needed the brawn and persistence of the unskilled and undereducated. The era that provided the first rung in the Horatio Alger ladder has passed. Nowadays there are few, if any, "janitor to corporation president" stories to be heard.

We are fast becoming a nation of skilled employees. Social and economic forces have demanded a change in perspective and have created an entirely new environment—new insights, jobs, industries, and national objectives. Some examples that graphically illustrate these transformations are the manpower shortages in the skilled and technical occupations, the high unemployment rate during peaks of prosperity, and, of great significance, the difficulty young people experience in entering the world of work.

In our present society most people will have to change occupations four or five times during their lives. Therefore, a long-range policy of preparing individuals with simple, specific job skills no longer makes sense. Yet, specific entry skills are required in order to join the labor force. This is the dilemma, and the challenge, facing educators, labor, industry, and business.

As our nation grows increasingly prosperous, our human resources must be developed to the fullest to ensure that as

111

few of our citizens as possible are left behind. Development can be accomplished only through education, which must include vocational education. This is the link between man and the world of work.

An educated person must have occupational skills as well as intellectual knowledge. Our society cannot survive unless each citizen has opportunities to prepare himself for entry into the work force at some point in his educational experience. *When this should take place is more a function of a person's individuality than of the organizational structure of a system.*

Since a person's status in our society is determined largely by his work role, occupational education is fundamental to every individual's well-being. Occupational preparation must now become a basic part of each person's educational heritage. This concept leads to the following conclusions:

1. Vocational education must become a part of every level of education to assist the individual in making the transition from school to work.

2. Educators must assume responsibility for helping students make this transition.

3. Schools and colleges must make learning how to work a part of their program by providing students with actual work opportunities with the cooperation of business, industry, and public employers.

The year-round school must then offer a whole set of new options:

1. The opportunity to take courses that students cannot get as part of the traditional curriculum. These might include skill courses, such as typing, machine shop, driver training, occupational guidance, guitar lessons, art, speedreading, literature, and a variety of courses to develop specific skills and expand interest areas solely related to the individual's concerns.

2. Specific entry-level skill courses leading to immediate employment for students who need to earn money to stay in school, for those who are leaving school and have not had vocational training, and for those who need work experience as part of their career plans.

3. Specific on-the-job training for money and educational credit directly related to the educational and career goals planned by the student.

4. Specific work experience for money and educational credit to gain employability skills and to explore an occupational area.

5. Career planning opportunities with students, parents, and school staff during vacation periods.

6. Youth volunteer programs for educational credit and activity credits in areas of career exploration or career-related work.

7. Transition from school work throughout the year so the labor market is not flooded with students all entering at the same time—June or July.

8. Specific planning for a continuing partnership between educators and employers. This should provide for an exchange between professionals in education and personnel from the work world during vacation periods which would occur throughout the year.

9. A prevocational orientation period of three weeks for all students, involving observation and work for students who visit plants and businesses as a basis for their career planning.

10. Special seminars, discussion groups, and group guidance related to the transition from adolescence to adulthood. These programs should not be structured or formalized and should be voluntary for students. Outside adults should be used to help broaden the discussion.

11. Opportunities for individual projects and study beyond the regular curriculum in areas of student interest, with teachers or other community adults acting as guides. These should be given credit and recognition by the school. Emphasis should be placed on the creative and "way out" approaches to learning.

12. A plan providing income through work and study in public institutions through the present federal programs, such as work-study and Neighborhood Youth Corps, should be made part of the total school program.

13. A full-time placement office open to all students and operating throughout the year as part of the school's program. These suggestions are presented in the belief that the school of the future must be seen by students as an active aid in helping them make the transition to adulthood. The school must learn to make work a functional part of the young person's

life, as it is now the major part of an adult's life. The school must become a bridge for youth rather than a barrier to his becoming an adult.

Two additional points need to be made. First, the exclusion of most young people from work experience causes them to miss the opportunity for adult-adolescent relationships which can give them a one-to-one contact in which they are responsible, useful, and necessary. The adult in this case treats the adolescent as an adult in the true meaning of the word; the work roles mandate it.

Research needs to be done in this area. It may prove that this kind of relationship is one which young people today have no way of experiencing unless it is part of the educational system. Surely it is needed.

Second, pressure on the schools to change has come solely from the academic community. The year-round school, truly aimed at broadening learning experience, particularly where a partnership with employers exists, could create a new pipeline of pressure on the schools. It might build into the educational system an effective change agent for the future.

Manpower Development

If America is to survive as a free democracy in this new, technological society in which we live, we must thoroughly re-examine our educational philosophy. We must overhaul our educational system and design programs which are calculated to prepare our citizens— and particularly our youngsters—for life in a world of work which demands skilled workers.

. . .

The Age of Technology is here. Its coming signifies a great new era of prosperity and, perhaps, unheard of leisure and luxury for many. But it also has tolled the death knell for the unskilled workers. Our general education high school diploma is no longer an adequate preparation for the skills which business and industry are looking for. It is no longer a ticket to success.

We do not lack for jobs in America. In any newspaper we find jobs aplenty for skilled workers. But we desperately lack adequately trained and educated people to fill those jobs.[3]

The obvious purposes of a manpower policy are full employment for every citizen who needs to work and provision of the necessary manpower to meet the needs of the economy. In 1946 Congress, anticipating the problem of a postwar depression, passed the Employment Act of 1946. This act made the goal of "maximum employment, production and purchasing power a national objective . . . with the assistance and cooperation of industry, agriculture, labor, and state and local governments."

Except during the depression, which spawned the Civilian Conservation Corps and the National Youth Administration, all federal legislation was aimed at improving education in order to provide the manpower necessary for the economy—for example, the Morrill Act of 1862, which made grants of land for agricultural colleges; the Smith-Hughes Act of 1917, which was to prepare agricultural producers, homemakers, and certain trade and industrial manpower; the Wagner-Peyser Act of 1933, which set up the employment service to match jobs and workers; the 1944 G.I. Bill of Rights, which provided education for veterans; and the National Defense Education Act of 1958, which made federal aid available to scientific and technical education.

It is interesting to note that during the whole history of an emerging national manpower policy the emphasis was on education as the development agent. However, the past decade has seen a reversal of this; that is, the emphasis has been on short, intensive skill training with a job as the main goal, even the provision of a job by the government as a last resort.

The provision of short-term jobs by the government as a last resort may be necessary, but the failure to provide a national program to educate and prepare all who need work to fill the manpower needs of a growing economy is inexcusable. Because of the changing nature of manpower needs in a technological society, the failure to prevent the flow of uneducated into the manpower pool or the failure to change the edu-

[3] From an address by Senator Wayne Morse (D-Oreg.), "Education for Jobs in a Technological Society," before the American Vocational Association, Dallas, Tex., December 10, 1968.

cational system so it can educate and train those who lack education or skills is a duplication of the "sorcerer's apprentice."

The relationship between education and manpower development—except in the professional, and now in the technical, areas—has been casual at best. Former Secretary of Labor Willard Wirtz stated the crisis in true perspective:

> Non-college bound youths receive little of the special attention given college bound youth during their school years, in the sense of preparing them for, and finding out where they will best fit into, the world of work. And when a young person leaves school even what little personal concern there was largely vanishes. To be sure, there exist some 2000 public employment offices throughout the country. But in a complicated system of thousands of hiring units, the disadvantaged youth is too often left to find, under his own steam, the job that fits his needs. The question then becomes how he can serve the economic system, not how it can serve him. The concern turns to what qualifications he has for jobs which already exist, not what kinds of job experiences should be structured to fit his needs. If he needs further training, it is up to him to secure that training. If he is younger than the age at which employers hire, it is necessary for him to "wait on ice" until another birthday rolls around.
>
> The Employment Act of 1946 did not distinguish on the basis of educational attainment when it established the National employment objectives. Society's obligations to see that there is an employment connection is the same regardless of how far a young person is able to go through the educational system.[4]

Such testimony led to the conclusion that one of the major purposes of our educational system is manpower development.

Dr. M. U. Enninger, president of Educational Systems Research Institute, prepared a paper for a Department of Health, Education, and Welfare task force on vocational edu-

[4] Wirtz, Willard. Testimony before the Senate Committee on Labor and Public Welfare, Subcommittee on Education, April 5, 1969, pp. 2571-72.

cation in 1969. In it, he attempted to develop a theoretical model of the school's role in manpower development. He called it a Manpower Conversion Model. It is included in the Appendix of this book as a basis for the school of tomorrow to effectively serve its role as a manpower producer.

At the present time, there is no accepted role for the school as an institution of manpower development; consequently, there is little basis for objective evaluation. The theoretical model by Dr. Enninger is presented on the premise that in the future the school's role in this area will no longer be a cause of embarrassment to educators, parents, or taxpayers.

The Best Investment of Public Funds

Prior to the late 1950's, it was generally believed that money spent for education was a cost or net loss to the economy of the nation. Hardheaded thinkers and businessmen were generally in the forefront of the effort to reduce school costs. During this same period, it was generally assumed that the way to increase national income was by capital reinvestment in property and equipment, that is, in factories, machinery, power production, and the hard goods that produced things. Therefore, a reduction in money for schools would provide more funds for those things that would increase the growth of national income.

As a result, in 1967 the United States was spending only 6.9 percent of the gross national budget on education, and the percentage of funds used to research improvements for education could hardly be measured, although business and industry were spending close to 10 percent of their income on research and development.

Modern economists virtually ignored the human resource factor in economic development, but within the last decade a number of economists have returned to look at the concept of human resources, specifically at investments in education. Theodore W. Schultz said in his presidential address to the American Economic Association in 1960:

The failure to treat human resources explicitly as a form of capital, as a produced means of production, as the product of investment, has fostered the retention of the classical notion of labor as a capacity to do manual

117

work requiring little knowledge and skill, a capacity with which, according to this notion, laborers are endowed about equally. This notion of labor was wrong in the classical period and it is wrong now. Counting individuals who can and want to work and treating such count as a measure of the quantity of an economic factor is no more meaningful than it would be to count the number of all manner of machines to determine their economic importance either as a stock of capital or a flow of productive services.[5]

The rediscovery of the significance of human resources and, therefore, education investments by Schultz and other economists has led to more efforts to include investments in education in the body of economic analysis.

The principle approaches have been the following: (1) determination of the relationship between expenditures on education and growth in income or physical capital formation over a period of time in one country, (2) the residual approach in determining the contribution of education to the gross national product (GNP), (3) calculation of the rate of return from expenditures on education, and (4) making intercountry correlations of school enrollment ratios and GNP.[6]

In the late 1950's economists began to examine the assumption that capital investment was the main source of increase in national income. They found that increase in the capital investment volume and changes in the size of the work force accounted for only 15 percent of the production growth in the United States. It is now generally assumed that wages and salaries, rent, interest, and the like are the other factors.

"When the work force of a country receives more education, the corresponding rise in their level of wages and salaries is translated directly into increases in the national income," writes Charles S. Benson. "And so economists . . . are asking what share of the nation's annual rate of growth in

[5] Schultz, Theodore W. "Investment in Human Capital." *American Economic Review* 51 : 3 ; March 1961.

[6] Horbison, Frederick, and Myers, Charles A. *Education, Manpower and Economic Growth*. New York: McGraw-Hill Book Co., 1964. p. 5.

national income can be attributed to educational investments. Current estimates indicate that between 20 and 40 percent of our growth is a result of expenditures on schooling." [7]

The sum of present thinking is that investments in education return at least one-third, or up to one and one-half more than investments in capital goods. Some of the increase is due to higher incomes of better educated people, but part comes from their higher productivity in the labor force.

The choice is between the concept of the prevention of human failure and the development of human resources and the concept of dollar investments in major programs of remediation and correction which come after the individual has failed to receive adequate education or skills. In the long run is it sound public policy to reject a public program—free public education—which is eminently successful for 90 percent of the population for a series of loosely connected programs which basically reject the use of the schools?

When we think of schools for tomorrow, we must think about their role in a total manpower development program. We must consider the school of the future with the conviction that it should serve all students and be successful in educating every child to his full potential and making his transition from adolescence to an adult role a constructive contribution to society.

The Comprehensive School

There may be excellence or shoddiness in every line of human endeavor. We must learn to honor excellence (indeed, to demand it) in every socially accepted human activity, however humble the activity, and to scorn shoddiness, however exalted the activity. An excellent plumber is infinitely more admirable than an incompetent philosopher. The society which scorns excellence in plumbing because plumbing is a humble activity and tolerates shoddiness in philosophy because it is an exalted activity will have neither good plumbing nor good philosophy. Neither its pipes nor its theories will hold water. [8]

[7] Benson, Charles S. "The Rationale Behind Investment in Education." *Education Age,* March-April 1967.

[8] Gardner, John W. *No Easy Victories.* New York: Harper and Row, 1968. p. 66.

The schools of tomorrow must above all become "inclusive" institutions rather than "exclusive" institutions. For too long our schools have had a hidden agenda, based on the concept that it was good if a certain percentage of the students failed. In fact, it has been thought for too long that the "good" teacher failed more than the "poor" teacher.

At one time this concept made some sense—at least while the work force acted as a second school system which took these transfers, entered them in low-level skill jobs, and gave them the chance to work up if they could. Today the work force no longer takes these students. They are left to the streets, the gangs, and the welfare workers.

People say, "The problem is that these students are lazy; they won't try." But literal application of the normal curve says the two at the bottom fail even if the class contains all geniuses. Students do give up. After receiving a report card every six weeks for eight years which says they are at the bottom, they don't have to be too smart to conclude that it is socially more acceptable to be lazy than to be dumb. Someone has said that the report card itself really isn't so bad. What makes it hard is that the parents have to sign the report card, and by signing agree to the facts as stated.

This is not an argument for doing away with failure (it could not be done) or for doing away with failing marks (the system would be false, and everyone would know it). This is an argument for providing options in our schools—areas of study and activity where each student can find success. Each one of us has areas in which we fail, but we would give up if we did not have things in which we could succeed.

At the junior high school and high school levels especially, we must develop activities and options which provide different ways to learn and to be successful. Vocational education is eminently useful because of its methodology of activities—self-study, problem solving, and nonverbal approaches to problem solving.

The school of the future should be truly comprehensive in its student body. It should have a no-reject philosophy insofar as race, color, creed, or previous condition of learning and achievement. It should be comprehensive in makeup and seek a diversified student body because students learn from their fellow students.

120

The school of the future should be truly comprehensive in program options. It should help every student find a curriculum that develops his talents and leads to a career of interest. Some students may go directly to work; others, to one or two years of postsecondary occupational study; and still others, to colleges and universities.

Tomorrow's school should be truly comprehensive in informing the student about the many kinds of career options available. Its programs and guidance should increase the choices available to the student in terms of knowledge about today and tomorrow. Choices should depend on the individual student rather than on the structure of the school.

The future school should be truly comprehensive in the methods available to learn. These include close alliances with other social agencies, business and industry, and with the total adult society.

The school of tomorrow should be truly comprehensive in the ways in which students may contribute to society. Limitations on in-school student activities, such as athletics and debate, must be eliminated and youth volunteer activities covering the whole range of society's needs must be made available.

The idea of free public education for everyone was radical. In practice, it still is, especially if it means the chance for every child to develop to the limits of his ability. A truly comprehensive school is a radical idea, but it would seem to be as natural as our concept of democracy and as hardheaded as the concept of economic growth and an increasing gross national product.

Continuing Education

Perhaps the most archaic term in education today is *graduation,* which is generally thought to mean completion of a certain level of schooling. Historically, it meant one had completed learning and was now ready to begin the process of living. This concept was once so firmly entrenched that many state constitutions do not provide for the expenditure of public funds for education for those over twenty-one. Some states find it extremely difficult to match federal funds for adult literacy programs, because they have not made changes in their laws which would allow state tax dollars to be used for basic education for adults.

Nevertheless, no person in the future, however formally educated, can ever escape the need to learn, the need to grow, and the need to keep up with the exploding quantity of knowledge in every field. An individual citizen's economic stability, personal fulfillment, and social responsibility are enhanced by ready access to educational resources and the opportunity for formalized continuing education.

For most people, continuing education has been a haphazard affair, producing a collection of skills, attitudes, and ideas learned at work, picked up from family and friends, read in the newspapers, seen on television, or pursued unsystematically in some self-designed study program. But self-education has its limitations and, as Benjamin Franklin recognized, some real dangers: "A self-made man hath a fool for a master."

For the world in which we live, most random attempts to educate oneself are inadequate. Few adults can successfully pick their way through the maze of facts and opinions to a learning objective, whether it be to speak English, write a simple sentence, fix a power mower, stimulate community participation in the democratic process, or make effective use of the "new knowledge" which is developing at a prodigious rate in the sciences and professions.

As a result, Americans are turning in massive numbers to systematically organized programs of adult education. Approximately twenty-five million men and women in this country participate today in various kinds of formal programs designed to help them explore areas of knowledge ranging from the practical to the abstract. They do so because they recognize that today's social, economic, and cultural trends clearly dictate the need for continuing education. Any individual who wants to participate fully in the life of his community and to grow in his occupation must absorb a striking array of information to guard himself against personal obsolescence. In addition, the country's continued social and political progress requires an increasingly sophisticated understanding of issues and events by each citizen. The "knowledge explosion" presents dazzling opportunities for individual development—but only to those prepared to take advantage of them.

Adult education (or continuing education; the terms are coming to be synonymous) can bring an extra measure of hope and pride to the disadvantaged adult, deprived during youth of the opportunity or incentive to learn such fundamental skills as reading and writing. Adult education can mean further advancement for the professional man whose knowledge and skills are steadily being made obsolete by the newest thinking and most recent literature. And for all Americans, whatever their level of learning or area of interest, adult education can bring freedom from ignorance and unfounded attitudes; it can enhance values and lead one to a more complete development of his potential for a satisfying personal and occupational life.

There is no time at which to "end" education. There is no point in a person's life when he has accumulated all the knowledge he wants or can use. General recognition of this fact, together with a remarkable response by public and private organizations, has made adult education one of the fastest growing segments of American education.

The school of tomorrow must make continuing education a major beneficiary of the public investment in buildings, facilities, and equipment. In a technological society, we cannot afford the present situation:

Over 23 million Americans 18 years of age and older have completed less than 8 years of schooling. Eight million adults 25 and over have completed less than 5 years. At least the latter and many of the former are likely to be, for all practical purposes, illiterate. Those who have not completed high school are only 46 percent of the total labor force; yet they account for 64 percent of the unemployed. Sixty-two percent of the jobless fathers of children receiving aid to dependent children have no education beyond elementary school. Forty-five percent of all families with less than $2,000 annual income have a family head with less than an eighth-grade education. The link between lack of education and the over $4.5 billion now spent annually on welfare payments to 7.25 million persons is beyond dispute.

123

Yet, of 15,200 school systems studied by the Office of Education, only 4,840 reported any type of adult education programs. Only 160, or 3.3 percent, offered any instruction whatsoever in adult basic education. Of 23 million educationally deprived adults, only 47,500 were being taught basic literacy skills and only 1.1 percent of the limited number of adult education courses offer such training. For the older worker who was deprived of educational opportunity in his youth, the nation as a whole simply has no education system.[9]

In 1966, Congress passed the Adult Basic Education Act, which allocated federal funds among the states to provide adult basic education. By 1968, this program had accomplished the following:

- 62,000 adults learned to read and write for the first time.
- 28,000 registered and voted for the first time.
- 3,500 used their public libraries.
- 87,000 found jobs, received raises, or were promoted.
- 48,000 entered job-training programs.
- 25,000 opened bank accounts for the first time.
- 27,000 became subscribers to newspapers and magazines.
- 8,000 left the welfare rolls and became self-supporting.
- 5,000 helped their children with school assignments.[10]

Adult basic education is the best guarantee of a flexible labor force which can adapt to shifts in the nature of job changes. Without basic literacy the adult is unable to learn the necessary occupational skills required of new, more sophisticated work. The illiterate and undereducated are not only out of the mainstream of society, but are unable to enter that society in an effective way unless they get a basic education.

The educational level of the adult is a highly predictive factor in the child's educational achievement. Continuing education can no longer be seen as competitive with the education of children. It is, rather, a necessary supplement to the education of all children.

[9] Mangum, Garth L., editor. *The Manpower Revolution, Its Policy Consequences.* Garden City, N.Y.: Doubleday and Co., 1965. pp. 469-70.
[10] Estimates based on 1968 annual report of adult basic education programs provided by state departments of education.

The comprehensive school of tomorrow must provide a program of varying educational opportunities for persons with varying educational needs. The following programs can be provided by the public school system below the baccalaureate level:

Adult basic education. This now refers to less than an eighth-grade education, but plans should be made immediately to carry basic education through the high school equivalency. In many cases, these programs should be worked out co-operatively between the school and employers, who would benefit directly from this service to their employees. Classes outside the school buildings—in factories, plants, and public facilities—should be fostered.

Occupational retraining and upgrading. These programs need to be expanded rapidly so that a significant percentage of the labor force is retrained annually. There is growing evidence that one of the most effective ways to retrain people —whether displaced by automation or unemployed because of social or personal disadvantages—is through cooperative education programs. The school develops instruction best suited to the classroom and helps a potential employer develop specific work skills at the job site.[11]

Continuing education for personal enrichment. Because of the increasing rate of change and the growing amount of leisure time, the school should provide a wide variety of courses, lectures, and programs aimed at renewing individuals' specific interests and updating their cultural interests.

Continuing education will become more and more a program of the future, both at the public school level and at the college level. It will build upon and supplement the full-time formal education process of youth. It should have two main thrusts: first, occupational upgrading; second, personal improvement and satisfaction. Activities should vary broadly, both as to location and form, although they generally would consist of courses (credit, noncredit, degree, nondegree); conferences, institutes, lectures, discussions, and workshops; independent

[11] Adapted from Matthews, Howard A. "Tomorrow Is Now." *American Education.* U.S. Department of Health, Education, and Welfare, Office of Education. Washington, D.C.: Government Printing Office, June 1967.

study; counseling and guidance; and on-the-job training and work experience with related instruction. The greatest possibility for success lies in the cooperative development of a continuing education program sponsored by the school and jointly financed and operated by the school, employers, and adult students.

The Problem of Transition

The prejudice in our schools for the college-bound student covers the gamut from special attention given by school authorities to special resources in the form of scholarships, loans, and grants, as well as to Selective Service System preference.

When it comes to assisting students to make the transition from school to a next step, most counselors find themselves spending most of their time writing letters and sending transcripts to colleges. What little time may be left is spent making arrangements for students to take the College Entrance Examinations or the Merit Scholarship Tests. This is one side of the problem of transition.

The other side of the problem is the situation the non-college-bound student faces. In 1967, the average unemployment rate for all teen-agers was 12.9 percent. The non-white rate was 26.5 percent, almost two and one-half times the white rate of 11 percent.

The seriousness of the problem is pointed up by the unemployment rate of teen-agers over the past three decades. In 1930 the teen-age unemployment rate was one and one-half times the national rate; by 1948 it had grown to two and one-half times the national rate; in 1963 it reached three times; and in 1967 it was almost three and one-half times the national rate. At the same time, we keep more of our youth in school longer than any other nation, presumably to prepare them for a useful life in our society and in our economy.

The fact is that about one-third of today's youth, about one million per year, find major problems and extended, serious difficulty in making the transition from school to work. The United States, the world's richest nation, with supposedly the best educational system, has the poorest record of all advanced nations in providing effective bridges between school and work for its youth.

The following hypotheses are possible reasons for this problem:

1. There has been a reduction in the proportion of low-skill entry jobs in the United States.

2. Recently the proportion of new young entrants into the labor force has been greater than in other countries.

3. There is some reluctance on the part of American youth to take low-paying, low-skill, or dead-end jobs.

4. In better-paying industries, high wages induce employers to give preference to more experienced, more responsible, better educated, and potentially more productive persons.

5. Residence and transportation barriers may separate many underprivileged youth from employment opportunities.

6. Finally, part of the problem stems simply from failure to give high priority efforts to assist disadvantaged youth in bridging the gap between school and work.[12]

There can be no question that we know a great deal more about the statistics of youth unemployment than about how we can help youth make the transition into the work force. The school of tomorrow must come to grips with this problem or many young people will continue to see the school as a barrier to their finding a decent job rather than as the best place to be to get a good job.

Apparently two-thirds of our youth are able to avoid the unemployment syndrome, but over 40 percent of the students who enter college do not graduate. Who helps these people make the transition to work? While the damage is not so obvious or painful, it must be true that many of these young people fail to find work which is up to their potential, and in many cases they may be doing work that could be done by less talented youth. This is a net loss to society, the economy, and the individual. (A more detailed presentation of this problem will be found in chapter 11.)

[12] For a full discussion of this problem, the reader may wish to refer to *The Transition from School to Work,* a Report Based on the Princeton Symposium, May 9-10, 1968, Industrial Relations Section, Princeton University.

The role of the school in solving this problem has been discussed at length in the past few years and some steps seem obvious. First, the school must assume responsibility for this problem. The fact that it never has, and that society has never before asked it to, does not change the situation today; the change is mandatory. Imagine the reaction of thousands of teen-agers if the school actually were interested in what happened to those who didn't go to college. Imagine the reaction of many parents who have been placed in the position of aligning themselves either with the school or with their child in the matter of work or education.

Second, the school of tomorrow must greatly increase vocational and career counseling for all youth, particularly for those who enter work directly from high school. The 1968 *Manpower Report of the President* noted that eight out of ten high school dropouts and four out of ten high school graduates had never received counseling on training or employment opportunities. Very few of the present school counselors have adequate, if any, preparation in occupational counseling. Occupational information is scanty and is generally not prepared for school use.

Third, the school of tomorrow must make work experience an integral part of education for career development. This program should include not only cooperative work experience but greatly expanded opportunities for youth volunteer activities. School credit and recognition of this method of learning as a part of education is necessary. If employment is dependent not only on preparation but also on experience, the youth with neither is bound to be locked out.

Fourth, the school must operate placement services for all students who need and desire this service. In a world where work provides the badge of adulthood for the adolescent, as well as the means of continuing learning while earning, matching a youth with a job is much more than a matter of obtaining employment. Since education is the bridge between men and work, what institution is in a better position to carry out this function than the school?

Fifth, the schools must follow up the success of students after leaving school. The results of this would form the best basis for evaluation of programs as well as a pressure to change to meet the needs of both the students and the labor force. This would probably be the best system of accountability available to the schools.

Other steps must be taken if education is truly to become a part of a national manpower policy. First, employers must be involved in providing work experience for youth in school. If this involves overhead costs to the employers, these costs should be borne by the schools, either through subsidy or some form of tax relief.

Second, a program is needed to bring employers into the schools for discussions with students on career potential, requirements, and experiences.

Third, employers need to secure new employees through the school placement office in order to emphasize and enhance the relevance of school, and in order to secure the best job-employee match, both in terms of the future and the immediate return to the individual and the employer.

Fourth, the development of a method of providing work experience to youth in high school, junior college, and college would result in a natural transition process from school to work. The benefits to both employers and students are obvious. The fact that the teen-age group at any time makes up only a fraction of the total work force negates the fear of some people that this program would work against those now employed. Eventually these same students find jobs, but the loss and inefficiency that accrues in the process creates dynamite which feeds much of today's social explosion.

Besides these considerations, the government must take positive steps to facilitate the process of transition from school to work. Funds must be made available for specific programs in the schools. Age restrictions which prevent fourteen- and fifteen-year-olds from acquiring work experience as part of their education must be removed. (The Department of Labor recently approved a two-year experimental reduction in order to allow this to be tried in the schools.)

The problem of minimum wages and a fair return for student work while in a training program has been widely discussed. The French legal minimum wage provides for reduc-

129

tions applicable to workers under eighteen years of age, according to the following scale:

Age Group	Percent Reduction from Minimum Wage, 1964
14-15	50
15-16	40
16-17	30
17-18	20

If we are to reach a large part of our youth while they are still in school, we must relate learning with earning. If we are really to develop a manpower policy which will help to prepare youth for entry into the work force in a sensible and efficient manner, we must have a youth wage policy consistent with the concept of earning while learning.

The most tragic trends appear to be the continued separation of educational programs from manpower needs and growing separation of human resource development from programs aimed at the undereducated and unemployed. These problems are discussed at length in the next chapter.

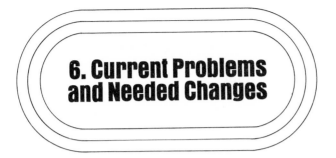

6. Current Problems and Needed Changes

The public school system has become a symbol of the power structure. Students in many universities and colleges are striking, demonstrating, and rebelling against the structure and the system. More and more high school students are following the lead of these older students and are also rejecting the establishment. Minority groups, the poor, and many liberal thinkers see the school as a symbol of conservative defense of the status quo. Many parents also see the school as a barrier to the future rather than as a road to success. Many of our most talented and able young people are leaving college before completing work on their degrees, which they say are phony symbols of learning, marks of subservience to the power structure, and proof of concern only for security, money, and material things. Young people, and many adults, feel the schools lack a commitment to the real issues which face the nation and the world. They feel school administrators and principals are afraid of their jobs, trying always to keep things the way they have been, being responsive only to the political and economic power in the community.

Why is it that so many believe these criticisms to be true? Our schools, compared to those in Europe and other parts of the world, have not adhered rigidly to obsolete curriculums and methods but have been responsive to the changing needs and technologies of the times. However, changes have lagged years behind the times and have been sporadic and often ineffective. Thus, the disparity between the schools that served the youth and community well and those that did not became even greater. This is true within single school systems and individual states as well as between parts of the country.

A few decades ago, the American free public school system was the hope of nearly every immigrant parent for the future of their children. The school was the true melting pot of our democracy, the carrier of a revolutionary spirit of hope, equality, and aspiration. The famous Bulletin 35 of the U.S. Bureau of Education, "Cardinal Principles of Secondary Education," published in 1918, spells out the spirit of the schools serving everyone, attempting to make them all successful, and, notably, speaking of things not required for college entrance. One of the unique things argued for at that time was the comprehensive high school, which today's community college may more closely resemble in terms of the present technology.

Where do we find comprehensive high schools today? Certainly not in the high-income, strictly white, college-bound, establishment-supporting suburban area. Certainly not in the small, rural, agricultural, black or white (but not both), low-income, nonindustrial or commercial, isolated community. Certainly not in the large city ghetto, whose residents have poverty-level incomes, high unemployment, and little hope of anything better. Certainly not in the all-white, privately supported schools which have been developed to avoid any comprehensiveness. Certainly not in the small high schools of the depressed areas where neither a job nor a future is forseeable.

The dropout rate is highest in the kind of communities just mentioned. The "selecting out" of students by the schools—by means of narrow curriculum, marking systems, or irrelevance from the viewpoint of the students—is creating a crisis of confidence in America. Unfortunately, it is still true that opportunities for higher education and occupational preparation are dependent more on parental income than on student ability and talent. College and vocational opportunities are more dependent on where one lives than on what one wants to do.

The school has become the whipping boy, the excuse, the rationalization for some of today's biggest problems. Both the extreme liberal and the extreme conservative assail the school systems—the conservative, because the schools are not more academic, more selective, and more traditional; the

132

radical, because they are too academic, too selective, and too traditional. The schools must try to be all things to all people.

There are two overriding objectives today which must be met by the schools, or we fail. First, we must give every child the minimum requirements of modern literacy, so he may continue his learning. We must reach and teach those children whose backgrounds have given them little or no basis for school work. To reach all or nearly all of these children is a first priority task.

Second, because of modern technology, we must make sure that every youth completes high school with the occupational skills needed to become employed or goes on to a program where these skills are taught. This has never been attempted before. These two new tasks are not additions to the basic function of the schools; they are the priorities of the times.

Separate School Systems

The fact that less than 8 percent of all expenditures for public elementary and secondary schools comes from the federal level accounts for some of the great disparities among schools in different parts of the country. One simple way to equalize educational opportunity would be for the federal government to increase its financial support to the schools and to distribute the funds on the basis of need. In effect, this is what has been happening in the educational programs funded through the Office of Economic Opportunity and in the Department of Labor's manpower training programs. In nearly all cases, these programs receive 100 percent federal financing and go directly to the community where the need is identified.

At the time the poverty programs and the manpower programs for the disadvantaged were started, the basic idea was to develop remedial efforts which would cause this group of people to disappear. This has not happened, of course.

The basic question today, then, is, how do we really solve the problem and prevent its recurrence? The trend appears to be toward a separate educational program, separately funded, outside the public school system. Since 1961, manpower training program appropriations have increased ninefold, with the bulk of these funds spent outside the public schools. Such programs have often been disassociated from

133

the schools on the theory that the schools are not concerned with the problem. There has been little, if any, increase in funds for occupational training in the schools relative to the increase in enrollments, and there has been no increase in the tax base by which the state and local financing of the schools could respond to the additional enrollments and rising costs, let alone the new thrust for occupational preparation.

The basic problem is illustrated by the fact that in 1968 the federal share of student costs in home economics was $5.09 per year; in vocational agriculture, $28.34; and in technical fields, $78.29. In comparison, Job Corps costs per enrollee were more than $8,000 annually.[1] This comparison is given not to criticize the costs of the Job Corps, but to indicate the trend of federal investments in solving the problem. However, the basic problem of why thousands of young Americans need these kinds of remedial programs is still unexplored—particularly the school's role in its solution.

The image of the schools as a scholastic community is so total that most research efforts in education, whether funded by the Office of Education or one of the many foundations in the nation, are almost totally concerned with the technology, methodology, evaluation, and improvement of *what is now being done*. The grand strategy is to improve the rate of learning, which, even if it could be done, still leaves unanswered the question, "What do we do about those who don't want to learn?" The problem is one of motivation, "education for what?"

Perhaps the schools are going to have to do some different things before they can learn how to do differently some of the things they now do. The net effect is that some people assume that the schools should not get involved; others, that the schools do not want to teach everyone; others, that the schools are unable; others, that it would lower the quality of education; and still others, that since the poor and indolent will always be with us, we should not contaminate our education system with them. For these reasons the thrust of the 1960's toward improved education and a comprehensive manpower

---

[1] Levitan, Sar A., and Mangum, Garth L. *Federal Training and Work Programs in the Sixties*. Ann Arbor: Institute of Labor and Industrial Relations, University of Michigan, 1969. p. 170.

policy drifted toward a separate school system—for those others.

There are many reasons why such an approach would be fatal to the development of a sound educational system and a truly comprehensive manpower system. First, the present trend is to put emphasis on the problem of remediation and correction. This tends to overlook the causal factors. Our attempts at preventing human failure and developing our human resources now reach only part of our citizenry. Concern is concentrated on the pool of uneducated, unemployed, and minority groups, not with the flow into the pool. If we do not stop the flow, we can never eliminate the pool.

Second, a separate school system would put the burden of funding on the federal tax-collecting structure for programs primarily for the few, which inevitably would bring a counter-resistance to raising federal tax levels. (There are already signs of this.) Yet, there appears no reasonable resource other than federal taxes, and taxation without benefit to the majority would be exacerbated. Direct federal funding has had its problems in the last few years not only for the reasons just mentioned but also because it tends to weaken the state and local governments' involvement and responsibility.

Third, under some present and some proposed federal legislation, an individual must prove that he is a failure, or that his parents are (in terms of income), in order to qualify for benefits. This is a glaring contradiction of our concept of equal educational opportunity. Yet nearly every piece of federal legislation calls for this kind of segregation, based on administration of the programs, selection of enrollees, and isolation of the trainees from the mainstream of American life. The necessity of having to wait for special federal funds until the society has manufactured failures is neither sound education nor sound manpower development. There is absolutely nothing to prevent the operation of such special education and training as part of the ongoing local educational program available to every young person. For example, the Neighborhood Youth Corps program provides income for needy youth in school and out of school—yet the ones who drop out are allowed to earn twice as much as the ones who stay in school. There is no incentive for the student to stay in school except long-delayed rewards for completing his education. He has no guarantee of a job, a scholarship, or a future. The only thing he is sure of is that he gets half as much money to stay in school instead of going to work.

Fourth, a separate school system, if carried far enough, will segregate people at some early age (twelve, thirteen, or fourteen), based on parents' income. Economic segregation may prove more disastrous than racial segregation in the schools. Certain Latin American countries have experienced some of the problems that can follow from this kind of segregation. Why can't federal funds for special manpower programs be used as a basis for integrating the schools? The basis might then be better education rather than solely social mixing. In many large cities today the federal programs are often nearly all black, while the public school programs are nearly all white.

Fifth, the separation of education and training based on need and source of funds tends to make the schools even more homogeneous and selective. The danger of the public school becoming "pure" ethnically, economically, and culturally is even more likely if certain students receive their education in a separate school. The long history of civilization attests to the genetic and social danger of constant intermarriage. It is true that our schools are too "pure" today, and the last thing we should do is hasten the process in an attempt to solve an immediate problem with a dangerous remedy.

Sixth, a separate program for occupational skills in federally funded and administered programs widens the gap between education and work at the very time technology calls for this gap to be closed. The concept of special programs for the education and training of the poor and uneducated is not new. It was tried in the big cities in separate vocational high schools and proved a dismal failure. There is even less reason to feel this approach would succeed today, especially if funded and operated entirely outside the local school system.

In addition, there is evidence that enrollees in the programs are not satisfied with simple skills and a job. They need and want self-improvement which will allow continued learning and career mobility, both vertically and horizontally.

Seventh, in the long run, there is a real danger that the

basic motivation for financing these programs will be employer needs rather than people needs. One approach is to use the nation's manpower needs as the basis for training programs and then add health, education, and social services as needed. Logically, however, the individual's talents, needs, and education would make a better base on which to build the necessary occupational skills, health services, and social services. The end result would be the same, with the added benefit that the system can adjust to the individual rather than forcing him to fit the system. We may be falling into the trap of thinking of our economic and social programs as completely separate. They cannot be in a technological age which is highly dependent on educated, confident, and skilled citizens.

Eighth, the worst danger of a separate program of education is that it would take the heat off our present educational system. It is extremely difficult to change the schools now, even in the face of violent attacks by "friends" as well as by those who would not hesitate to destroy them completely. We have too many educators, school boards, and taxpayers ready to say, "Yes, let the federal government take care of those others. In fact, we have some more in the schools I would like to send them." There are those who would make the schools accountable only for those who fit the present curriculum and methods. To relieve the schools of responsibility for those who most need education would, in the long run, be the surest way to guarantee the eventual decay of our educational system.

Ninth, if the major thrust for manpower development is allowed to take place outside the educational mainstream, it would further separate the schools from the employers, removing from the schools another important pressure for change. A closer relationship with business, industry, and public employers would result in new approaches to education and occupational skill training. This would do much to make schools more responsive to student needs and to changing labor market demands.

Tenth, a separate school system would make it even less likely that the year-round school, with a variety of approaches to learning, work experience, youth participation, and integration of all kinds of persons into the school program, will come into being.

137

New Roles for the Schools

Society today judges a man's worth by what he can do, his ability to live effectively, earn a living, and to achieve his own purposes. Society judges the school more by how well it helps each student achieve his goals than by how well a few have done. To meet today's manpower requirements and to help everyone become a contributor to our society, the school must perform several new functions.

Occupational orientation and guidance programs must be installed in our school systems, beginning at the elementary or junior high school levels. To offset the dropout rate, students must be acquainted with the wide variety of jobs that employers have to offer, with the skills needed for each occupation, and the compensations that training and a job offer. Some experimental efforts along these lines are already underway, and others should be encouraged. Clearly there is need for a bridge from junior high school to high school vocational programs so that young people will benefit from efforts to motivate them to think about work and the relationship of education to work.

Schools, in cooperation with business and industry, must offer work-experience programs to students so they can develop skills, earn scholastic credit for the work experience, and earn money. Work experience is as important to the high school student as it is to the college student. Cooperative school-work programs are a real asset to the youngster seeking entry into the job force. Limited work-study and work-experience programs in distribution and marketing, some of the trades, and a few other fields have been in operation at the secondary level for many years. Such opportunities need to be extended to as many students as possible and should not be restricted to a few vocational fields or to needy students. These programs should be planned and operated by local school officials who would be responsible for developing contacts with local industry and business and for placing high school youngsters in jobs pertinent to their studies and interests. Initially such programs could be limited to students who need the money to help them stay in school. However, introducing youngsters to the world of work has an educational as well as an economic value, and work-experience programs should be extended to all high school students who need or wish to participate in them.

New links must be forged between business, industry, and education. In today's technological world, classroom instruction is of little benefit without an opportunity to apply what is learned. Youngsters must understand job application forms, learn the importance of interviews, learn good work habits, know how to get along with supervisors, how to dress properly, and how to develop skills on the job. Business and industry can play a vital role by informing schools of specific requirements and perhaps supplying instructional material, machines, and even part-time instructors. They could also accept pupils for part-time work and supervise them in the work-experience programs.

Job placement bureaus must be operated in high schools. Teachers are better acquainted with the interests, abilities, and characteristics of pupils than anyone else. Therefore, the schools are in the best position to place a student in the kind of job that suits him best, that he will be happiest in, and that provides a step in his career development. Schools should be responsible for the transition of all noncollege-bound students from school to work. The school cannot ignore these responsibilities if it is to be effective and give direction to the entire educational process.

There is another issue which has been buried in our practices, times, and problems—the educational level of the nation's adults. This country, at this time, has several million adults eighteen years of age and older who, by accident or intention, have been denied the opportunity to fulfill themselves, achieve personal goals, and build into their lives the values and aspirations of a free society. A meaningful work role for them is out of the question. They have not learned the basic skills—reading, writing, computing—to make them employable. These people help fill the welfare rolls and the unemployment rolls.

We have learned that the investment a nation makes in developing human talent determines its character. For a free society this investment may be the key to survival. The planning process in a free society always involves the adult, because he has the franchise. No technological tool has been

139

invented that can replace him or his ability to make judgments. Yet in the past we have always emphasized education for the child, who neither participates nor contributes to public affairs, and we have neglected the adult who is the decision maker. There are, however, opportunities for help—opportunities through federal assistance and opportunities through local and state programs in each community where business and employers are located.

There is a great need for strengthening the business-employer-school partnership at the local level. Basic education can best be promoted through joint efforts between the local school and the employer. We must develop a plan which provides continuing education for adults in basic education programs and which is responsive to changing conditions, individual needs, and the needs of the labor market.

The concept of education as being finished when a person is prepared to become a full-time participant in the labor market does not have the validity it had in the past. The future requires a meaningful dialogue between industry and education and specific development of a plan for continuing education for everyone. With what is known as "the tight labor market," many employed persons today stand a chance of joining the hard-core unemployed, of becoming just another statistic on the welfare rolls.

A National Manpower Policy

There have been dozens of books and hundreds of articles written and published during the sixties which have spoken to, about, and around the question of a manpower policy. Yet in none of these has a specific role for the educational structure of this nation been spelled out or even considered a major component of a comprehensive manpower policy. The dilemma posed by this fact is clearly defined in an article by Stanley Ruttenberg:

> The Labor Department looked at the status of the hard-core of unemployed youths and adults in the Nation and suggested more than a decade ago that we had to do something about the source of this unemployment. The source, it was pointed out clearly and graphically, was the continuing and growing rate of dropouts or pushouts

140

from our schools, as well as advancing technology and automation. The decade of the sixties, we said, would produce more than 10 million jobseekers who would not have finished high school. We also pointed out that the number and types of jobs such persons could fill were diminishing rapidly with each year, even as the dropout rate increased.

The seeds of the dilemma are with us today. The school system, at great expense, keeps turning out ill-prepared persons for the labor force; and the Federal Government, at great expense, attempts to mold these persons into productive citizens with the aid of private industry, using the same basic training which was available in the school system.

But, the school system, both vocational and academic, has tended to recede from the realistic needs of the present and the future. Learning for the sake of learning, arbitrary academic requirements, and poor teaching tools have taken their toll of pupils. Systems that insist on the standards of the past, the hoary traditions, have tended to inspire apathy and total disinterest among the young recipients. This glaze of apathy seems to have reached upward into the curricula and to those who teach them.

. . .

Manpower programs have not found all the solutions. Neither the Labor Department nor any other Federal agency is capable of finding anything more than a short-range solution for our manpower problems. The answer lies in the hands of our educational system—a system that has been the foundation and the strength of our country. The task of that system today must be to improve the school curricula to prevent the school pushout, dropout, and hordes of unprepared persons from descending on the job market, unskilled, untrained, and unwanted.[2]

[2] Ruttenberg, Stanley. "Manpower Training—The Seeds of a Dilemma." *Manpower*, January 1969. p. 13.

If we are going to develop a manpower policy that is more than a piecemeal approach to various crises and political or economic fluctuations, it must be based on principles stemming from long-term people needs and economic growth potential.

If a national manpower policy is to provide the necessary manpower from the professions to the low-skill jobs and is to make sure that everyone is employable and employed as spelled out in the 1946 Employment Act, then a set of criteria must be developed. The following list is neither definitive nor necessarily valid in all respects. It does not speak to the problems of job development or economic factors, but rather to the basic components of people and manpower needs in a rapidly changing technological society.

1. Provision of a basic education through the high school level which provides the tools for continued learning and retraining is necessary for everyone.

2. Everyone must receive occupational skill training at some level of his education—in high school, postsecondary schools, college, or graduate professional schools.

3. Work experience should be provided as part of this education, preferably prior to the time the student enters on full-time employment.

4. Special basic education and skill training must be made available to those who find themselves unemployed or underemployed.

5. Since this program of education and training cannot entirely take place within the educational structure, provision for private and public employers to participate in the program is mandatory.

6. Supportive services, such as health, and rehabilitation services for handicapped and disabled persons should be part of the total program.

7. Opportunities for student assistance at the technical and paraprofessional levels must be available to all who qualify in order to meet more rapidly the growing demands of technology.

8. Income support should be provided to those who need it during training and retraining periods prior to employment.

9. Incentive payments of federal funds should be made to local and state educational units that make the most rapid

142

progress toward full employment, reducing school dropouts, and upgrading the labor force. These payments should be based on local rates of change and not on national criteria.

10. Contractual arrangements between local education (and training) agencies and private businesses should be encouraged when this is the most inexpensive method of financing.

11. Full-time utilization of public facilities and equipment should be a goal of the program.

12. Assessment and evaluation of the program should rest upon a follow-up survey of students on the job after one, two, and three years of experience and a reduction in the size of the flow as well as of the pool.

13. There should be public review of plans and programs by independent advisory groups and open citizen hearings.

14. The long-range policy should provide incentive to coordinate, consolidate, and reduce the number of agencies and the resulting heavy overhead.

15. Incentive for greater federal, state, and local cooperation should be provided.

16. The neediest person's ability to be responsive to changing manpower needs should be increased.

17. The policy should be responsive to immediate needs, but also to future needs in terms of manpower requirements, population patterns, and disadvantaged people.

18. The policy should be comprehensive, embracing both prevention and correction.

7. A History of Manpower Development

America's strength and affluence is basically the result of human achievement, stemming from men's ideas and brought into being by their experience, initiative, talents, and skills. Thus, in a very real sense, the progress of a free society is determined by the investment made in helping its people discover and develop their potential.

For well over a century, this nation has invested in a succession of strategies to develop the minds and skills of its people. Today, the effort is called "manpower development"; the strategies are called "manpower programs," supported by "manpower legislation."

This chapter focuses on federally supported programs which promote the development of professional, technical subprofessional, and skilled nonprofessional manpower; why these programs came about; and why objectives changed.

The Professions

As early as the 1860's the industrial potential of America began to emerge and change the nature of work, especially in agriculture and engineering. Professional competence and skills were in demand, but the colleges and universities, traditionally confined to educating the elite, had not produced the professional manpower needed in agriculture and engineering.

[1] Much of the information here has been adapted from published reports of federal agencies responsible for leadership in manpower development (see Tables 1 and 2) and from Levitan, Sar A., and Mangum, Garth L. *Federal Training and Work Programs in the Sixties.* Ann Arbor: Institute of Labor and Industrial Relations, University of Michigan, 1969.

TABLE 1. Funding Federally Supported Manpower Programs—Fiscal Years 1961-1968 (Millions of Dollars)

	1961	1962	1963	1964	1965	1966	1967	1968
DEPARTMENT OF LABOR								
U.S. Employment Service	112	144	162	173	182	226	277	296
Bureau of Apprenticeship and Training	4	5	5	5	6	7	8	8
Bureau of Labor Statistics (Manpower Statistics)	4	5	5	6	7	8	9	9
Manpower Development and Training Act	—	—	70	130	397	435	421	416
DEPARTMENT OF HEALTH, EDUCATION, AND WELFARE								
Vocational Education	50	54	57	57	187	261	285	296
Vocational Rehabilitation	75	88	103	128	146	231	328	387
Adult Basic Education	—	—	—	—	19	36	29	39
OFFICE OF ECONOMIC OPPORTUNITY								
Neighborhood Youth Corps	—	—	—	—	132	272	373	281
Job Corps	—	—	—	—	183	310	211	285
Work Experience and Training	—	—	—	—	112	112	100	45
Operation Mainstream	—	—	—	—	—	—	36	36
New Careers	—	—	—	—	—	—	36	36
Special Impact	—	—	—	—	—	—	20	20
CAP Manpower	—	—	—	—	6	28	29	30
TOTALS	245	296	402	499	1377	1926	2162	2184

Source: Departments of Labor; Health, Education, and Welfare; and Office of Economic Opportunity.

To accommodate the new era's demand for professional manpower in specialized fields, Congress passed the Morrill Act of 1862. This legislation encouraged states to set up land-grant colleges and universities by providing each state with

146

TABLE 2. Summary of Federally Supported Manpower Programs, 1968

Program	Agency [1]	Level of Operation Fiscal 1967 (Thousands of Persons)	1968 Appropriation (Millions of Dollars)	Services Provided
U.S. Employment Service	USES	5,815 [2]	296	Recruitment, counseling, testing, placement, employer services and limited labor market research
Vocational Education	OE	4,823 [3]	296	Vocational education
Vocational Rehabilitation	RSA	174 [4]	387	Medical & psychiatric assistance, prosthetic devices, skill training, education & other services needed to enhance employability
Adult Basic Education	OE	411	39	Rudimentary education
MDTA Institutional Training	USES OE	177 [5]	386	Remedial and skill training; basic education
OJT	BWTP	110 [5]		Subsidies to employers to cover training costs
Experimentation and Demonstration	MA	[6]	30	Research and wide range of services
NYC In-School Out-of-School	BWTP	446 [7] 172 [7]	281	Work experience including limited counseling & some education
New Careers	BWTP	9	36	Training, subprofessional and employment
Special Impact	BWTP	6	20	Low income area investment to improve employment opportunities
Operation Mainstream	BWTP	8	36	Work experience, limited counseling, basic education, skill training
Job Corps	JC	39 [8]	285	Skill training, conservation work, and basic education
Work Experience	APA	46	45	Work experience, including limited supportive services and basic education
CAP Manpower	CAP	NA	30 [9]	Any service enhancing employment & employability of the poor

Eligibility Criteria	State and Local Program Administrators or Contractors	Allowances
All workers but the bulk unemployed	State Employment Security agencies	None
State determined	State Vocational Education agencies	Limited allowances (56,000 participants in fiscal 1967) provide $45 per month not to exceed $350 per year for poor youth 15-21.
Physically, mentally or "socially" handicapped	State Rehabilitation agencies	Limited to 36 special workshop projects in 27 states as of July 1968. Provides $25 per week for an individual with $10 per dependent to a maximum of four.
Over 18 years of age	State Education agencies	None
Mostly unemployed, but some upgrading	Public schools or skill centers and private schools	Adult—$10 above average weekly unemployment benefits in state plus $5 for each of 4 dependents.
Same	Employers, state apprenticeship agencies, trade associations, unions, and nonprofit community agencies	Youth—$20 per week None
Same	Public, nonprofit or private institutions	Same as institutional

Key to Agency Abbreviations

Department of Health, Education and Welfare	Department of Labor	Office of Economic Opportunity
APA—Assistance Payments Administration	BWTP—Bureau of Work-Training Programs	CAP—Community Action Program
OE—Office of Education	MA—Manpower Administration	JC—Job Corps
RSA—Rehabilitation Services Administration	USES—U.S. Employment Service	

[1] See Key to Agency Abbreviations.
[2] Non-farm placements calendar 1967.
[3] Preliminary estimate, excludes home economics students.
[4] Rehabilitated during the year.
[5] Enrolled during the year.
[6] Some 40,000 to 50,000 persons were "involved." However, the wide variety of services provided makes a total operational level meaningless.
[7] Enrolled September 1966-August 1967.
[8] As of June 1967.
[9] Excludes wages paid to indigenous poor.
NA—Not applicable.
Source: Levitan and Mangum, *op. cit.,* pp. 18-19.

14-21 years of age, family income below poverty level Mostly 16-21	Same	$1.25 per hour Maximum 15 hours per week $1.25 to $1.60 an hour Maximum 32 hours per week
Disadvantaged adults	Public or nonprofit institutions	Employment at minimum wage
NA	Public or nonprofit institutions	NA
Disadvantaged adult (rural area emphasis)	Public or nonprofit institutions	Employment at minimum federal or prevailing local wage
Same as NYC but school dropout	Urban centers—private industry and education institutions Conservation centers—Depts. of Interior & Agriculture and state agencies	$30 to $50 per month plus $50 a month adjustment allowance, half of which can be allotted for family support with matching by Job Corps
Public assistance recipients and other needy, including farm families with annual income of less than $1200	Public welfare agencies, nonprofit agencies and private employers under special waiver	Basic needs, as defined by state
Income below poverty threshold	Public, nonprofit or private organizations	Determined by project

federal land for support of at least one college. These institutions were to teach "without excluding other scientific and classical studies . . . such branches of learning as are related to agriculture and the mechanic arts . . . in order to promote the liberal and practical education of the industrial classes in the several pursuits and professions in life."

Congress then passed the Hatch Act in 1887 so that land-grant institutions could establish agricultural experiment stations for research and for diffusing "useful and practical information on subjects connected with agriculture." Three years later, the Second Morrill Act stipulated permanent annual appropriations to support the institutions and the Smith-Lever Act, passed in 1914, added agriculture and home economics extension services.

One hundred years after the Morrill Act of 1862 this country had land-grant institutions in the fifty states and in Puerto Rico. Although the sixty-eight institutions account for

149

only 3 percent of American colleges and universities, they include several distinguished universities and five of the nation's seventeen schools of veterinary medicine.

In 1963, land-grant institutions enrolled 21 percent of the college population, awarded 20 percent of all baccalaureate degrees, 25 percent of all master's degrees, and 40 percent of all doctorates. The following year they conferred 74 percent of all baccalaureates in agriculture, 37 percent in engineering, and 47 percent in home economics.

On the one hundredth anniversary of the Morrill Act, Oliver C. Carmichael wrote: "Undoubtedly the scientific, technological and technical development of the past 100 years has been largely due to the emphasis on science and technology in American higher education which in turn stemmed largely from the land-grant college movement." [2]

The Morrill Act, with its modest beginning, virtually set the pace for federal leadership and support in the development of professional manpower. Since then, the continuing shortage of professional manpower in the fields of education, science, medicine, and engineering has stimulated a series of legislation to support education and training for professional careers. Among the most notable are the Sputnik-inspired National Defense Education Act of 1958, the Health Professions Educational Assistance Amendments of 1965, the Education Professions Development Act of 1967, the amendments to the National Defense Education Act, and the Higher Education Amendments of 1968.

Skilled and Technical Manpower

Since colleges had assumed responsibility for supplying professional manpower, it seemed logical to expect that eventually high schools would provide the skilled and technical manpower needed for the nonprofessional occupations. But no such development took place, that is, not without federal legislation.

Pressure for vocational training, or a useful and practical education, at the high school level reached a climax in the

[2] Carmichael, Oliver C. "A Hundred Years of the Land-Grant Movement." *Saturday Review,* April 21, 1962. p. 59.

early 1900's. The need for skilled workers had become critical. Although the population increased from seventy-six million to over ninety-two million between 1900 and 1910, too few possessed the skills or training required by the changing economy.

The National Society for the Promotion of Industrial Education, organized in 1906, concentrated its efforts on gaining leverage to push for passage of federal legislation.[3] It favored federal-state assistance to vocational education in secondary schools, an idea which teetered in the balance. In 1916 vocational education legislation became a "national preparedness factor" in the training of manpower for a war effort. In this setting, Congress passed the Vocational Education Act of 1917—better known as the Smith-Hughes Act—which President Wilson signed two months before America entered World War I.

The Act authorized $7.2 million, an amount that is still being appropriated yearly. Dominant allotments went to vocational agriculture and home economics, but provisions were included for training in trades and industry. Between 1917 and 1956, several other pieces of vocational education legislation added some $40 million to the annual appropriation of $7 million.

The George-Reed Act of 1929 added $1 million annually to expand the agriculture and home economics program; the George-Ellzey Act of 1934 upped the supplementary funds to $3 million and provided additional support for trades and industry; and the George-Dean Act of 1936 added $14 million, authorized funds on a continuing basis, and added support for vocational education in the distributive occupations.

World War II and the 1950's

During World War II, Congress put more than $100 million into the Vocational Education for National Defense (VEND) program. VEND provided preemployment and supplementary training for seven million war production workers between 1940 and 1945, received just praise, and influenced Congress to supplant the $14 million George-Dean

[3] In 1926 the Society became the American Vocational Association (AVA), the leading professional organization in vocational education.

151

Act with the $29 million George-Barden Act of 1946. Funds were authorized for the same four service fields (agriculture, home economics, trades and industry, and distributive occupations), but states were allowed greater flexibility in programs.

A more direct move toward an active manpower policy came that same year. The Employment Act of 1946 made the achievement of "maximum employment, production and purchasing power" a national objective and a specific concern of the federal government, "with the assistance and cooperation of industry, agriculture, labor, and State and local governments." But in the years following, government efforts toward its objective took the form of limited fiscal and monetary measures to prevent recessions or stimulate business recovery. There was little public demand for more affirmative action. This period of complacency and inaction about manpower problems came to an abrupt halt in the 1950's.

The early 1950's were years of beleaguerment for vocational education. The federal school-aid controversy was at its peak, and vocational education was caught up in the argument. The Korean War began, demanded heavy spending, and the cries for cutbacks in domestic spending grew louder. States' righters said the government should drop the vocational education program altogether; labor and business support had become lukewarm. The American Vocational Association rallied its allies against these forces and helped the program to scrape through yearly congressional battles with little damage, most of which was repaired between 1955 and 1957.

The 1958 National Defense Education Act (NDEA) brought the first significant addition to the vocational education program since 1917. Under Title VIII, it made funds available for training persons for employment "as highly skilled technicians in recognized occupations requiring scientific knowledge . . . in fields necessary for the national defense." [4]

---

[4] Congress made Title VIII of the NDEA a permanent part of the Vocational Education Act of 1963, in recognition of the increasing need for technical education and for trained technicians.

The Vocational Education Act of 1963 [5]

Vocational education needed a boost forward, but it also needed a stronger base upon which to operate and expand in the complex space age of the sixties. On February 20, 1961, President John F. Kennedy, in his message to Congress on American education, recommended that a panel of consultants be appointed to review and evaluate the current program and submit recommendations for improving and redirecting it. The consultants deliberated from November 1961 through November 1962 and concluded that the national program of vocational education had been insensitive to economic and social change, to labor market demands, to the impact of change on education and education for job preparation, and to the diverse vocational needs of various population segments.[6] This report was used as a basis for drafting the Vocational Education Act of 1963.

Passage of the 1963 Act was spurred by the high levels of unemployment among young people. It recognized the need for a flexible educational system which could provide prevocational training, saleable skills, and work experience to high school students. It focused on services to people without respect to predetermined occupational groupings and, in effect, suggested that funds would be available to take care of all training needs except training for occupations requiring a baccalaureate degree. The Act authorized federal funds to be used for:

1. Training persons attending high school.

2. Preparing high school graduates or dropouts available for full-time study for job entry.

3. Training or retraining persons in the labor market for advancement or job stability.

---

[5] Text adapted from *Vocational Education—The Bridge Between Man and His Work: General Report of the Advisory Council on Vocational Education*. U.S. Department of Health, Education, and Welfare, Office of Education, OE 80052. Washington, D.C.: Government Printing Office, November 1968.

[6] U.S. Department of Health, Education, and Welfare, Office of Education. *Education for a Changing World of Work*. Report of the Panel of Consultants on Vocational Education. Washington, D.C.: Government Printing Office, 1964.

4. Developing special programs for persons with academic, socioeconomic, or other handicaps that prevent them from succeeding in the regular vocational education programs.

5. Supporting the ancillary services and activities needed for teacher training and supervision, program evaluation, special demonstration and experimental programs, development of instructional materials, state administration and leadership, and the conduct of periodic evaluation of all programs and services in relation to projected manpower needs and job opportunities.

The Advisory Council on Vocational Education reported on the achievements and progress which the 1963 Act had made possible, but also discovered that vocational education programs and services under the 1963 Act had not expanded rapidly enough to help students with special needs, the culturally and economically disadvantaged in depressed rural areas, and young people in the slum and ghetto neighborhoods of large metropolitan areas.[7] The total of federal vocational education funding had been entirely too small to expand and develop programs in accordance with need. In addition, all youth did not receive the benefits of vocational guidance because of a lack of commitment among schools to include vocational guidance in the total education process. The Council's report included a comprehensive series of recommendations for dealing with these inadequacies and other problems and suggested that all federal vocational legislation administered by the Office of Education be combined into one act.

Vocational Education Amendments of 1968

The 1968 amendments to the Vocational Education Act embodied most of the Advisory Council's recommendations. Highest priority was given to the training and educational needs of the rural and urban disadvantaged, the mentally and physically handicapped, and those seeking training at the post-secondary level. The legislation permitted great flexibility in programs, authorizing large resources which would be at the

[7] *Vocational Education—The Bridge Between Man and His Work,* op. cit., p. 197.

disposal of state and local educational agencies. It earmarked one-third of the home economics funds for development of special programs to improve the quality of family life in economically depressed areas and placed stress on consumer education in home economics curriculums. It also authorized new and enlarged programs of combined school and work and other promising innovations which, if fulfilled, will aid greatly in building a bridge between school and employment.

The 1968 amendments call for profound changes in vocational education. They offer the public schools great resources with which to make the changes, but they also impose on them equally great responsibilities for developing the vocational and educational potential of the nation's citizens.

Manpower Development and Training Act

Early in 1961 the federal government took action to stimulate recovery from the recession that had begun in 1960. In addition to monetary and fiscal measures, the government moved to reduce social and economic waste among its human resources.

The country had, and still has, large manpower resources which could be drawn on to meet its manpower needs—women who want suitable jobs, not the traditional "women's jobs"; a greatly underutilized, and sometimes unused, work force of Negroes, Mexican-Americans, Puerto Ricans, and American Indians; and disadvantaged teen-agers in rural and urban areas. The totality of wasted manpower has almost always included, in addition to the unemployed, large numbers of people who have given up the search for work, who no longer have will or purpose. In addition, there are those who are confined to the least desirable, lower paying jobs because of poor education, poor health, and discrimination—especially, but not exclusively, racial.

The training of jobless workers in depressed areas began under the Area Redevelopment Act of 1961. A considerably larger undertaking was launched under the Manpower Development and Training Act (MDTA) of 1962 which aimed at achieving full employment. Manpower programs were charged to train persons who were unemployed because of automation, shifts in market demand, and other economic

155

changes and conditions. In addition, the programs were to equip jobless workers with needed skills and to aid in matching workers and jobs.

Since the passage of the MDTA more than one million persons have enrolled in training programs—nearly 715,000 in institutional programs, the remainder in on-the-job training or in some combination of the two. Over 600,000 persons have completed both institutional and on-the-job training programs during the first six years of operation under the MDTA. Nearly 450,000 in this group were in institutional training, and about 85 percent of those who completed institutional training obtained jobs. This degree of success is especially remarkable in that over two-thirds of those trained were classified as disadvantaged and over one-half of this group were school dropouts.

The Department of Health, Education, and Welfare (HEW) and the Department of Labor share responsibility for administering the MDTA. HEW arranges for institutional training, either directly or through state agreements, in public and private education and training institutions. It is responsible for classroom instruction, including adequacy of curriculums and facilities and the provision of manpower instructors. The Department of Labor designates the occupations for which training is to be provided and selects and refers individuals to manpower training programs. Upon completion of training, the Department of Labor is responsible for placement of trainees and for periodic follow-up on the employment progress of former trainees.

Changes Since 1962 and Emerging Patterns

The manpower training program has changed considerably since 1962, though its objective—prompt placement in jobs—remains the same. The MDTA was originally designed to solve the paradox of high unemployment and the inability of employers to hire workers in skill-shortage occupations. Even with the decline in unemployment, manpower underutilization remains highly concentrated among specific population segments—nonwhite teen-agers and adults, older workers, the culturally underprivileged from urban slums and rural areas, the illiterate, and the physically and mentally handicapped.

In an attempt to make the manpower program a more effective instrument, Congress passed several amendments to meet the complex needs of these groups. During the first year of operation under the Manpower Development and Training Act, Congress authorized an enlarged program of youth training because of the high rate of youth unemployment. Since lack of education was prevalent among the hard-core unemployed, provisions also were made for basic education.

Additional amendments to the MDTA in 1963, 1965, and 1966 were aimed at further increasing the effectiveness of the program by authorizing special training programs and services to equip the disadvantaged for employment. These amendments led to a redirection of the program in 1966 with a decision to concentrate 65 percent of the manpower effort toward training the disadvantaged and the other 35 percent toward meeting the need for trained personnel in occupations with skill shortages.

The JOBS (Job Opportunities in the Business Sector) program, launched in 1968, represented another new partnership between business and the federal goverment in training and employing disadvantaged workers. It ranks with the on-the-job training program, established six years before by the MDTA, as an innovative undertaking by industry and government in the training of manpower. The JOBS program differs from the on-the-job training program in that it (a) serves only disadvantaged workers; (b) is targeted to the fifty largest urban areas; (c) relies on employers to provide not only jobs and training but also the full range of supportive services required to help disadvantaged workers make a satisfactory job adjustment; and (d) utilizes the services and support of businessmen to help develop and promote program efforts. This program, spearheaded by the National Alliance of Businessmen, reaches out to tap an unused and long-ignored reservoir of manpower.

The Trainees

Each change in program direction has been reflected in changes in the characteristics of enrollees. The most radical change has been the rapidly growing proportion of disadvantaged persons enrolled in the institutional program. Per-

157

sons classified as disadvantaged—those least likely to be employed or, once hired, able to keep a job—constituted 69 percent of the total institutional enrollment in 1968.

The Manpower Administration of the Department of Labor, for manpower program purposes, defined a disadvantaged individual as a person having two or more of the following characteristics: nonwhite, less than twelve grades of education, unemployed at least fifteen weeks, under twenty-two or over forty-five years of age, handicapped, or a public assistance recipient. This definition has been changed somewhat for current data collection purposes, chiefly to include the poor who lack suitable employment.

Throughout the years more men than women were school dropouts and more nonwhite than white trainees were dropouts. Although white trainees were less likely than nonwhite trainees to drop out of school before graduation, they were more likely than nonwhite trainees to drop out in pre-high-school years. Of the 56 percent of all the white trainees who were school dropouts, 22 percent had never entered high school. On the other hand, although 62 percent of all the nonwhite trainees were school dropouts, only 16 percent had dropped out prior to the high school years. The trainees with the lowest level of educational achievement were the most likely to have been unemployed at the time of enrollment for training (see Table 3).

Nonwhite trainees increased from just over 27 percent of all institutional trainees in 1967 to 49 percent in 1968 (see Table 4). They represent a much larger proportion of the trainees than nonwhite persons are of the unemployed in the nation's labor force.

TABLE 3

Years of School Completed	Percent of 1968 Enrollees Unemployed at Enrollment
Less than 9 years	86
9-11 years	83
12 years	77
Over 12 years	64

Source: Manpower Report of the President, January 1969.

TABLE 4. Percent of Manpower Trainees with Stated Characteristics
Enrolled in Fiscal Years 1968 and 1967

	Institutional		On-the-job	
	1968	1967	1968	1967
Trainees enrolled	100	100	100	100
Dropouts from high school or grade school	60	58	50	45
Nonwhite	49	41	36	27
Unemployed	80	81	67	61
Underemployed	17	16	30	36
Public assistance recipients	13	12	5	3
Eligible for allowance	83	81	24	16
Unemployed 15 weeks or more	45	41	36	33

Source: Manpower Report of the President, January 1969.

In October 1968, Congress extended the authority for administering the manpower training program to June 1972. At the same time, it acted to strengthen institutional training, giving particular attention to manpower training skills centers. The fifty-five manpower training skills centers, recognized as a major resource for training the unemployed and underemployed, offer great promise for the speedy training of persons in need of employment or upgrading. They also have potential as a community-wide resource for retraining and developing new skills.

The Role of the Schools

Progress in developing this country's human resources will depend, in large measure, upon the educational system. Manpower development programs impose heavy demands on educational institutions at all levels. Given the resources, the schools can take on these new tasks. The schools' responsibilities for manpower development are threefold. The first is essentially remedial—to provide education and training for people who lack marketable skills or are employed below their capabilities, while job vacancies remain unfilled for lack of qualified workers. Second, the school must give students the best preparation for work and life. This responsibility involves education at all levels, from preschool to postgraduate. Third, schools must provide for continuing education and updating of skills throughout the individual's working life.

159

Conclusions

In assisting the unemployed to find jobs, the MDTA program contributes not only to the welfare of the trainees and their families but also to that of the nation. Unemployment involves heavy costs in terms of lost productivity and purchasing power, welfare payments, crime, and delinquency. Estimates show that the MDTA training programs returned to society within one year more than the total cost of these programs to the federal government.[8]

The War on Poverty [9]

In his State of the Union Message in 1964, President Johnson said: "It is, therefore, the policy of the United States to eliminate the paradox of poverty in the midst of plenty in this Nation by opening to everyone the opportunity for education and training, the opportunity to work, and the opportunity to live in decency and dignity. . . ." Congress confirmed his statement later that year by passing the Economic Opportunity Act, which described its intent "to mobilize the human and financial resources of the Nation to combat poverty in the United States."

The Job Corps

The Job Corps was created as part of the Economic Opportunity Act in order to prepare youths, aged sixteen through twenty-one, "for the responsibility of citizenship and to increase [their] employability . . . by providing them in rural and urban residential centers with education, vocational educa-

---

[8] All studies to date indicate that the benefits of manpower training programs exceed their costs. For example, a recent pilot study by the Department of Labor comparing the costs and benefits of MDTA institutional training indicates the value of the training as a federal investment. This study concluded that the average net federal benefit-cost ratio, defined as the direct and indirect benefits to society (exclusive of increased taxes paid) compared to the federal investment per trainee was 1.78 to 1 in the first year after training. Thus, even though no one knows how long the differential benefit may last, or whether it may increase or decrease, the desirability of the program is clear.

[9] This section draws heavily on the information compiled by Sar A. Levitan and Garth L. Mangum, *op. cit.*

tion, useful work directed toward conservation of natural resources, and other appropriate activities." The underlying assumption was that many youths from impoverished homes should be removed from their home environment before they could be rehabilitated through training and education.

Although antecedents of the Job Corps may be traced back to the Civilian Conservation Corps (CCC) of the thirties, the contrasts between the two institutions are significant. The CCC was a product of the Great Depression, when deprivation and need were widespread, and the one and one-half million enrollees represented a broad cross section of the population. It was terminated when the armed forces absorbed the bulk of its clients, and acute labor shortages developed from wartime conditions. The Job Corps, on the other hand, focuses upon the special needs of a small minority of youths who, because of educational deficiency and debilitating environment, are at a competitive disadvantage in the labor market. The CCC was essentially a job creation program which emphasized conservation work. The Job Corps stresses the needs of the individual Corpsmen—though the work experience of enrollees in conservation centers is also devoted to "useful social work."

It is difficult to estimate the size of the Job Corps' potential clientele. In 1967, there were about one million out-of-school, unmarried youths from poor families, most of whom were eligible to enroll in the Job Corps. Even under ideal conditions, the majority of these potential candidates might not have been interested in residential centers or even required such costly training. In fact, the Job Corps has had to maintain a continuous promotional effort to fill the available facilities, which by mid-1967 could accommodate 43,000 youths.

It must be left to speculation whether the difficulties in attracting enrollees were caused by lack of interest on the part of potential clients, the quality of training and education offered in the centers, or inability to "reach" the youths. In large part, the problem may be traced to the decision of the Job Corps administrators to stress the needs of the most poorly educated, those who needed the Job Corps facilities most desperately. The Job Corps could have avoided a great deal of criticism and unfavorable publicity if the administration had decided to attract the "cream" of the disadvantaged youths. Whether they could have filled their quotas this way is also open to speculation, since the expanding labor market and armed forces provided ample opportunities in most areas for "good," well-motivated youths. The initial negative image of the Job Corps, which still persists, may also have hindered recruiting. It is probable, therefore, that the Job Corps had little attraction for youths who were able to obtain jobs on their own.

The record of the Job Corps is clear: it tried to attract youths who had difficulty finding employment even in a tight labor market. Two out of every five enrollees in May 1968 had completed eight years of education or less. Actual educational achievement was much lower than the formal education indicated and had not varied much since the second year of the Job Corps. Reading and arithmetic comprehension for half of the enrollees was at about the fifth-grade level. Nearly one out of every three was unable to read a simple sentence or solve a third-grade arithmetic problem. Three out of every five came from broken homes and two out of every five from families on relief (see Table 5).

Ethnic mix. A major problem of the Job Corps has been the continued increase in the proportion of Negro and other nonwhite enrollees, a factor which has contributed to tensions

TABLE 5. Corpsmen Characteristics as of May 1, 1968

	Men			Women
	Total	Urban	Conservation	
Highest grade completed (%)				
8 grades or less	38	33	51	24
9-10	42	50	38	38
11-12	20	17	11	38
Median educational attainment				
Reading	5.2	6.0	3.6	6.3
Arithmetic	5.2	6.3	3.6	6.1
Family (%)				
Broken home	60	NA	NA	NA
Unemployed head of family	63	NA	NA	NA
Relief	39	NA	NA	NA

Source: Job Corps, Office of Economic Opportunity.

in the centers and to the early departure of some enrollees. During the first year of the Job Corps, whites constituted a majority of the enrollees. By July 1967, the ethnic distribution of enrollment was 32.3 percent Caucasian, 58.5 percent Negro, and 9.2 percent others. The ethnic distribution did not differ greatly according to type of center.

Even a more experienced and knowledgeable staff might have found the problems of achieving the proper balance between discipline and freedom of Corpsmen difficult, if not insurmountable. Inducing southern whites, for example, to live with Negroes in racially integrated dormitories on a voluntary basis and motivating them to train and learn together on an equal basis would be no mean accomplishment, even for an expert in social psychology. Few of the Job Corps staff, at least in the early days, were fully prepared to handle such problems. But they learned quickly; plagued by strife and violence during the first two years, only a few racial incidents in Corps centers have been recorded since then.

Program evaluation. According to a June 1968 follow-up study of 161,000 youth who had left the Corps six, twelve, and eighteen months before, about seven out of every ten former Corps members are constructively occupied—in jobs (79 percent), in school (10 percent), or in the armed forces (11 percent). The three out of ten who were not accounted for in these ways included many who had spent less than six months in the program, as well as some girls who had withdrawn from the work force for marriage and other reasons. Overall, unemployment was still high, but the proportion usefully and gainfully occupied represented a great increase over the 44 percent who had had jobs, either full- or part-time, before they entered the program.

Among former Corpsmen who were still unemployed, about one out of four said the chief problem was lack of transportation to work; another one in four said racial attitudes barred him from jobs; and most of the others attributed their failure to obtain work to lack of high school diplomas. The Job Corps is attempting to minimize employer demands for high school diplomas by working through the National Alliance of Businessmen and its job-finding program for the hard-core unemployed. At the same time, Job Corps efforts at general education development have been intensified; to date, 7,000 Corpsmen have passed the high school equivalency examination. Cooperative arrangements have also been worked out with the Department of Labor, in which youths who drop out of the Job Corps are referred to the Neighborhood Youth Corps (NYC) or MDTA training projects.

To assist Job Corps enrollees interested in employment in the federal government, representatives of the U.S. Civil Service Commission and other federal agencies visit Job Corps Centers to provide counseling and guidance, including information on recent policy changes with respect to disclosure of arrest records. A system has been devised which will permit each enrollee to receive consideration for federal employment in his home city or any other location of his choice. Through December 1968, the Department of the Interior and the Department of Agriculture alone had hired about three hundred Corpsmen.

Neighborhood Youth Corps

From its inception in 1964 until mid-1968, the Neighborhood Youth Corps (NYC) enrolled nearly 1.6 million young people from low-income families and placed them in varied work activities. As a first step in overcoming handicaps to employment, NYC youth gain genuine work experience in a supervised work setting, thereby beginning to establish work habits and attitudes that will stand them in good stead for their whole working lives.

The NYC program has three separate components with somewhat different objectives—an in-school program for youth of high school age (not necessarily in high school grades), an out-of-school program, and a summer program designed to encourage high school students and dropouts to return to school in the fall.

For the nearly 200,000 disadvantaged youth served by the in-school program during fiscal 1968, the objective was to make it easier to remain in school through financial assistance earned by part-time work.[10] In order to encourage rather than

[10] It should be noted that this figure and others for "individuals served" represent the total number enrolled in the given program during the fiscal year, including both first-time enrollments and individuals already in the program at the beginning of the year.

impede continued education, in-school enrollees are limited to a maximum of fifteen hours of work per week. The pay is $1.25 per hour.

Wages help to cover basic necessities such as clothing and school supplies and perhaps help out with family expenses, thus facilitating school attendance as well as furnishing a work incentive. For youths in poverty-stricken families financial pressure at home may be a critical factor in deciding between further education and immediate entry into the job market. Low-income families are notable for their frequent disinterest in long-range personal plans, probably because of a pervasive feeling of futility about sustaining such plans. The availability of the NYC program is thus a strong positive factor for school continuation in the face of an often negative home environment. The minimal pay the enrollees receive is tangible support of their individual efforts. Furthermore, the NYC—with its counseling services and working relationships with the U.S. Employment Service and other government agencies, industry, and labor—gives youths guidance beyond the capability of most poor families.

The NYC's out-of-school program served more than 160,000 disadvantaged youths in fiscal 1968. In addition to furnishing work experience in preparation for the competitive job market, this program encourages youths who dropped out of high school to resume their education on either a full-time or part-time basis. Project sponsors also refer youths, for whom further education may be difficult, to vocational training programs and assist them in obtaining regular jobs. Besides paid work up to forty hours per week, out-of-school programs provide supportive services, including remedial education, counseling, and medical assistance. Compensation for time spent receiving supportive services, within the forty-hour workweek, is a new and important feature of the program. It is designed to overcome resistance to participation in supportive activities on the trainees' own time.

The out-of-school program has a relatively small Work-Training in Industry segment, in which sixty-six private firms participate. The six hundred enrollees in this program are paid by the employer, who is reimbursed by the NYC for part of the training costs. As in other NYC out-of-school job arrangements, the enrollees' workweek may be adjusted to include time for supportive services. The counseling and remedial education provided by NYC builds a foundation for future work, training, or educational experiences.

Like the in-school program, the summer NYC program bolsters youngsters' financial resources to help them to continue their schooling in the fall. During the summer of 1968, 364,000 boys and girls across the country performed many different tasks. They worked in beautification projects; improvement and maintenance of school buildings, parks, and recreation facilities; and with young children in Head Start projects and in Operation CHAMP, a summer recreation program for children and teen-agers sponsored by the NYC, the President's Council on Physical Fitness and Sports, and the Office of Economic Opportunity.

Several program changes have facilitated recruitment and swelled the number of NYC enrollees. One change made by the 1966 amendments to the Economic Opportunity Act extended the scope of the in-school program, qualifying students in grades 9 through 12. Transportation to and from work sites was also authorized—a matter of particular importance in rural areas. It is highly important that the NYC succeed in helping youth from the ranks of school dropouts and poor families, many of whom would otherwise be likely to continue the cycle of poverty. More than one-fourth of all enrollees are on welfare rolls or from families receiving public assistance.

A recent in-depth study of 2,000 youths formerly enrolled in the NYC out-of-school program found that, on the average, this group did not have a significantly better employment situation than a control group of non-NYC enrollees, nor did they return to school in larger proportions. Nevertheless, the overwhelming majority of participants expressed satisfaction with their work experience while in the NYC. The findings suggested that the program be bolstered with closer links between training and real jobs, more effective techniques for motivating return to school, and possibly more emphasis on remedial education. Some fundamental restructuring of the program along these lines is in process.

166

Furthermore, it is necessary to look beyond the statistical averages, which often conceal highly important accomplishments. Many individual projects have a high success rate in terms of enrollees returning to school, entering vocational training, or going to work in steady jobs. There have been instances where college potential has been identified, and the NYC counseling staff has steered a few enrollees into college preparatory courses.

Moreover, many cities have credited the NYC with decreases in juvenile crime rates. In San Antonio the rate dropped 12.6 percent in the low-income area where the NYC was operating, while climbing 5.5 percent in the higher-income sections. A juvenile court judge in Dayton credited the NYC with a 30 percent drop in juvenile crimes in 1967. A Los Angeles newspaper reported that only 1 percent of 2,000 enrollees had been convicted of crime since joining the project, although 50 percent had criminal records.

Changes Since 1963

Amendments to the Economic Opportunity Act in 1965, 1966, and 1967 made significant changes in the Neighborhood Youth Corps, authorizing programs to provide part-time employment and on-the-job training for young people from low-income families. In addition, these programs were to make maximum use of programs operating under the Manpower Development and Training Act, as amended, and the Vocational Education Act of 1963. Later amendments to the Economic Opportunity Act defined the objectives of the Job Corps more explicitly, added programs known as Operation Mainstream, New Careers, and Special Impact, and emphasized coordination and consolidation of these programs in specific areas.

The 1962 Amendments to the Social Security Act

The 1962 Amendments to the Social Security Act were designed to ease public criticism of relief given to persons able to work and to create work-relief projects to help train relief recipients for jobs. In other words, these amendments introduced the concept of rehabilitation by establishing a Community Work and Training Program for persons eighteen years or older who received assistance from the Aid to Fami-

167

lies with Dependent Children Program. The objective was to instill better work habits in enrollees in order to enable them to get and hold a job.

Under Title V of the Economic Opportunity Act of 1964, this concept was expanded and the program was made a part of the "war on poverty." The Work-Experience Program (as it was then called) served not only those on welfare but also other needy persons who would have been eligible for public assistance except for certain technical problems. The focus continued to be on unemployed adults, primarily the parents of dependent children.

The Work-Experience and Training Program, as it was renamed in 1966, had an enrollment of about 85,000 during that fiscal year. Subsequently, enrollments dropped somewhat because of reductions in funding. At its peak, the program reached only a very small proportion of all persons on welfare rolls.

The Work Incentive Program (WIN), a comprehensive manpower program designed to really break the cycle of poverty for public assistance recipients, was made mandatory in 1967 (Title IV, Social Security Act, as amended). The WIN program is administered jointly by the Department of Labor and the Department of Health, Education, and Welfare through state agencies. Its national goal is to restore to economic independence all employable persons sixteen years of age and over in families receiving Aid to Families with Dependent Children.

All states were required to enter the WIN program by July 1, 1969; only fifteen states were still operating Title V projects beyond the end of 1968. Under WIN, the enrollee retains his welfare status, until he proves his ability to succeed in the regular job market. Furthermore, although WIN began with a limited appropriation, the authorizing legislation is open-ended with respect to client referrals. Referrals by welfare agencies to WIN manpower services proceed under three priorities.

Priority I is for persons who can be identified as job-ready when their case is first reviewed. Intensive efforts are made to find them suitable jobs or on-the-job training opportunities and to provide the supportive services needed to keep them on the job; allowing participants to retain a considerable part of their earnings (the first $30 of their earnings per month, plus 30 percent of all additional earnings) without affecting their welfare benefits furnishes an incentive to work.

Priority II is for those who are not job-ready but can be made so through work orientation, basic education, skill training, and work experience. After this, intensive efforts are made to persuade employers to hire these individuals, and services are provided to ensure their retention on the job. During the training period, $30 per month is added to welfare benefits as a training incentive.

Priority III enrollees are judged not ready even for the kinds of services provided for the priority II group. For these people, special work projects are arranged with public or private nonprofit agencies. Their potential for training and regular employment is reassessed at three-month intervals, and at each reassessment they may move into the priority II or I group. Priority III enrollees are guaranteed a total income equal to their public assistance grants, plus 20 percent of their wages.

The $10 million appropriation in fiscal 1968 funded WIN programs for 8,200 enrollees in eleven states. The $118 million appropriation in fiscal 1969 provided for an estimated 100,000 enrollees and child day-care services for a limited number of enrollees.

The federal government is the nation's largest employer of WIN graduates. Operating under guidelines issued by the U.S. Civil Service Commission, federal agencies are to employ person who complete training in WIN programs and serve as hosts to program enrollees who need work experience to develop skills for employment. From November 1965 through September 1968, federal agencies provided more than two and one-half million hours of work experience and training to enrollees under the Work-Experience and Training and Work Incentive Programs.

Vocational Rehabilitation [11]

The vocational rehabilitation program began as an adjunct to vocational education, sharing with the latter a common

[11] Levitan and Mangum, *op. cit.*

coauthor and a similar method of financing. The Smith-Fess Act of 1920 added moneys for training the industrially disabled to the matching grants for vocational education begun under the Smith-Hughes Act of 1917. However, the inauguration of rehabilitation services for disabled veterans at the end of World War I was impetus for federal support of rehabilitation efforts already under way in several states.

The program at first operated under the independent Vocational Education Board and later under the Education Division of the Department of the Interior. It maintained a precarious existence during the 1920's but during the 1930's managed to shift its image to that of a relief program, ever escaping the early economy measures of the Roosevelt administration.[12] When the Federal Security Agency was established in 1939, the vocational rehabilitation program was transferred to it, along with most other New Deal social service programs.

Financial support remained limited to training the physically disabled, with no provision for medical or other services. Some states provided medical care, supportive services, and subsistence funds but, lacking federal support, these declined as a proportion of all rehabilitation expenditures from 13.7 percent in 1922 to 4.4 percent in 1938. As a result, those states most involved in rehabilitation efforts demanded unshackling from the federal vocational education program and the broadening of federal support.

War production manpower shortages and disabled returning veterans focused new attention on vocational rehabilitation early in World War II. Efforts to consolidate both veteran and civilian rehabilitation programs under a common jurisdiction were unsuccessful. However, out of these debates came the LaFollette-Barden Act of 1943, which established the current vocational rehabilitation program. The federal tie to vocational education was severed, and an independent Office of Vocational Rehabilitation (OVR) was organized in the Federal Security Agency.

Client eligibility was expanded to include the blind and mentally handicapped. Rehabilitation services were to include

[12] Obermann, C. Esco. *A History of Vocational Rehabilitation in America.* Minneapolis, Minn.: T. S. Denison & Co., 1965. pp. 240-42.

170

medical restoration and all services necessary to return the disabled to remunerative employment. Rehabilitation clinics and cooperative rehabilitation activities were established to help meet the manpower needs of defense industries. The number of rehabilitated clients nearly doubeld from 22,000 to 43,000 in one year (see Table 6). In the process, the country became more aware of its large disabled population and the shortages of rehabilitation personnel to provide the needed services.

General sympathy for the disabled and bipartisan support for vocational rehabilitation was sufficient not only to protect it from the cutbacks in social service activities in the 1960's, but also to bring it major expansion during that period as well. The 1954 amendments authorized a strong research program and federal grants for university support and indi-

TABLE 6. Number of Persons Served and Rehabilitated by State Vocational Rehabilitation Agencies in the United States (Selected Fiscal Years)

Year	Served	Rehabilitated
1921	NA	523
1930	NA	4,605
1940	65,624	11,890
1942	91,572	21,757
1943	129,207	42,618
1945	161,050	41,925
1950	225,724	59,597
1954	211,219	55,825
1955	209,039	57,981
1956	221,128	65,640
1957	238,582	70,940
1958	258,444	74,317
1959	280,384	80,739
1960	297,950	88,275
1961	320,963	92,501
1962	345,635	102,377
1963	368,696	110,136
1964	399,852	119,708
1965	441,332	134,859
1966	499,464	154,279
1967	569,907	173,594

Source: Department of Health, Education, and Welfare, Rehabilitation Services Administration.

vidual fellowships to train professional rehabilitation personnel.

Recent legislative treatment of the vocational rehabilitation program reflects both the growing public concern for those handicapped in competing for jobs and successful efforts on the part of the program to build political support. This development of a firm political base has been particularly successful under the direction of Mary E. Switzer, who became director of the OVR in 1951, commissioner of vocational rehabilitation in 1963, and administrator of the newly created Social and Rehabilitation Service (SRS) in August 1967.

It is, of course, difficult to be against rehabilitating the physically and mentally handicapped. But the Vocational Rehabilitation Administration has established a reputation for competent administration and skirted the troublesome federal-state relations issue by giving the bulk of its money to the states in largely unfettered grants. But these are more ways of avoiding criticism than of fostering aggressive support. On the more positive side, the federal agency, as well as state agencies, have cemented relationships with universities through research, fellowship, and training grants. Support for research on medical restoration has developed friends in medical circles.

The National Rehabilitation Association functions as an effective spokesman for a broad range of vocational rehabilitation agencies and groups, both public and private. The Association has been deeply involved in legislative activities and often acts as liaison between Congress and the rehabilitation groups. It provides technical expertise in the development of legislation, organizes grass roots support, and maintains relations between the states, the Congress, and the federal agency. National associations of sheltered workshops and volunteer rehabilitation facilities have also won federal support for their activities and have become strong supporters of the vocational rehabilitation program.

In addition to engendering widespread support with no entrenched opposition, the agency continues to effectively exploit current public policy emphasis. Miss Switzer sees a definite pattern in the evolution of social philosophy and has chosen to ride with it: "Vocation Rehabilitation, like many other aspects of human affairs, has evolved through three

172

stages of public attitudes—compassion without action, followed by willingness to act for economic reasons, followed by willingness to act for social reasons." [13] In response, the agency developed cost-benefit analysis as a political argument before other agencies had begun to experiment with it as a management tool. Vocational rehabilitation expenditures are never spoken of as costs but as high-return investments. Traditionally the argument has been not that rehabilitation makes people happier but that it makes them self-supporting.

In keeping with the times, emphasis shifted from economics to humanitarianism in 1965. Amendments that year contained four major provisions: (a) liberalization of federal financing and case service eligibility, (b) federal support for the new construction of workshops and other rehabilitation facilities, (c) an intramural research activity including a data-processing facility, and (d) a concerted program for the removal of architectural barriers to the handicapped. However, vocational rehabilitation's contribution to the "war on poverty" was a predominant theme in the hearings and floor debate on the bill. Eighty percent of entering vocational rehabilitation clients are reported to be poor because they had no income when they applied for services. Supporters within and outside the agency suggested reassignment of the total antipoverty effort. Such inveterate economizers as Congressman H. R. Gross suggested expansion of vocational rehabilitation as a "proven antipoverty program instead of pouring money into new untried programs." Final passage of the legislation was achieved by a standing vote in the House and a similar show of unanimity in the Senate.

The 1965 amendments changed the matching ratio for the basic support of state rehabilitation activities from between 50 and 70 percent to a 75 percent federal share and resulted in a doubling of federal expenditures in the following two years (see Table 7). Innovation grants were added with 90 percent federal support in the first three years to encourage development of techniques not previously used in the state. Also provided were 90-percent-supported expansion grants to encourage an increase in the number of rehabilitants receiving

[13] Switzer, Mary E. "Rehabilitation a Decade Hence." *Rehabilitation Record* 5: 19; July-August 1964.

TABLE 7. Vocational Rehabilitation Expenditures (in Thousands of Dollars)

Fiscal Year	Basic Support				Federal Grants *		
	Total	Federal Grants	State Funds	Federal Share	Research and Demonstrations	Training and Traineeships	Research and Training Centers
1921	285	93	192	32.6%	—	—	—
1930	1,700	740	960	43.5	—	—	—
1940	4,108	1,972	2,136	48.0	—	—	—
1945	9,856	7,136	2,720	72.4	—	—	—
1950	29,347	20,340	9,007	69.3	—	—	—
1954	34,902	21,762	13,140	62.4	—	—	—
1955	39,254	24,463	14,791	62.3	299	637	—
1956	49,461	31,003	18,458	62.7	1,181	1,990	—
1957	57,684	36,054	21,630	62.5	2,000	2,668	—
1958	67,517	42,178	25,339	62.5	3,600	4,156	—
1959	74,712	46,530	28,182	62.3	4,600	4,651	—
1960	80,548	50,059	30,489	62.1	6,390	6,117	—
1961	89,264	55,321	33,943	62.0	8,163	7,106	—
1962	103,823	64,008	39,815	61.7	9,450	9,427	723
1963	117,050	72,099	44,951	61.6	10,994	12,108	1,700
1964	140,098	86,779	53,319	61.9	15,179	16,442	2,965
1965	160,771	99,285	61,486	61.8	17,069	19,770	4,084
1966	232,143 **	158,852	73,291	68.4	20,568	24,520	7,574
1967	330,214 **	248,184	82,030	75.0	21,015	29,717	8,575

* Excludes international research grants.

**Data include funds for Sections 2, 3, and 4.

Source: Department of Health, Education, and Welfare, Rehabilitation Services Administration.

current services. Private nonprofit as well as public rehabilitation groups were made eligible for the latter program. Full federal financing was provided for planning grants for the development of statewide comprehensive plans. The 1954 federally financed training grants and individual trainee fellowships for development of professional rehabilitation personnel were also expanded. The 1965 amendments also provided for the first authorization of moneys to construct new rehabilitation facilities and workshops. Grants were also made available for initial staffing or to upgrade existing staffs.

The work of the National Commission on Architectural Barriers is a further indication of the many-sided attack by vocational rehabilitation on the problems of the handicapped. The Commission's coordinated public relations program is designed to make architects and builders aware of the special needs of the handicapped. It provides technical assistance to ensure the handicapped of ready building access and the use of drinking fountains, telephone booths, and other public facilities. Efforts are also being made to obtain official action through legislation or state and local building code revisions to achieve necessary reforms in architectural planning.

The amendments of 1967 and 1968 authorized federal funds to be used for vocational rehabilitation of handicapped individuals who are both deaf and blind and authorized the training of professional and allied personnel needed to provide specialized services to the deaf-blind.

For more than thirty years, the Rehabilitation Services Administration of the Social and Rehabilitation Service has administered the Randolph Sheppard Vending Stand Act, passed in 1936. Under this Act blind persons are given preference to operate vending stands on federal and other property. In 1968 there were 2,920 stands on federal and private property, providing employment for 3,259 operators. These operators averaged $5,580 in annual earnings.

The 1968 amendments added a grants program which allows contracts or jointly financed cooperative arrangements with employers and organizations for projects to prepare handicapped people for employment in the competitive labor markets.

175

Other new programs include projects to recruit and train manpower, including the handicapped, for careers in rehabilitation; grants to public, private, and rehabilitation agencies to encourage development of special programs to recruit and train handicapped individuals for career jobs in health, welfare, public safety, and law enforcement; and a program to help the disadvantaged, including those *without* physical or mental disabilities *but with employment handicaps* as a result of environmental deprivation.

The rehabilitation process has proved its ability to serve the physically and mentally handicapped. This same process appears applicable to the new dimension of the program—helping the economically and socially handicapped to become employable. During fiscal year 1968 alone, 208,000 handicapped individuals were rehabilitated, compared with only 110,000 in 1963. This is particularly noteworthy since over one-fourth of all rehabilitants are classified as mentally ill or mentally retarded, about double the proportion of five years ago.

Federal-state vocational rehabilitation services are aimed at:

1. Handicapped youth in school rehabilitation programs.

2. The mentally retarded, through the public schools and their special education components.

3. Public offenders and juvenile delinquents, through integration of vocational rehabilitation services with the rehabilitation services of correctional institutions.

4. The mentally ill, through integration of state hospital services with local rehabilitation agency services.

5. Alcoholics, beneficiaries of Social Security Disability Insurance, disabled public assistance recipients, selective service medical rejectees, and target areas of highly concentrated social and economic need.

Vocational rehabilitation has demonstrated that many with serious physical and mental handicaps can be made economically self-supporting by intensive services and a favorable public and employer reaction and that the rehabilitation effort pays off in both economic and humanitarian terms. It suggests that the same could be true with the most seriously socially and environmentally handicapped. It also demonstrates that even a proven payoff and an apparent federal willingness to supply large amounts of matching funds cannot attract support for services for more than a fraction of those eligible.

The Federal-State Employment Service

The preamble of the Constitution contains the philosophical basis for the existence of the U.S. Employment Service which has been renamed the U.S. Training and Employment Service (USTES). According to the preamble, one of the purposes for establishing the federal government was to promote the general welfare, and failure to develop and use properly its human resources has a negative influence on the "general welfare." The Federal-State Employment Service system has as its major function the facilitation of the employment process for all workers and employees who seek its assistance.

Therefore, fundamental to all federal manpower development efforts is the conviction that maximum use must be made of the Federal-State Employment Service system. Its resources—a national network of state and local offices and trained manpower staff—are unmatched and make the Employment Service the logical agent for local implementation of national manpower policy. However, in order to fulfill this role the Service has undergone basic changes to redefine its place in a changing economy.

In the drive to achieve full utilization of the nation's unused or underutilized manpower resources, ever-increasing demands have been placed on the Employment Service at all levels—federal, state, and local. During the 1960's the list of new legislation passed in which the Employment Service had a role is indeed formidable. In addition to the basic legislation authorizing employment and training programs, such new legislation as the Farm Labor Contractor Registration Act of 1964, the Civil Rights Act of 1964, the 1965 amendments to the Immigration and Nationality Act, and the Veterans Readjustment Benefit Act of 1966 have added heavily to Employment Service responsibilities.

Before 1962, the Employment Service functioned primarily as a labor exchange and as administrator of the work tests for unemployment insurance claimants. The agency was limited in its placement functions by the types and numbers of jobs offered by employers and listed voluntarily with the local office, and by the workers and unemployment insurance applicants who found their own way to the office. Today, its role is no longer limited to job placement but has been broadened to include identification of people who need employment assistance, improvement of the labor exchange in matching people to jobs, and development of an employment structure that is free from discrimination and artificial hiring requirements.

To deal with these varied functions, funds for the Federal-State Employment Service more than doubled over the five-year period from June 1963 to June 1968 (from $153 million to $341 million), and the number of local offices increased by nearly one-fourth (to 2,147).

The State Employment Service agencies first moved toward reorientation when, under the Area Redevelopment Act of 1961, they assumed new responsibilities which included careful surveying of area training needs, development of training proposals, the selection and referral of individuals for training, and placement of these individuals after they were trained. In 1962, with the passage of the Manpower Development and Training Act, the role of the Employment Service was further expanded. In 1966, after a searching analysis of responsibilities for meeting the manpower needs of the country, the Employment Service developed the Human Resources Development (HRD) concept—the most significant change in the orientation of the public Employment Service during recent years.

Begun on a demonstration basis in Chicago in 1965 and adopted as a basic part of Employment Service operations in 1966, the Human Resources Development concept is addressed directly to the most critical present and prospective manpower problem—that of hard-core unemployment and underemployment in urban slums. The implementation of the HRD concept brings together all Employment Service efforts to serve individuals in the various groups that have difficulty in obtaining suitable employment, i.e., youth, older workers, handicapped, members of minority groups, hard-core unemployed, and the urban and rural poor.

The HRD concept recognizes that active efforts to seek out the disadvantaged must be made. The background of alienation and discouragement characteristic of slum residents often

178

means that those who need help most will not seek it, even if they know it is available—and many do not. HRD therefore starts with an effort to identify and reach out to those most in need of employment services through new avenues, including the use of community workers, staff in small neighborhood centers, and mobile units. Wherever possible, individuals who reside in the community to be served, or who are representatives of the groups to be served, are utilized in these outreach efforts.

A second basic premise of HRD is the belief that people who are disadvantaged need special kinds of services to help them prepare for and adjust to the modern world of work. These services include special counseling and testing, instruction on the requirements of a regular work situation, referral to occupational training, and continuing contact with the worker after he is employed to help him adjust to his new work environment. A team approach to assisting workers is presently being introduced, using counselors, coaches, and other trained Employment Service personnel. This approach provides continuity in carrying out the individually tailored plan which is developed for each of the HRD clients to chart his progress from unemployment to a job situation which matches his interests and capabilities. In addition, special efforts are made to obtain employers' cooperation in hiring these disadvantaged workers.

Direct linkage with the outreach efforts of other community action, welfare, and education agencies and neighborhood programs is an integral part of HRD. For example, Employment Service personnel are stationed in community action agency neighborhood centers and in other accessible locations.

Human Resources Development is not itself a program but provides the rationale and methodology for Employment Service participation in a number of programs. The new HRD approach has enabled the Employment Service to become the deliverer of manpower services to urban and rural slum areas in the Concentrated Employment Program (CEP). Area residents are being recruited as community service trainees on the employment offices' own staffs, in order to provide a bridge to the target communities and, it is hoped,

179

give convincing evidence to these communities that the Employment Service has a true commitment to serve their best interest. Maintaining contact with private employers through the JOBS program and other, more traditional channels also enables the Employment Service to provide necessary linkages in the employability-employment process.

In addition to the Concentrated Employment Program a major operating base for the HRD concept is the network of centers which has evolved from the Youth Opportunity Center (YOC) program. The YOC program was initiated in 1964 in response to the growing concern about youth unemployment. The national network of centers has now been expanded to provide services to the disadvantaged of all ages.

The Employment Service's concern with youth is based on more than twenty-five years of service in many of the nation's school systems. The cooperative schools program, designed to assist youth in the transition from school to employment, was developed voluntarily by the staff of local schools and local Employment Service offices to supplement school guidance programs. It provides placement and employment counseling services to seniors entering the job market and to school dropouts, with the objective of helping them find suitable jobs. During the 1966-67 school year, local employment offices served nearly 10,000 high schools, close to one-half of all the high schools in the country.

Working with school officials in inner cities, small towns, and rural areas, the Employment Service is now reorienting its cooperative schools program in line with HRD objectives. Emphasis will be on providing employment assistance to actual and potential dropouts as well as to high school seniors and recent graduates who, because of unequal educational opportunity, are inadequately prepared to bridge the gap between school and work.

The expansion and transformation of the Employment Service have not been accomplished without problems. The Employment Service has struggled through major difficulties occasioned by local differences in both needs and program approaches, delayed legislative action on funding, and different program demands and priorities from the national offices of the various federal agencies seeking to carry out the programs required of them under different pieces of legislation. Inadequate staffing, the rigidities of state merit systems, and the slow development of rapport with minority groups in many states have also contributed to the problems of growth and readjustment.

Under the Wagner-Peyser Act no groups or individuals may be denied the services of the public employment offices. Furthermore, nearly all services applicable to one group are needed to some degree by other groups. One of the greatest difficulties of the Employment Service has been how to stretch its limited staff resources to meet the needs of residents of depressed rural areas and urban ghettos; of unemployed and underemployed persons; of employed applicants who expect to be laid off; of jobseekers who meet the criteria of disadvantaged and those who do not; of veterans and nonveterans.

State Employment Service agencies hope to alleviate some of their staffing problems and at the same time provide job opportunities for the unemployed and underemployed through the TIMS (Training in Manpower Services) program, which was developed to help staff priority manpower programs with newly trained people who were previously unemployed or underemployed. TIMS guidelines call for recruitment of people who live in the community to be served, waiver of written merit system examinations as a selection requirement, establishment of a career ladder of preprofessional job classifications, and a firm commitment on the part of the state agencies to hire those who satisfactorily complete the training. Six TIMS programs are underway, and a number of states are considering this kind of training to help staff their manpower programs.

As the development of a national manpower policy moves into the next phase, the Federal-State Employment Service—strengthened by the addition of new manpower tools and with increasing ability to respond to local needs—can assume an even larger role in the implementation of manpower programs.

Adult Basic Education

About 17 million Americans eighteen years of age and over have less than eight years of formal schooling. They represent 13 percent of the population in this age group. A large majority of these individuals are still of working age: two out of every three are under 65, and one out of every four is under 45 years of age.[14]

The Adult Basic Education (ABE) Program, initially authorized by the Economic Opportunity Act of 1964, represents a national effort to remedy the education deficiencies which limit the employment opportunities of this large segment of the population. The program is now administered by the U.S. Office of Education under the Adult Education Act of 1966. It operates through state departments of education and, mainly, local public school systems, although private nonprofit educational agencies may also apply to the states for funds for local programs. Classes are offered free of charge to undereducated adults and are now available in all states, the District of Columbia, and several territories.

Adult basic education can take place almost anywhere. The principal concern is to bring education to the people wherever they are—in homes, churches, union halls, hospitals, or prisons. Formal adult learning centers have been established in school buildings in a number of areas, but many basic education classes are conducted in open-air settings of migrant labor camps and Indian reservations.

Subject matter usually has to do with occupational, social, or family activities. Reading, writing, arithmetic, speaking English, and other fundamentals come first, followed by practical instruction in such down-to-earth matters as answering an advertisement by telephone, using the classified telephone directory for job leads, and making out an application blank. The curriculum may include consumer education, home and family life, and other subjects necessary to carry out adult responsibilities. Television and radio are used as instructional aids; in one case, a traveling language laboratory is bringing advanced instructional techniques to Spanish and American Indian settlements where English is unknown.

ABE students are as ethnically varied as America itself— white, black, Oriental, Mexican-American, American Indian, Puerto Rican. More are married than not, and nearly half are the heads of families or the main wage earners, though

[14] *Manpower Report of the President,* including a *Report on Manpower Requirements, Resources, Utilization, and Training,* January 1969. p. 80.

the wages they earn are usually minimal (more than half the ABE students recently surveyed reported annual incomes below the $3,000 poverty line). One out of five was on public assistance.

Altogether, 1.3 million people—nearly two-thirds of them under forty-five years of age—have been reached by the ABE program in the past four years. Though nearly one-fifth reported that they had nine to eleven years of formal education, their actual educational accomplishment was below the eighth grade as required for participation in the program. One out of every five enrollees had never gone beyond the third grade.

Most of the people in the program enrolled without a definite occupational goal in mind, seeking simply to better their education. However, about 10,000 each year go into job training under the manpower training programs. The Adult Basic Education Program thus supplements the more limited MDTA provision for remedial education for those who need this extra help in order to profit from occupational training.

Efforts have been underway to strengthen the program. Training institutes have been held for teachers and administrators, chiefly in summer sessions at colleges and universities across the country, to acquaint them with the special problems of the disadvantaged and to improve their techniques for teaching this group. Several demonstration projects also have been sponsored by the Office of Education to aid in developing new and more effective teaching methods and materials. Other special projects aim at recruiting and enrolling the under-educated, the hard-to-reach and hard-to-teach, in remedial education and job training programs.

The level of funding for the ABE program will largely determine the pace of progress in eliminating adult illiteracy in the United States. Since fiscal 1965, Congress has appropriated nearly $109 million for this program. Annual appropriations have more than doubled during the past four years: in fiscal 1965, the appropriation was $19 million; for fiscal 1968, nearly $39 million. However, the scale of program operations is still far below that required to quickly reduce the educational deficiencies which now contribute so heavily to the national problems of poverty and hard-core un-employment.

8. A Manpower Development Approach

Emerging Trends

During the 1960's certain trends were evident from the standpoint of a national manpower policy:

1. The trend toward making manpower policy synonymous with programs for the unemployed and the disadvantaged.

2. The trend toward sole concern for the pool of disadvantaged and little concern for the prevention of the causes of unemployment and individual failure.

3. The institutionalization of emergency measures into permanent operating programs funded solely by the federal government.

4. Failure to recognize lack of education as the root cause of individual failure and the substitution of job skills as a corrective at a time when technology has been moving the nation and the work force in precisely opposite directions.

5. A practice of isolating the administration of federal programs from other levels of government to the degree that the federal government is seen by many as having sole responsibility for the disadvantaged.

6. A trend to respond only to the crises and not to the long-term need of rebuilding and restructuring established institutions to reduce the flow into the pool of disadvantaged.

7. A practice of noninvolvement of state or local officials in the planning of federal legislation and administrative regulations until the legislation or regulations have been fixed, with the force and effect of law.

8. A trend to reduce the pressure for state and local response to their responsibilities for the disadvantaged.

9. A trend to force a partnership between the federal government and business rather than to encourage a state and local partnership with individual employers.

10. A trend toward establishing a system, rather than developing a plan, for coordination and supplementation. The core of this problem is in the bureaucratic establishment at the federal level where cooperation is penalized and incentives for separation are provided by appropriations.

Funding and Legislation

In general, budget requests have tended to become institutionalized in proposed legislation. Support for remedial manpower training has been an administration priority during this decade, with little thought given to prevention. However, Congress has promoted both vocational education and manpower training, as shown by passage of the Vocational Education Amendments of 1968 and the budget increases voted for both vocational education and manpower training in fiscal year 1970.

Appropriations for vocational education stabilized shortly after an initial small increase when the Vocational Education Act of 1963 was put into effect in fiscal year 1965. Between 1966 and 1969, appropriations varied by no more than $32 million over the 1966 level, reaching in 1969 a figure only about $13 million above 1966. Budget requests usually came close to final appropriations, since authorization levels were so low.

During this same period, the states responded swiftly to the additional funds provided under the 1963 act. While only a 50-50 matching effort by the states was required to meet federal funding requirements, most states overmatched the federal dollar by large amounts and continued to increase expenditures for vocational education in spite of spiraling state and local taxes and the uncertainty of federal appropriations.

In October 1968, Congress passed the Vocational Education Amendments of 1968, authorizing basic grants of $2.9 billion to the states for the first five years of operation. Parts of the act have separate authorizations for exemplary programs and projects, cooperative education, consumer and homemaking education, residential schools, and work-study. The amendments placed high priority on meeting crucial needs and provided stiff requirements to ensure that efforts to help the disadvantaged would be made: 15 percent of the basic grant allotment must be spent on the disadvantaged, 15 percent on postsecondary programs, and 10 percent on the handicapped.

The 1970 budget request of $279 million was considerably lower than authorizations provided in the Vocational Education Amendments of 1968, but it did represent an increase of about $31 million over the previous year's request and appropriation. The administration decided to include vocational education in budgetary restrictions to reduce inflation, but the House, responding to mail from concerned citizens, passed an allowance of $488 million, almost doubling the 1969 appropriation of $248 million. This indicates the obligation House members felt concerning the Vocational Education Amendments of 1968, which authorized up to $565 million in basic grants in 1970, as well as Congressional support of the strongly expressed demand to increase funding for manpower development through public education. The Senate also increased appropriations for vocational education.

Administration support of vocational education has been limited to minor increases. The conflict of philosophy between present manpower legislation and vocational education centers on delivery systems. While vocational education is primarily a decentralized program administered through states and thus subject to Congressional influence and control, manpower training programs are more centralized, requiring direct federal decision by the executive branch.

Comparison of the vocational education budget with those of the Manpower Development and Training Act and the training programs under the Economic Opportunity Act shows that during the 1960's the executive branch has generally supported manpower training more than vocational education. In a year in which much concern was expressed about the effect of additional expenditures on inflation, the federal budget request for the Manpower Development and Training Act increased almost $290 million over the previous year's appropriation. Most of this increase will go to on-the-job training programs in JOBS and CEP. Total requests amounted

187

to $689 million for 1970, as compared with $279 million for vocational education.

The 1970 projections for JOBS and CEP came to $316 million, leaving the states only $208 million with which to conduct their MDTA training programs. Since about 60 percent of the $160 million allocated for institutional training under MDTA goes to the state employment services for the payment of allowances to trainees, the institutional programs were reduced relative to on-the-job training.

General trends in MDTA budgets include increased support for on-the-job training programs and for subsidizing employers who provide basic education as well as job skill training. During the mid-1960's policy was redirected from serving the less disadvantaged—those who were motivated and willing to learn and work but who were lacking in skills and opportunity —to providing manpower training for the hard-core disadvantaged, the functionally illiterate, and the alienated.

The actual programs which were promoted in redirecting MDTA, however, reduced emphasis on institutional education programs and gave greater priority to on-the-job training, which is lower in initial cost and guarantees an entry job but which gives no guarantee of continued employment if job skills shift. The proof lies in the fact that the number of people in the pool of disadvantaged remains about the same.

The hard-core disadvantaged frequently need basic education before they are able to accept skill training. Difficulties experienced by many employers in training disadvantaged people has led to federal subsidies to employers for locating plants near slums and for hiring and training the disadvantaged, including providing them with a basic education. Although this is a good program, the flow of disadvantaged to the pool has not been reduced.

Both vocational education and MDTA appropriations show a pattern of initial rise to a level maintained from 1966 through 1969, then great increases provided in the House allowance for fiscal year 1970. The budget request, however, varied considerably for 1970, with vocational education rising only slightly, while manpower training increased by about 70 percent. The House approved almost all of the administration's request for MDTA, including the increases for JOBS and CEP, both fundamental on-the-job training programs.

188

Training programs under the Economic Opportunity Act include the Job Corps, the Neighborhood Youth Corps, and several other programs administered by the Department of Labor. The administration's budget asked for decreased funding from 1969.

Adult basic education received increased budget requests which were approved by the House. The amounts involved were small compared to the need, but adult basic education was one of the few educational programs increased in President Nixon's budget. Since all of these funds flow directly into programs for the hard-core disadvantaged, the value of this program could not be disputed.

Considering overall budget trends since 1965, support for vocational education seems to have come chiefly from Congress, while manpower development and training has been pushed by the executive branch. Increases in funding have gone to on-the-job training, increasing direct training by private employers and resulting in more subsidy arrangements for employers and smaller responsibilities for public education —even though many facilities and skill centers located in schools and colleges are not in full use.

Since many of the on-the-job training programs are administered by the Secretary of Labor through a direct grant system, there has been greater federal direction of manpower training programs with less involvement of state and local governments. The greater involvement of private employers has reduced the role of education in manpower training to the extent that if administration budget trends are approved by Congress, the Secretary of Labor and private industry will have the major administrative and program responsibility for manpower training.

The result of the emphasis on manpower training programs means concentration on remediation at the expense of prevention. On-the-job training and even regular institutional training programs under MDTA and OEO help those people who failed to receive proper education and skill preparation. Vocational education should be developed into a well-coordinated system extending from junior high exploratory programs through skill training, with levels of instruction from basic education through advanced postsecondary programs. Then in cooperation with private employers, vocational education could reduce the flow of the unskilled and alienated into the unemployment pool as well as effect some permanent pool reduction. Budget requests, however, indicate a tendency to settle for remedial, short-term manpower programs as the solution to current problems of unemployment, without coming to grips with long-term needs for education and training.

Efforts to institutionalize trends in budget requests concerning education and manpower training have been made in proposed legislation. Some of the proposed legislation reduces the role of the educational system in manpower development and training, tending toward a completely federalized manpower program under the control of the Department of Labor. This, in effect, would establish a dual system of education with separate programs for the disadvantaged after they have been denied the help they needed during their development years in school.

On May 5, 1969, Representative Steiger introduced the Comprehensive Manpower Act of 1969 in the House. Its declared purpose is "to develop and strengthen a systematic National, State, and local manpower policy and provide for a comprehensive delivery of manpower services." Structure of the bill includes authorization of $2 billion for fiscal year 1971, increasing to $3 billion for 1974. The appropriations are to be divided: 30 percent reserved by the Secretary of Labor for direct grants for educationally oriented programs, with the remainder to be apportioned among the states. To administer the program, the Secretary of Labor is to enter into an agreement with the governor of each state, in which a planning group is to develop a comprehensive manpower plan for the state. Responsibility for carrying out the plan rests with the governor. If the comprehensive plan is not approved by the U.S. Department of Labor, the Secretary is to formulate a plan for the state together with the Department of Health, Education, and Welfare. Long-range plans are to be submitted to and approved by the Secretary of Labor, and the Secretary of HEW must approve sections of the plan relating to institutional training and operation of skill centers.

The Steiger Bill is aimed at providing training and assistance to those from poverty-level families, unemployed and underemployed persons aged sixteen or older, students in grades nine through twelve from low-income families who need part-time employment and useful work experience, and persons eligible for the Job Corps.

Programs acceptable for funding include counseling and testing, skill training, basic education, medical examinations and treatment, on-the-job training, work-study, public service employment, family and supportive services, recruitment and placement services, research, employer incentives, experimental programs in correctional institutions, relocation payments, evaluation of state programs, cooperative training, and training allowances.

The involvement of the educational community is limited to participation in the planning group by the state educational agency, a requirement that institutional training be provided through the state educational agencies where possible, requirements that the Secretary of HEW approve aspects of the plan relating to institutional centers and approve direct grants for educationally oriented programs, plus joint participation of the Secretaries of Labor and HEW in formulating a plan for a state without one.

Representative O'Hara also introduced a bill in May 1969, entitled The Manpower Act, with the purpose of ensuring "an opportunity for employment to every American seeking work." In this bill, the Secretary of Labor has total responsibility for providing manpower services either directly or through contracts with public or private agencies and organizations. He selects the most appropriate mode of operation; state plans are not authorized. No state apportionments are provided for; authorization of appropriations includes such sums as would be necessary to carry out the act.

Those eligible for training and services are much the same as in the Steiger bill, with the addition of persons in correctional institutions. Persons between eighteen and sixty-five who are unemployed or underemployed, but able and willing to work, are eligible for public service employment.

Approved activities are similar to those in the Steiger bill, with the addition of residential training programs and development efforts to solicit job opportunities for the disadvantaged, occupational training in industry through contracts for upgrading programs, and public service employment for those not likely to find employment in the private sector. Neither the educational community nor the Secretary of HEW is to be involved directly in this proposed manpower program. The Secretary of Labor is authorized to use any type of appropriate institution.

On August 12, 1969, Senator Javits introduced the administration bill on manpower training, the Manpower Training Act of 1969, in the Senate and Representative Ayres presented it in the House. The bill was intended to "establish a comprehensive manpower development program to assist persons in overcoming obstacles to suitable employment and for other purposes." Other purposes include creation of a comprehensive manpower service system with a single administrative channel through the Secretary of Labor, governors of states, and mayors of cities and incorporation of innovations to improve the manpower delivery system, such as advisory councils, computerized job banks, incentive opportunities, and provisions relating the amount appropriated under the act to the national unemployment level.

The administration bill authorizes continuous appropriations of the amount necessary to carry out the act, with 75 percent of the funds (except for job bank and economic stabilizer funds) to be apportioned to the states in a uniform manner. Three stages of decentralization are proposed: states having an approved plan would receive 25 percent of their apportionment (the Secretary of Labor would control the rest); states having a comprehensive manpower agency, a state manpower planning council, and an approved plan could use slightly over 66 percent of their apportionment; and states with exemplary plans and processes of implementation could control 100 percent of their funds. The Secretary of Labor could spend 20 percent of the total funds appropriated as he found necessary, and the remaining 5 percent of the appropriation would go to states which were making additional contributions to activities under the state plan.

The job bank has a separate authorization. The bill also declares that an active manpower policy should be used as an economic stabilizer and provides for an automatic increase in manpower program funds, equal to 10 percent of the amount appropriated, which would be used by the Secretary of Labor when the ratio of national unemployment reached 4.5 percent.

Each state must establish and maintain a comprehensive manpower agency—with representation from all agencies having responsibilities for manpower training—to be eligible for control over its funds. The Secretary of Labor administers all funds a state does not qualify for and determines when a state has an acceptable manpower agency and plan.

The groups this bill would serve are similar to those in the other two bills—the unemployed, underemployed, and disadvantaged, sixteen years or older. In addition, the Secretary of Labor can designate persons eligible for participation or can impose additional qualifications if he determines it necessary for the implementation of the act. Programs and services which can be funded under the state plan include most of those in the other two bills. The Secretary of Labor also determines other programs which could be funded.

Direct involvement of HEW is limited to concurrence by the Secretary of HEW with respect to programs, standards, rules, and regulations, and to representation of all agencies administering manpower training in the manpower planning organization and in area advisory bodies.

Any of these bills would substantially reduce the role of education in manpower development and training. They would permit control of all occupational training by a delivery system of direct federal contracts, establishing a dual system of education in which the disadvantaged "have nots" go to federalized private industry schools and the "haves" go to regular public institutions.

Specific effects of the trends in budget requests and in proposed legislation include the following:

1. Control over program administration by the Secretary of Labor and state governors.

2. Elimination of real participation by the Secretary of HEW and the educational community in manpower development and training.

3. Lack of real coordination of all the diverse programs now providing manpower training.

4. Development of a separate school system.

5. Permanent establishment and institutionalization of short-term, remedial manpower training.

6. Emphasis on training to reduce unemployment rather than on educated, participating citizens who would be able to

choose from a broad range of occupations in the world of work.

We must either do new things in education or develop new institutions to meet the need for manpower training. Education is the underlying base for manpower development, and integration of the educational system with manpower policy is essential for successful operation. The concept of skill training can be dehumanizing; development of human resources requires more than narrow preparation for a job. The schools must accept responsibility for manpower development or new institutions will be developed which emphasize remediation rather than prevention, isolate the disadvantaged from the mainstream of society, and, even worse, reduce the pressure on education to develop the necessary programs to serve those who most need education.

Present and proposed manpower legislation provides 100 percent federal funding for the programs, including services and individual income not provided in any educational legislation. This puts states and local agencies in an impossible position. State and local taxes have risen sharply during the sixties, to the point where it is difficult to provide matching funds under vocational education legislation. Thus, it is very easy to give up and let the federal government carry the load.

Since federal programs tend to utilize private industry or skill centers rather than educational systems, a manpower development policy will have to be developed to include education as its basis and to coordinate the diverse federal, state, and local programs which attempt to meet the multitude of needs. Manpower training programs are generally highly effective for people who have entered the labor market and need remedial help to develop specific skills. Vocational education prepares youths for job entry and adults for long-term upgrading with great success, preventing failure and reducing the flow into the unemployment pool. The disadvantaged can benefit from both types of programs, depending on their individual needs. A manpower policy must be developed which provides a structured plan with programs for all of these people.

In neither the short- or long-range time span does it appear likely that those most in need are anxious to be trained outside the mainstream of society. Surely a way can be found which will allow these people to be integrated into a public system of education and skill development open to all.

A National Manpower Development Commission

Thomas Jefferson said, "If a nation expects to be ignorant and free, in a state of civilization, it expects what never was and never will be." The people of this country have long held to this basic concept—more than have any other people. We are now the oldest political unit among the nations. Yet today, as never before, we are aware of the horrendous danger of having some of our citizens without an education. It is obvious that those who are ignorant are not free in a technological age. Our efforts in manpower policy development have tended to overlook this fact and to focus instead on remediation and job skills. This has resulted in a manpower policy geared more to jurisdictional organization than to functional need.

At the same time education in this nation has tended to expand on the basis of a concept which emphasized only one side of learning. Alfred North Whitehead, the Harvard mathematician and educator, said that some educational trends were fallacious. He wrote:

> The antithesis between a technical and a liberal education is fallacious. There can be no adequate technical education which is not liberal, and no liberal education which is not technical; that is, no education which does not impart both technique and intellectual vision. In simpler language, education should turn out the pupil with something he knows well and something he can do well. This intimate union of practice and theory aids both. The intellect does not work best in a vacuum. The stimulation of creative impulses requires, especially in the care of a child, the quick transition to practice . . . .[1]

In both the short- and long-run approach to manpower policy the end is the person and the means is his development through learning. Supply of labor, reducing unemployment,

[1] Whitehead, Alfred North. *The Aims of Education and Other Essays.* New York: New American Library, July 1949.

195

job development, economic growth, fiscal effectiveness and organization, and administration are but means which must stem from a basic purpose and a basic premise regarding human development goals.

It is doubtful that anyone would quarrel with either the purpose or means. The arguments, the conflicts, and the failures grow out of the secondary means and procedures. Yet if there is no basic philosophy or scheme, the building of a sound operation will neither solve the problem nor accomplish the secondary goals. At any one time a secondary goal, such as unemployment or poverty, will take precedence in operating; but, if this is not built on a sound premise, it will surely fail. Some progress has been made, but the pool of unemployed and those in poverty have not been substantially reduced in terms of actual numbers.

A recent paper prepared by Walter Reuther spells out some of the major goals which a national manpower policy should consider. Reuther says in effect we must consider the following in a manpower policy:

Regarding Employment

1. Full employment; how do we create it and maintain it.
2. A job as rewarding work, for every person to his highest capacities.
3. A good work environment, which will promote individual dignity and self-respect.
4. A chance to learn and advance for every person.
5. A decent wage and income insurance between jobs.

Regarding the Nature of Work

6. Strive to eliminate the uselessness of certain work.
7. Prepare all for creative and contributory work.
8. Allow for the enjoyment of leisure.
9. Develop means for the transition from one job to another in a technological society.

Regarding the Equality of Opportunity

10. Special help for the disadvantaged individual and community.
11. Elimination of the barriers of prejudice as to race, creed, or sex.
12. Opportunities for the handicapped.

196

13. Preventive and therapeutic medicine for personal or area distress.

Regarding the Worker as a Human

14. Eliminating the use of people as "manpower" and their purchase in a "labor market."

15. The human as a contributor to society rather than as an instrument of production.

16. Education and training for people as more effective participants in, and for enjoyment of all, aspects of living.[2]

This is a tall order. Yet we cannot wait to act upon the broader, more human aspects of manpower policy. It is thus sound philosophy to make education the cornerstone of manpower policy as human problems arise from technological changes. Such changes must provide benefits and protection for all, and any policy which simply aims at eliminating the symptoms of unemployment and poverty without focusing on the causes cannot be good enough today.

There are basic problems to be encountered in accomplishing our goals, many of which grew out of what appeared to be sound solutions in the past. The first of these problems is the unplanned overlapping of federal agencies involved in some aspect of manpower policy implementation. We cannot immediately eliminate these agencies of course; such a cure would be more drastic than the disease. Many people needing help would be lost in the shuffle, and the time factor alone would be disastrous to many. We must, therefore, provide incentives for cooperation and coordination among agencies at the federal level. This is difficult to do by taking away responsibilities (politically at least), but it might be done by substituting new or more important responsibilities which would be needed in a comprehensive manpower policy.

The second problem is the multiplicity of governments involved in some aspect of manpower policy implementation— federal, state, local, and intermediate. Again, we should not eliminate the responsibilities of these various levels and forms of government. In fact, it may be argued that this would be the worst thing to do. If the smallest government unit sees no

[2] Reuther, Walter P. "The Human Goals of Manpower Policy." *Manpower Tomorrow.* (Edited by Irving H. Siegel.) New York: August N. Nelly, Publishers, 1967. p. 31.

responsibility, we cannot expect that sound solutions will be formed, because it is at this level of government that the opportunity for direct involvement with people is greatest. The solution rests more on how these government levels and units may supplement each other's efforts than on the elimination of responsibility for the problem at any one level. Incentives for planning together and incentives for helping each unit do what it can do best appear to be the best places to start.

Third is the variety of funding levels available in various pieces of federal legislation. There are now laws which provide a variety of support levels to the needy depending on the program in which they participate. To accomplish manpower training, one federal agency may supply 100 percent money, another 90, another 80, another 50, and some none at all. Incentives to compete rather than complement are built into federal laws. On top of this, the ability of various areas, governments, and private employers to match federal funds is so diverse that it prevents some from even making an effort. A program must be developed which tries to build equality among support programs for similar responsibilities. The question is constantly raised as to how schools can carry out programs of manpower training or provide related services when their funding level is 50 percent that of another local agency receiving federal funds to do the same thing. Federal funds in manpower should be used to stimulate support from local and private sources and to increase their desire to be responsible.

Fourth is the instability of federal funds and their late arrival, preventing—often eliminating—sound planning and administration. Unusually high overhead and start-up costs keep recurring because of this instability, which is rooted in the fact that there is no basic manpower policy.

Fifth is the constant change in laws on the books which causes confusion within all agencies involved. In the beginning it was hoped that after a few years the need for permanent programs to aid the needy would disappear. Since that is not likely to happen in a technological society, constant changes in the laws are bound to create ineffectiveness. This is not an argument to keep the same laws but rather to develop a long-range plan within which change may occur. How many of the states which must submit long-range plans for federal approval are aware of any long-range plans of the federal government?

Sixth is the variety of local conditions and environments which dictates the failure in many places of any overall federal set of regulations. Obviously, greater reliance is necessary on the people and elected officials in these areas as to how to carry out such operations. This, of course, must be done within the framework of a national policy.

Seventh is the fact that the solution of manpower problems lies with the development of people—each of whom is different. No single approach to each person at any level is likely to create the self-development of each individual, which should be the first goal of any manpower policy. Perhaps we need to consider a policy which provides greater options and choices to the individual after adequate personal help and assistance. This approach argues that there are several ways for an individual to gain competence and several social institutions which may serve him. The concept that it is necessary to have one all-encompassing agency may be unsound.

Eighth is the common problem of protecting the senior worker in each craft, skill, or profession. Those who have achieved some security because of their own skills or professional organization greatly fear the technological change which may replace them with less well-educated and skilled people. Overcoming this fear or upgrading these people to higher level work has got to be part of the solution. Simply ignoring it will create future problems faster than the present ones can be solved.

Ninth is the lack of emphasis on monitoring or assessing the effectiveness of new programs. The inability to evaluate by state and local governments, either through lack of funds or manpower, seriously delays program change at these levels. There is practically no money at the operating level in the federal government to get the facts needed to improve administration. It may be well to assign the evaluation of programs to a different level, but to prevent the local, state, and federal administrators from monitoring and assessing their own programs guarantees administrative and jurisdictional defensiveness.

Tenth is the competition for political "brownie points" among the various government levels. Who will get credit for the program that works seems to be of great concern to elected officials at each level and often prevents organization and administrative changes. The swing vote at all levels or the minority of voters that can control an election often become the basis for action because there is no comprehensive policy.

The last problem is that there is no stimulus to continue innovation or improvement. There must be rewards built into a manpower program to provide incentives for effective results. At present, the overriding emphasis is on the development of new approaches, with little emphasis on providing funds to flow to the state or local agencies doing the best job. The belief that simply knowing about good practices will cause change is considered to be a change agent in itself. The gap between research and development and program operation is especially obvious at the federal level. Federal funding at present bypasses the state and local government units as change agents and relies on so-called competition with other private or nonresponsible organizations to use the change money. It is not working.

The previous analysis indicates that there should be a better approach than those discussed. The following ideas are presented as a basis for such an approach. They are grounded on a few principles which should be outlined first.

1. Fiscal incentives for cooperation and coordination are necessary at the federal and state levels among the various agencies responsible for program administration.

2. One single manpower agency cannot do the job, nor is there any likelihood that one could be formed at either the federal or state level.

3. Parts of the manpower job should be assigned to those agencies, at federal and state levels, that have the talent and experience in particular areas.

4. An overall planning group is necessary which is not responsible to any agency that administers programs. This group must consider both flow and pool problems.

5. There must be citizen participation at all governmental levels in an advisory role, independent of any personal benefit or government connection.

6. Special funds for long-range planning and agency plan review must be provided.

7. Education is the underlying base for manpower development; thus the educational agencies at all three levels must be a fundamental part of the overall operation of the policy.

8. Public hearings are necessary prior to the adoption of any plan at all three governmental levels.

9. Prevention should have equal priority with correction.

10. Plans must involve business and industry in the development of manpower, as well as its utilization. This must be done on a permanent basis.

The most glaring defect in the present piecemeal approach is the failure to develop manpower and correct failures at the fringes of society's mainstream.

The most urgent need is a planned approach that meshes the variety of programs which are now separate. This includes general education, vocational education, manpower development and training, adult education, poverty, rehabilitation, welfare, and on-the-job training.

The most feasible process is to use those agencies now established rather than build additional ones.

The most effective way is to provide incentives to coordinate rather than compete.

This is the way to start. In the long run this effort may lead to the development of a new agency, the elimination of others, and the changing of practices; but this is not likely to come about just because someone suggests it.

The first step in developing a truly comprehensive manpower policy would be to establish, by Congressional action, a National Manpower Development Commission, independent of Congress, federal agencies, and the executive branch. The Commission members, to be appointed by the President, would have overlapping terms of service so the Commission could not be dominated by any administration. The Commission would administer no programs, make no federal grants, and control no federal agency. Its primary purpose would be to review the operation of the total manpower development effort and report to Congress, the executive branch, federal agencies that operate programs, and parallel state agencies. Its recommendations should be made public and be available to any concerned agency or unit. In addition, this Commission should have at its discretion an incentive fund which it could make available only to federal agency operating units.

The Commission should consist of eleven voting members representative of organized labor, business and industry, education, urban planning, rural development, state planning unit, along with citizens knowledgeable in manpower, vocational education, poverty, welfare programs, and health fields.

In addition, there should be seven ex officio, nonvoting members appointed from the Department of Housing and Urban Development—Model Cities, the Department of Commerce—Area Development, the Office of Economic Opportunity—Community Action, the Department of Labor—Manpower Administration, the Department of Health, Education, and Welfare—Health, Vocational Education, and Social Services. The Commission would be free to invite representation from other agencies when it wished, but it could not mandate any specific task to be done by the agencies. Agency compliance would be voluntary.

Funds to operate the Commission would come from Congress, limited by law. There would be no appropriations, however. The funds would be set aside from each agency's appropriation.

The independence of the Commission should be so protected that it would not appear before the Bureau of the Budget or committees of Congress in support of programs or funds for itself or any agency of the federal, state, or local governmental units. Governmental units might ask it for information, but the Commission would provide it only within the operating funds it is allowed and at its sole discretion.

The incentive fund which the Commission would have available to it would come from 1 percent of the appropriations of each of the following federal agencies—Department of Labor; Department of Health, Education, and Welfare; Office of Economic Opportunity; Department of Commerce; and Department of Housing and Urban Development. The money could then be allocated to any single agency, or a combination of agencies, through a coordinated plan sub-

202

mitted to the Commission by the combined agencies. Criteria for selection of agency grants would be:

1. The urgency of expanding a single program or plan to meet a current crisis.

2. Programs which promote and actually cause agency co-ordination in expending their own funds.

3. New program approaches which appear to the Commission to offer promise of stemming the flow of youth and adults into the pool of disadvantaged.

4. Programs that grow out of joint planning between and among federal agencies.

5. Such special programs as the Commission feels merit trial funding and which include the commitment of redirection of agency funds by the applicant agency.

The basis for awarding the funds to any federal operating unit or combination would be the submission of an application and a five-year plan by the agency to the Commission. No funds would go to an agency refusing to outline its future plans. The agency's plan would include consideration of plans submitted to it by the individual states.

The National Commission would report annually—or through special reports as it deemed advisable—only after a review of federal departmental plans and upon receipt of reports from each of the state commissions recommended in this proposal.

It is further suggested that the Commission, in its annual report, outline a plan for the federal departments to consider in developing their own operations. A public hearing of the Commission's plan would be held prior to the final draft, at which time written questions could be raised by concerned federal departments and written comments could be submitted to the Commission within ten days. The Commission would consider these comments but in no way be held accountable for including them in its own plan or recommendations. Each state commission could also comment in writing on the Commission's plan within ten days following the hearing date, in no more than five written pages. The annual report would also include the awards of incentive funds and a brief outline of the proposal and the reasons for funding each proposal.

State Manpower Development Councils

The proposal for a start in developing a comprehensive manpower plan includes a State Manpower Council operating in similar fashion to the federal Commission. The State Council would operate from funds set aside from federal grants made available to each state by each of the federal departments. A state incentive fund would be available, in the same manner as the federal incentive fund, for the State Manpower Development Council to distribute among the state agencies administering funds for manpower development. It is suggested that 2 percent be set aside for the State Council. Each State Council would then have not less than $200,000 or more than $400,000 to operate its own activities.

Each State Manpower Development Council would be appointed by the governor for overlapping terms which exceed the term of office of the governor, except that the first appointees would be staggered. First appointees to the Council would draw lots to determine their length of appointment. The State Council would consist of sixteen members representing the state employment agency, vocational education agency, state welfare agency, state health department, state employment security, state education agency (if different from vocational education agency), state economic opportunity agency, organized labor, business and industry, urban planning, rural development, state planning office, along with citizens with special competence in employment creation, disadvantaged planning and services, local education functions, and industrial development.

The duties of the State Council would be:

1. To develop a state Comprehensive Manpower Plan after review of the state plans prepared by each of the state operational units receiving federal-state grant funds, including vocational education, public health, state welfare agency, state employment agency, vocational rehabilitation agency, and office of economic opportunity.

2. To allocate incentive funds to each of the state administrative units or any combination thereof which meets the criteria established for such grants to improve the operation and plans of state manpower development programs.

3. To hold a public hearing, at which time the incentive grants would be made and the preliminary state plan presented. Twenty days should be allowed for comments from state agencies and local units before a final plan is presented to the governor, the legislature, and the National Manpower Development Commission.

4. To develop an annual report which would include an evaluation of and recommendations to each of the operational state units represented on the Council. These would be based on a review of the state plan submitted by each agency to its federal counterpart or funding unit.

5. To act as an advisory council to the state agency designated to administer the Manpower Development and Training Act in the state. (*Alternate*) To be the state board which administers the corrective and remedial manpower funds from the Department of Labor.

6. To comment on the National Manpower Development Commission's annual report and recommendations.

7. To make specific recommendations to the governor, the state legislature, and the state board regarding changes needed in the individual state agency plans. These would include recommendations for changes in legislation and organization necessary to improve the operation and development of the state's total manpower efforts.

8. To prepare and disseminate guidelines for cooperative local manpower planning.

9. To evaluate and assess progress and state plans developed by the state manpower agency.

9. Education and Manpower Policy

We have talked a great deal in this country about manpower policy and manpower development, but there is still no real national manpower policy. Under the heading "manpower development," we have essentially produced a not-too-sophisticated approach to welfare and to the poor. This approach, and all present proposed legislation, is concerned almost completely with programs aimed at the poor and the disadvantaged. The major premise of this book is that programs which isolate the poor and the disadvantaged from education and services which all other citizens use to gain individual success will not work.

A national policy which provides an approach for the disadvantaged that is separate from the main programs for other citizens is de facto segregation of both groups and therefore of less quality and less value. In both the short run and long run, such a policy rigidifies present institutions and multiplies the need for even greater isolation. No citizen of this country wants to be branded a failure in order to gain the extra help he needs to become a successful person. No institution or program will long be supported if it is seen solely as an increasing burden to the rest of society.

What Is Our Present Manpower Policy?

The present definition of the target group to be served by manpower programs includes the unemployed, especially those out of work for fifteen weeks or more; the nonwhite; youths, especially those with less than a high school education; those over forty-five years of age; those receiving public assistance; the physically, mentally, and socially handicapped; the residents of inner city ghettos; and members of families having an annual income of less than $3,150 per year for a family of four.

Our manpower policy is thus simply a special program for the "others" in our society. It has become increasingly an experiment in designing an approach to welfare for the most disadvantaged members or potential members of the labor force. The original emphasis of the Manpower Development and Training Act, to upgrade those in the labor force to move into shortage skill areas, has been almost totally replaced by the emphasis on the submarginal labor force groups and handicapped individuals. At the same time, public funds to train and retrain for shortage skills have become a smaller and smaller percentage of the federal investment.

There has been little concern for the concept of job development as a function of manpower policy. While we now know that mere economic growth will not provide jobs for all, the overall function of manpower policy is to develop a total approach to a stable and increasingly productive economic foundation for national strength and development. While the development of labor supply and its placement is fundamental for all, our present policy has focused only on the poor and disadvantaged part of the supply, a loss to both the poor and the rest of society. At the same time, this narrow focus has placed nearly all efforts in the hands of one federal agency. It is obvious that the solution to the problem cannot be achieved unless other agencies and other levels of government are given responsibilities and funding under a total manpower policy umbrella. The lack of an umbrella becomes the basis for agency conflict and competition in order to avoid the rain of criticisms that follows from continuing problems.

These remarks are not made to question the necessity of immediate efforts and emergency programs to aid the poor and unemployed. They are not made to criticize the value of the present objectives, but rather to ask if this is a wise or broad enough base for a true manpower policy, either for today or tomorrow. We have become so "hung up" on this goal that we are unable to develop a true comprehensive manpower policy. In the long run a manpower policy must become an integral part of all government efforts at all government levels in the areas of economic, educational, and political policies which *are aimed at all parts of the nation and all of its citizens.* If this is not done, the support and the resources needed will not be produced, nor will public funds be invested at a sufficient level. If the present manpower programs continue in the direction they are headed—simply doing more of what has been done and trying to do it better—they will be in the same kind of trouble that the educational system is now in.

What Is a Comprehensive Manpower Policy?

A comprehensive manpower policy should contain several elements, including adequate job opportunities (demand); qualified and motivated people (supply); and a process for bringing people and jobs together (placement). Of course to these must be added the concept of economic stability and growth with special help for the disadvantaged.

Unfortunately, very little effort has been made, in terms of money, in the area of job demand. Very little has been done, in terms of money, relative to placement—at least for youth and in response to the mobility of people. The major emphasis has been on the supply of labor and has been almost totally related to the poor and unskilled. Since all poverty programs began without any overall manpower policy, their policy has evolved in practice, bit by bit, amendment by amendment, and dollar by dollar. In effect, manpower policy has become direct aid to the poor, minimal skill training, and an entry job.

The action developed where the money was, and the Department of Labor became the largest educator of one group of citizens—the disadvantaged. As time passed, the Department of Labor took over many of the OEO programs involving education and training and greatly expanded its own role in the education component of training the unemployed. The situation now has reached the point where this effort has become the public image of the major role of manpower policy and the Department of Labor. In effect, the evolved purpose of manpower policy is service to the poor, and this has become institutionalized in the Department of Labor. The provision of the necessary supportive services required to make an individual not only employable at the entry level but capable of upward mobility in the labor market has been reduced and confused in the emphasis on simply getting a job. While the demand increases for workers at the highly skilled and technical levels, those most in need of work are trained at lower levels of skill. This simply clogs the entry openings and creates a scarcity at the technical levels. In the preoccupation with the supply side, the need to relate supply to demand has been largely overlooked. If job creation efforts were part of the manpower policy and programs, and were marked by attempts to improve the quality of labor supply, there could be a demand component, which manpower policy now lacks.

The limited purpose of present manpower policy and practice is most clearly shown in the federal budget entitled Federal Manpower Programs. The scope of the concept is found in the following statement:

This five-fold increase [in the federal budget for manpower programs from 1964 to 1970] reflects the increasing emphasis on manpower programs as a method for increasing the employability of the disadvantaged— "poor persons who do not have suitable employment and who are either (1) school dropouts, (2) under 22 years of age, (3) 45 years of age or over, (4) handicapped, or (5) subject to special obstacles to employment." [1]

Further evidence of constricting the purpose of manpower policy to one area is a "list of new aids to the competitively disadvantaged which have emerged from the experiments of recent years." [2]

1. Remedial education for the children of illiterate parents and the victims of deficient schools.

2. Outreach to seek the discouraged and undermotivated in their native habitat and to encourage them to partake of available services.

[1] U.S. Bureau of the Budget, *Budget of the United States 1970,* January 1969. Special Analysis K, pp. 134-47.

[2] Levitan, Sar A. and Mangum, Garth L. *Making Sense of Federal Manpower Policy.* Policy Paper in Human Resources and Industrial Relations No. 2. Ann Arbor: Institute of Labor and Industrial Relations, University of Michigan-Wayne State University, and National Policy Task Force, 1967. pp. 4 ff.

3. Adult basic education to remedy the deficiencies of those left behind.

4. Prevocational orientation to expose those of limited experience to alternative occupational choices.

5. Training for entry-level skills for those unprepared to profit from the more advanced training which takes for granted the mastery of rudimentary education.

6. Subsidization of training costs to induce employers to accept less attractive employees for on-the-job training.

7. Training allowances to provide support and incentive for those undergoing training and residential facilities for youths whose home environment precludes successful rehabilitation.

8. Work experience for those unaccustomed to the discipline of the work place.

9. Job development efforts to solicit employer support and uncover job opportunities in keeping with the abilities of the disadvantaged jobseeker.

10. Creation of public service jobs tailored to the needs of jobseekers not absorbed in the competitive labor market.

11. Supportive services, such as medical aid, for those who need corrective measures to enter or resume positions in the world of work, or day-care centers for mothers with small children.

12. Relocation allowances for residents in labor surplus areas and special inducements to employers to bring jobs to those stranded in depressed areas.

Nearly all the above items are related to the problem of labor supply and only two to the problem of demand and two to the problem of matching people and jobs. It may be well to pose some questions at this point. Since labor supply in a technological society is most closely related to education, what social institution should be provided the resources to serve those not now served? Many of these "new aids" require resources (money) not now available to the school. Should not federal manpower policy be such that program operation puts the money where the people are and where facilities already exist? Again, the flow and pool problem; why not use more funds to prevent people from getting into the position where they are required to prove their failure before they qualify for special help?

This kind of analysis must raise the fundamental question of what would be the best role for each federal agency to carry out and which governmental level can best do the job. It also poses the question of whether any one agency should do the job. Even more importantly *can* any one agency do the job? Finally, we must ask if a national manpower policy which originated and developed as a welfare service concept should continue to be so oriented.

Alternative Approaches

Many persons have become disenchanted with the variety and overlapping of approaches to this problem during the 1960's. What was often tried as an alternative to the "failures" of established social institutions has been in operation long enough to provide evaluations of the new institutions. The same questions still arise as were posed in the early 1960's, and the pressure is not on the new programs—OEO, MDTA, and a host of other experiments. They were certainly not all failures, but we still lack a policy for a continuing effort which now is recognized as necessary for the well-being of the nation. It surely is obvious that there can be no "six-day war" to win the victory over poverty, injustice, and unequal opportunity.

The essential question is whether we are going to be concerned with all manpower development as a public policy. Today the answer must be yes, because one level of the problem cannot be solved in isolation from the other levels of the problem. In a technological society no person can remain in a static, unchanging work role; therefore, what is done at one level of manpower supply is affected by what happens at other levels.

If one level of the manpower problem, the education and training of the disadvantaged, for instance, becomes the responsibility of one agency and one level of government, the disastrous result will be that no one is charged with the proper relation between the two levels of manpower needs. An escalating competition develops for public funds for one manpower level against the needs of other levels with tragic

212

results for both. The opportunities for vertical mobility of individuals is reduced and the investment at one level may multiply the problems at the other level.

The isolation of segments of the manpower supply component from the total picture of manpower development is destructive both to helping the disadvantaged and reducing manpower shortages of higher skill demands. A total approach would be one of preventing unemployment, instead of combating unemployment. Another aspect of a comprehensive manpower policy is that it is not a policy limited to special groups. It concerns itself with all human resources, all groups of people, and all kinds of demand. A comprehensive policy also provides for adjustments during economic change rather than after change has occurred. Because of the growing rapidity of changing manpower demands due to technology, a fast way of responding is necessary at all levels of manpower supply. The approach which needs to be considered is the assignment of functions of the total manpower picture to governmental agencies under a comprehensive policy which is concerned with all manpower components.

Manpower Supply

Responsibility for the supply of manpower, that is, the education and training of individuals for employment, should rest with the federal agency which has experience and personnel in the field of education and training and which is presently responsible for the education of all youth as well as skilled, technical, and professional manpower through institutions at the state and local levels of government. The necessary resources and services should be provided through this system of federal, state, and local agencies, to serve the disadvantaged as well as the rest of the nation's citizens. A permanent relationship with employers must be established, not as an emergency measure, but as a permanent pattern of manpower development. At present the needed extra resources and services required by the disadvantaged are delivered through a multiplicity of other agencies, yet most state laws require youth to attend the public schools which do not receive this type of federal support.

Manpower Demand

Manpower demand is, of course, fundamental to the successful utilization of a trained manpower supply. It is also the most directly affected by changes in the total economy brought about by new knowledge and improved efficiency in production and services. Yet this is the component of manpower policy which has had little attention.

It would seem that the federal agency most concerned with analyzing and anticipating new demands and reduction of old demands would be the Department of Labor. There is a major need to project labor demand and, in cooperation with other federal agencies concerned with economic policies, to determine the demand for labor supply far in advance of present conditions. Without a better system of planning for change instead of reacting to change, the preparation of a qualified labor supply is likely to be always too little and too late. The assignment of this function to the federal agency with experience and personnel in this field of manpower need is more reasonable than to expect the development of an education and training system for a fraction of the total manpower resources outside the system which now serves the majority of citizens.

If this component of manpower policy could be integrated with plans for economic growth and stability, with industrial development, and with growing needs in public services and social services, a more rational approach to developing manpower supply could be developed. The lack of adequate projection of labor needs related to other government planning prevents adequate planning by the supply component. In addition, the expanding need for informational material regarding future employment opportunities at all levels of education—elementary, secondary, postsecondary, college, and adult—is so great as to hinder planning by individuals as to the best way to prepare for their future work roles. If these two needs—better future projections of manpower needs and job opportunities and information as to educational and skill requirements—were more adequately met, the job of schools and business and industry would be much easier.

Matching Supply and Demand

Finally, there is the matter of bringing together the qualified person and the job vacancy. This is now left largely to private efforts of workers and employers. Those who most need this service are likely to get the least help. In terms of a healthy manpower policy, placement should be a great deal more than merely finding a job; it should be a matching process which provides hope for learning while earning so the individual looks to the future with hope for improvement. Up to this time, the Federal and State Employment Service has functioned (and it began this way) as an office providing income insurance during periods of unemployment. Few individuals or employers tended to use the placement service since it was not related to institutions concerned with preparation of qualified manpower but primarily served those least well qualified. Since the matching process requires demand as well as supply, such a service cannot function isolated from preparation.

It also has been consistently demonstrated that a placement function directly related to the education and training institution provides rapid feedback for creating change as well as motivation to the learner involved in preparation for employment. There has been little effort to integrate placement with the schools of the nation; in fact, the argument has become one of institutional and agency jurisdiction. What is needed are joint efforts which serve the individual while he is in the training process.

The present mobility of job demand and industry location as well as population shifts due to technological change indicate that a new national emphasis must be placed on the creation of a job bank information center which can be used by regional and local placement centers. The correlation of future labor demand patterns with immediate demand specifics in terms of jobs becomes mandatory if a good matching process is to be developed. Localized placement efforts are not adequate for today, let alone for the future.

Again the Department of Labor would appear to be the logical federal agency to provide the plans and data so sorely needed to serve the entire manpower supply spectrum. This, however, does not mean sole jurisdiction over the placement process; this must be tied to the supply and demand com-

215

ponents through the institutions that prepare and the employers that use manpower. In effect, it must be clear that bringing supply and demand together in specific employment should not be the sole responsibility of the federal agency or its state components; rather the necessary information and services should be available to the supply and demand programs so they can integrate their efforts for maximum human resource development and utilization.

A Hard Head and a Warm Heart

Up to this time, the major thrust of manpower efforts for the unemployed has come from a moral concern and a long-held ethic of responsibility for the poor plus the growing militancy of the poor and the blacks to organize as a political and social force. The time has come to approach the manpower effort with a hard head as well as a warm heart. The welfare of every citizen is dependent on the ability of each person to become successful. We can no longer assume that most citizens do not need any help but rather that everyone needs special preparation for employment as well as a good job which uses his talent and a network of information and services which allows the best match to be made.

A manpower policy related only to the poor shows a failure to recognize the conditions of the time. A new approach is needed. E. Wight Bakke has stated it well:

> The parting of the ways came after World War II. In Western Europe, as we have seen, there occurred a modification in emphasis and objective in the direction of positive and preventive measures, and the target population was beyond the disadvantaged unemployed.
>
> In the United States, after a brief start toward a full employment objective and the development of positive labor market activities to support it, we continued on the remedial road characterizing our traditional approach, albeit with an emphasis on remedies focused on the most fundamental cause of human distress in a working world—the lack of employability.[3]

[3] Bakke, E. Wight. *The Mission of Manpower Policy.* Kalamazoo, Mich.: W. E. Upjohn Institute for Employment Research, 1969. p. 48. This book is recommended to all those who wish to obtain a lucid analysis of what is needed in a comprehensive manpower program.

216

Bakke goes on to outline the development of a de facto manpower policy in the United States with a list of reasons for our emphasis on the disadvantaged portion of our population to the exclusion of the rational development of a total manpower program as a foundation for a stable economy with particularized employment for all.[4]

Lip service to full employment. Until recently, we never had to face up to the inflationary consequences of attempting to promote full employment and economic growth by expansionary fiscal and monetary policies.

Evidence of those hardest hit by unemployment and poverty. There was clear evidence from experience and from our monthly employment and unemployment statistics that we faced a problem of *class* rather than *mass* unemployment. The persistent youth unemployment rate of three times the general average and a nonwhite rate double that of white youths pointed up the necessity for efforts to help disadvantaged youth, particularly nonwhite youths.

The "war on poverty." A third factor was the decision of President Johnson to make the "war on poverty" a major part of his domestic program. The idea was bold and in the best tradition of every American earning what he gets. It also did not take much savvy for Congressmen to sense that a war on poverty focused on benefits to disadvantaged individuals had more appeal to American voters than economic planning and a rational distribution of services and funds to achieve economic growth and stability. No one was much concerned that manpower activity and social welfare activity were becoming the same in the public's mind. One can give hearty support to the intent, if not the results, of the poverty war and at the same time warn of the danger of a manpower policy if the mission and operational field are restricted to the least employable.

The civil rights movement and riots. When special attention was concentrated on the Negro, a host of problems pertaining to health, education, family and community life, extralegal occupations, and adaptation to urban and industrial life arose, indicating the need for services normally considered the province of social welfare but obviously required to develop satisfactory employability.

[4] *Ibid.,* pp. 56-66.

217

Supply and demand. The current government-sponsored manpower program in the United States focuses largely on activities useful in improving the supply of labor and devotes limited effort to demand. This is supported by tradition. Vocational education, the G.I. Bill, and the National Defense Education Act all are aimed at supply. The potential of compensatory enlargement or reduction of particularized demand for labor falls into the class of politically oriented activity known as "pork barrel." Public works, distribution of government contracts, and regional development are looked upon by Congressmen, who have sectional interests to serve and a political acceptance to preserve, as something to get for their constituents. To plan and to distribute such particularized demand-producing measures of the public works and contract variety rationally and in the interests of balanced economic stability and growth as part of an overall labor market policy would run into sectional political interests. For example, in the 1967-68 school year the average annual salary of elementary and secondary instructional staff varied from $4,735 in Mississippi to $9,450 in California, while expenditures per pupil during this same year varied from $413 in Mississippi to $1,125 in New York. At the same time federal support to equalize educational opportunity was about 8 cents of the total dollar expended nationally and amounted to $96 per child in Mississippi and just under $13 per child in New York, which hardly made an equalizing factor, yet was politically difficult to move that far.[5]

The attitude toward planning. The constant and continuing fear of federal control on the part of large numbers of people and individual institutions militated against any real initiation and follow-through of a comprehensive, preventive, and positive manpower policy.

The Result Today

Primary emphasis in the 1960's on the disadvantaged, to the exclusion of other basic elements of manpower policy, has limited, if not prevented, the potential of a manpower policy

[5] U.S. Department of Health, Education, and Welfare, Office of Education. *Digest of Educational Statistics.* Washington, D.C.: Government Printing Office, 1968. pp. 33, 55.

more broadly conceived to strengthen the nation's economy and to increase the economic well-being of *all* American people —especially the disadvantaged. The flow continues and the pool is again getting larger. This is certainly not intended to criticize the efforts made, but rather to point up that concentration on one part of the problem cannot solve the problem or even the part most in need of solution.

The net effect of today's policy can be best stated by posing the following questions:

1. Are benefits for the uneducated, unemployed, underemployed, and minority groups actually limited by the narrowness of the present concept of manpower policy?

2. Can skill shortages and unsatisfied manpower demands continue without harm to the availability of public income to support the crisis of the disadvantaged?

3. Will failure to be concerned with upgrading the presently unemployed prevent entry-level jobs from becoming available to the less skilled?

4. Will the continued lack of attention to the prevention of unemployment for adult members of the labor force act to increase the pool of unemployed even faster?

5. Isn't preventive action in every way more desirable and much less costly?

6. Doesn't concentration on the primarily disadvantaged, after the fact, result in even less job development and adoptive preventive action?

7. Can overall economic stability and growth be achieved if the ever-growing pool of unemployed is not reduced?

8. Can human dignity and self-respect be better developed by preventive rather than corrective means, and can it be achieved at all except in a system of manpower development in which both preparation and skill training is coupled to and supported by the work of those possessing what has been called "higher-level" responsibility and talent?

The Challenge to Education

Throughout this chapter, I have challenged the failure to include prevention as a first-order priority if the most needy are to be served in a way that is more than a patriarchal approach from the federal government. Such an approach, it seems to me, requires three things:

1. Education's involvement and prime responsibility in providing occupationally salable skills and work experience at all levels.

2. A reversal of the trend toward separation of education and training of the disadvantaged from the mainstream of society. This would mean an emphasis by other governmental agencies on those areas of manpower policy which must be expanded if manpower development is to be more than sophisticated welfare.

3. A plan whereby the necessary services and resources needed by the education and training institutions, to prevent failure, are available through the institutions which have the first responsibility for preparing youth for employment. However, up to this time there has been a failure to consider such possibilities on the part of the educational community as well as the welfare and manpower fraternities. This failure has resulted in noninvolvement of state and local governments; noninvolvement of those concerned with fiscal, monetary, health, education, trade, investment, urban and regional development, and military policies; the definition of successful manpower policy as one which gets the unemployed jobs (regardless of their future or value) ; and a public image that manpower policy is simply assistance to the poor in the form of short-term skills for immediate employment.

Putting the matter positively, measures to meet particular employability and employment needs of the disadvantaged necessarily support and are supported by, concurrent measures to train, upgrade, make more productive, allocate, and utilize more effectively the entire labor force including the employed; and to deal with the factors, processes, facilities, and organization of the entire national labor market. Putting the matter negatively, a consequence of concentrating predominant attention on the disadvantaged unemployed, to the relative neglect of manpower effort in the more comprehensive sense, is to reduce the possibility of adequate service *even for the disadvantaged.*[6]

[6] Bakke, *op. cit.,* pp. 89-90.

The growing awareness of blacks and other disadvantaged of their right to equality of treatment makes them aware that they have been set aside as objects of special treatment and marked as a special class rather than given extra help to get into the mainstream. *The actions of any government should be perceived as provided for all citizens, if the hope is sincere to integrate all into the mainstream of American life and to develop within those with special needs a sense of unity with, rather than separateness from, the national mainstream.*

In the final analysis, a comprehensive manpower policy or program must deal swiftly and strongly to help all those who suffer from poverty and social degradation move into a respected role in American society. But the mission and operation of a manpower policy cannot be constrained to the relief of poverty. The necessity of the development of all citizens, from the unskilled to professional and administrative, is the function of manpower supply; and it cannot be centralized and separated from the total manpower program. To deemphasize the new role of education in a technological age can only delay the final solution for those most in need of assistance.

10. Major Issues in Education and Manpower Development

The forces of change are demanding a review of long-held American attitudes toward the utilization and conservation of the country's human resources. The evidence has become concrete on the connection between the education of every citizen and our strength as a society. It has become obvious that there must be a comprehensive national manpower policy, and such a policy must be based on education and training. It has also become apparent that no single agency or level of government can do the job.

In major national crises—such as World Wars I and II— the nation has turned to the educational community for help, and it has responded with the education and training of skilled manpower. Most observers contend that today's problems of youth in a new world of work is a "major national crisis." We must have, almost immediately, a national policy decision which sets a direction toward solutions. This policy must speak to the nature of the change and not just to the specific symptoms of the problem as has been done thus far. The responsibility of the educational community, as well as others, is to see that the role of education in a manpower policy is clearly defined. The relationship between education, the individual, and his adult work role must be more than a temporary "flirtation"; it must be a permanent "love affair." The responsibility of Congress and the executive branch is to set the policy in regard to national problems, finance, and special needs and to involve all levels of government in the effort to solve the problems. Thus far it has been a case of frittering away time and money because we lacked a policy or puttering with the visible symptoms. We must have fundamental change in our established institutions.

223

Those who formulate policies must be aware of several major issues that demand understanding and the involvement of education before they can be solved. The constant barrage of criticism of education for failing to do things that nobody wanted education to do must be replaced by a sober assessment of how education can do those things that must now be done. Those who must consider how this is to be accomplished must look at some major issues.

Prevention Versus Correction

How can preparation for a career or an occupational role become a major purpose of American public education in order to prevent terrible future damage to people and excessive costs for remediation?

The absence of this function in the American schools comes from two basic American values. The first is the ideal of preventing class distinction in our society. We thought this would come about if we offered all children the same curriculum and the same methods. The second is the status of college and advanced educational degrees as the hallmark of achievement. In the past, the nature of work allowed most of our educational failures to be absorbed into the work force and educated on the job.

Unfortunately, the response has been to create new institutions which are not concerned with the prevention of failure, but rather are solely directed at short-range correction. This has tended to neglect the emphasis that must be given to prevention. There are those who now believe that education is a failure. They argue that American public education cannot change; thus, during the 1960's major federal funds were spent on programs which relieved the schools of responsibility for those who need education the most. Those whose own education and philosophy were developed in institutions with the platonic concept of learning have pushed for even greater separation between education and work. Emphasis on more and better of the same education has really prevented educational change. This emphasis has tended to move us in the direction of a dual school system and, in many ways, has created even greater inequality of opportunity.

The Generation Gap

How can we involve youth in a relevant and contributory role in a technological society?

Our young people are essentially excluded from any significant role in the welfare of the home, the community, and the school. They are truly nonessential in today's society. The symptoms of this exclusion from society are a matter of daily record in every newspaper and news magazine in the nation. Those who suffer most are the poor, the minorities, and, often, the most educated.

The patterns of transition from adolescence to adulthood have disappeared for many young people. For some, the inability to find work because of a lack of education and training is a permanent rejection by society. For others, the pattern of preparation for living and involvement lasts so long it is intolerable. In the past, involvement for nearly all youth was real, necessary, and recognized by their parents, friends, and themselves. The youth who wanted could make his own way, become economically independent, choose several patterns, and plan several approaches to self-dignity and independence. Most of all, young people were needed. They could find employment easily, or they could earn their own way while in school.

Our youth today yearn to make a difference, improve society, and contribute to a better world. Unless we find ways to use our young people in the solving of societal problems, we can expect an increase in the generation gap. The schools of the country must become the social institution which provides ways for youth to become involved; unless they do this, they will lose relevance for more and more young people.

Unemployment and Underemployment

How can schools become a pathway to employment and career improvement for all those who enroll and for those who need more education or retraining?

The nation with the highest level of educational achievement also has the highest level of youth unemployment. In addition, we have manpower shortages in many skilled and technical areas. The relationship between education and employment is greatest in a technological society; yet we have

225

less involvement of our educational system in occupational preparation than do other industrial countries, particularly for the unemployed or underemployed. At the same time, we appear to have the greatest commitment to education as a method of individual development and self-improvement. We have learned that simply having a job with little hope for upward mobility is not adequate satisfaction in an affluent society.

Although all these conditions are known, we still have failed to involve the schools in any major effort to reduce the hopelessness of the unemployed. There are approximately 24 million adults over sixteen years of age, yet we have launched no major effort to reduce adult illiteracy. Our schools are not seen as relevant institutions by those in greatest need of education, and the connection between adult basic education and preparation for employment is casual at best. Our school facilities and equipment are used less than half of the year and almost not at all by employers and other social agencies as a way to attack the unemployment and underemployment problems.

Educational Change

How can schools offer the diversity of educational options necessary to serve all the youth of the nation?

The image of education is firmly implanted in most people's minds. Most Americans have attended twelve years of school or more; hence, concepts held by most citizens tend to define the purpose of the schools in relation to their own experience. Because most people have been successful in school and as adults, the pressure is to maintain, expand, and improve the schools as they are today. The concept of excellence in education is one of selectivity and narrowness.

Up to this point educational research and experimentation have been mainly devoted to teaching methods, curriculum content, technological aids to instruction, and to activities within the walls of the school. Essentially, efforts have been devoted to changing the methodology of what is already being done. The basic assumption seems to be that if we do more of what we are doing now and do it better, we will solve the problems.

1. One must question the assumption that doing the same thing better will reach those that were not reached in the past.

2. One must raise a more fundamental question: how can the schools motivate some to learn in the first instance?

3. One must question whether such tinkering will bring basic changes.

4. One must question whether knowing how to do better causes one to do better.

5. One must question whether the resources for research and experimentation should be used mainly by those not responsible for operational programs in education.

6. One must question if less than 1 percent of each educational dollar spent on research can have much impact.

7. One must question whether large investments for new learning carried on by institutions apart from the educational structure will change the structure of education or will relieve the schools of any necessity to change.

8. One must question whether funds for educational change which do not require commitments for new uses of state and local funds will change the use of the ninety-two cents raised by nonfederal taxing units.

9. One must question whether the failure to involve local and state educational leaders in planning for change develops a climate for cooperation or for competition and conflict.

10. One must question whether increasing investments for research will bring as much immediate change as will investments in new program diversity.

The essence of this argument is that we are failing to try new educational approaches because we have too clearly defined the role and function of the schools. The present role of the schools was set decades ago and to simply adjust what is now being done fails to consider the possibility of new activities by the schools as an approach to change. Until the schools get involved in doing different things, there is little pressure to change what they are now doing.

Transition From School to a Next Step

How can the educational system develop a continuing relationship between its students, its programs, and the world of work?

Young people today have little opportunity to learn about career options and the many kinds of work available. They have little opportunity to learn about or explore emerging occupations of the future. There is little material available in the usual school curriculum that describes the work to be done or the relationship between education and a work role. This is particularly true at the elementary and junior high school level; it generally is late in college or in professional school before the instructor concerns himself with the occupational function of education. Thus, 80 percent of young people fail to receive guidance and assistance in selecting a career area. Furthermore, there is almost no opportunity for first-hand experience when the student makes a choice; he is most likely to be influenced by occupations which he has encountered.

The complexity of the work world today is such that even if the student is prepared the problem of placement in an entry job related to a career goal is likely to be purely accidental. The more the individual needs help the less likely he is to get it. Today an entry job must provide both earning and learning, yet there are those who argue that placement is not a function of the schools. The real test of any educational experience is what happens to the individual after he leaves. If we need a way to assess the quality of education, a follow-up of the student should provide a quick and definitive evaluation. It may also be the simplest way to determine what change should occur as well as the pressure to make change take place.

We have known for a long time that a reward for learning increases learning. Can there be any greater reward for a youth than a job which challenges him and provides income, independence, and a chance for upward mobility? Is there a better way for the schools to become accountable? The time has passed when education can avoid responsibility for transition assistance to young people who enroll as students.

At the same time, government agencies with know-how and experience in developing occupational projections, labor market information, and manpower needs must concentrate their efforts on the development of materials of this kind to be used at all levels of education. The concept that one agency can do all things and should have sole jurisdiction is fallacious.

228

The Undereducated

How can the schools cooperate with business, industry, public employers, and other social agencies to help the uneducated succeed in a technological society?

The relationship between poverty and lack of education is well documented. For the poor, lack of education means loss of seniority rights; technological displacement from jobs; first-fired, last-hired; loss of self-dignity; and a lack of hope in the future. Often the side effects on people are more serious, since they affect the educational achievement of their children, and a new round of failure, despair, and nonparticipation in society is the result.

Schools can no longer avoid the responsibility to offer aid in the form of direct education to these people. An even greater opportunity exists in the development of permanent relationships between local educational units and local employers. The advantages are apparent to employers in business, industry, and government in the form of greater productivity, stability, and loyalty from employees. There is no place in the nation where people work which does not have schools and school personnel.

Education and retraining must become a continuous pattern in our technological age. This partnership at the local level represents the best opportunity for an efficient, responsive pattern to the problem. The development of this relationship could bring about a new image of schools and their role in the minds of many people. This kind of partnership has long been in effect at professional and managerial levels with higher education; it has now become necessary that a similar program be developed at the level of greatest need. The alternative is the development of additional institutions and programs at greater cost while much of our school facilities, personnel, and materials are only partially used.

Lack of Relevance in Education

How can the schools provide optional ways to learn and a choice to those who do not wish to go to college?

When nearly one million young people fail to complete high school each year in this nation, one must conclude that many do not believe that schools are helping them very much. When

229

nearly 40 percent of the high school graduates each year enter four-year colleges to obtain baccalaureate degrees and only half of them succeed, we must ask if the choice was relevant. When 50 percent of the high school graduates drop out before completing two years, something must be wrong.

The most amazing thing is that so few people see this as a problem. College enrollment has become the end for so many people that a student has little choice. Today a person must have an advanced degree or be considered a failure. This societal worship of higher education as a symbol has become so great that it dictates the program of the high schools; prevents the definition of quality in education; downgrades the concept of the work role of adults; dictates the kind of personnel that can work in the schools; determines schools' accreditation regardless of purpose; and prevents the development of multiple learning approaches and multiple education goals for the students.

The net effect of this parental snobbery, administrative fear, and professional featherbedding has been the development of a galaxy of fully funded federal education programs which begin to develop their own clientele and vested interests. The development of this educational system has created a new, closed, class-conscious educational structure.

We must have the development of a multiplicity of goals in the schools. Such a development would lead to a multiplicity of learning approaches, many of which could use talents people have that schools today seldom strengthen and never reward. It would appear that each of us in a democracy must find an adult role which makes a contribution to society through some form of work.

The school must forget the curriculum which was college prep, vocational, and general and move to a program aimed at career preparation and development. This would mandate certain basic educational skills with related theory and knowledge for a career and an adult role, plus specific occupational skills at some level of competence. For some, this might occur in high school; for some, in one or two years of education following high school; and for some, in college; but in every case there must exist the chance to exit and reenter the educational system for more learning and retraining. The purpose would be to broaden options rather than to make early choices of job training, general education, or college preparation.

Lack of a National Manpower Policy

How can the nation develop comprehensive manpower policies responsive to the needs of people and to the market demand for more skilled, technical, and professional manpower?

The absence of any manpower policy has created immense confusion. For example:

Question: Can one get tax dollars in order to attend school to prepare for a job?

Answer: Yes, if you are going to college to prepare for a paraprofessional or professional job. No, if you are in high school—unless you can prove you are a failing student, your parents are poor, or you have a police record. In this case we have a special school for you; in fact, if you are bad enough we have a school where you can live, get paid, receive clothing, and get transportation home during vacations.

Question: If I get a National Merit Scholarship, may I learn to become an auto mechanic?

Answer: No, these can only be used for college degrees.

Question: If I can finish high school, I plan to go to a special school to become an oceanographic technologist. I need money to stay in high school; where can I get it?

Answer: You can earn $21 per week by working in the Neighborhood Youth Corps, but you can earn twice as much if you are a dropout. In fact, you would then become eligible for Manpower Development and Training, which will provide up to one year of training with pay, transportation, and certain health care. You must be over sixteen, but we will also help you get a job at the end of the year.

Question: What am I eligible to receive while in high school?

Answer: Nothing, unless you can prove you are a failure.

Question: What about my little brother in the sixth grade? He needs glasses.

Answer: You should go see the welfare people; if your parents aren't on welfare, there is nothing the school can do since you are in a school which has less than the average disadvantaged.

Question: Can I get help to retrain my employees prior to closing the plant?

Answer: No, we can't do anything until they are unemployed.

Question: My greatest skills are in the electrical field; can I get training under MDTA at the local school?

Answer: No, because we have no shortages in this area for electricians. The course the school is running is not eligible for federal funds, and you will have to pay the tuition.

These are admittedly overdrawn positions, but they illustrate the lack of concern for a manpower policy. Legislation now being prepared in Congress is aimed at the pool of disadvantaged, undereducated, unemployed, while at the same time ignoring the flow into that pool. If this does not become part of a national policy which involves other levels of government, other federal agencies, and the educational system, we are simply engaged in a game of perpetual motion.

The question of manpower needs simply comes down to paying the difference between the cost of basic education and occupational preparation. We now do it for the professions, such as law, medicine, engineering, and teaching. Are we going to do it for other occupational areas and for those people who do not want to become lawyers, doctors, or scientists? Maybe the real prestige and status problem comes from the fact that the taxpayers pay most of the cost for professional manpower and practically none of the training costs for the nonprofessional.

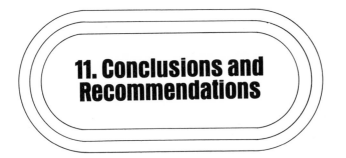

11. Conclusions and Recommendations

A veneer of progress in the form of technological advancements covers the societal distress in America—a functional disorder symptomized by youth rebellion and unemployment, severe pockets of poverty, increasing racial tensions, drug abuse, rising crime rates, increasing welfare rolls, widening gaps in educational opportunity and quality, disagreement over our military posture, manpower shortages, and a nation divided over goals and solutions. In the middle of this crisis is a system of education unresponsive to the needs of many of its youth and most of its adults.

Regardless of the achievements of any individual or group, the greatest resource of the nation is the sum of the individuals available and the diversity of their talents. It is obvious that the nation has no policy for the development of this resource either in its education or its manpower programs. Its maximum development must become a first priority of education and manpower policies. Each time a person fails to achieve this maximum potential, to whatever degree, there is a loss to the nation and to the world.

Education for the assumption of a contributory adult role is not the only solution to our social crisis. It is in the schools and colleges, however, that the prevention of this waste must begin. It is through the schools, in cooperation with other social agencies, that the tragic cycle of poverty, discrimination, inadequate education, and youth rebellion can best be reversed, for it is by learning that skills are acquired, attitudes developed, a desire for knowledge born, and hope created or aborted. The often quoted statement of Alfred North Whitehead made in 1917 seems especially applicable today:

In the conditions of modern life the rule is absolute,

233

the race which does not value trained intelligence is doomed. Not all your heroism, not all your social charm, not all your wit, nor all your victories on land or at sea, can move back the finger of fate. Today we maintain ourselves. Tomorrow science will have moved forward one more step, and there will be no appeal from the judgment which will then be pronounced on the uneducated.[1]

Conclusions

From the prior chapters, some basic conclusions have been drawn which are fundamental in planning the role of education in the development of a comprehensive manpower policy. Conclusions have also been drawn about the need for a manpower policy which is fundamentally based on education. In each case we are speaking primarily to that part of a manpower policy which is concerned with the provision of needed manpower in the labor market, the education and training of those not employable, and the continuing education and retraining of present workers. There are no conclusions or recommendations on job creation or economic growth and employment.

Technological change will continue at an increasing rate as a benefit to all or as a threat to many in our society. The overriding necessity of our time is to educate all youth and adults to use technological change for the benefit of every individual and for the strengthening of our total society.

A comprehensive national manpower policy must be as concerned with the development of human resources as it is with correction of failures. If the sole or major effort of a national manpower policy is concerned only with the pool of unemployed and disadvantaged and not with the flow of uneducated and unskilled youth and adults into the pool, then the problem can never be solved. In the long run, the goal of a manpower policy should be to eliminate the pool of disadvantaged and unemployed and to prepare everyone for employment.

A test for insanity used in New York State at the turn of the century illustrates the flow and pool problem. The person to be tested was taken to a room which contained a bucket, a

[1] Whitehead, Alfred North. *The Aims of Education and Other Essays.* New York: New American Library, 1949. p. 25.

dipper, and water running into the bucket. He was told to empty the bucket. If he used the dipper and never emptied the bucket, they sent him to an institution. If, however, he turned off the spigot and then emptied the bucket, he was declared sane.

In a technological age of constant change, education must be the basic foundation of a comprehensive national manpower policy. A manpower policy which does not provide a direct linkage with the public school system assumes that work and jobs are unchanging and man is only interested in economic returns. Education must provide the basis for continual learning as well as skills which are transferable among a variety of jobs and which provide for the vertical mobility and flexibility every person must have in a changing work force, which is increasingly becoming automated. The essence of increasing economic growth is found in the more efficient use of our human resources. Such efficiency comes from an educated citizenry.

The threat of a dual school system in the nation has become a real possibility. We, as a people, decided long ago that we wanted a society designed for people. This society must provide equal opportunities for every young person to fulfill his potential; equal opportunities for every person, young and old, to live his life with a measure of dignity; and equal opportunities for every person to be free of want, ignorance, disease, and discrimination. Some of our present policies and proposals actually require a declaration of failure before a person can be eligible for certain education. The danger of a separate school system based on family income, ability to be employed, past educational achievement, or certification of failure could be more destructive of the fabric of our society than our dual school system based on race. Separate cannot be equal in our concept of democracy.

In a technological age, occupational preparation must be a fundamental part of everyone's education and a specific task of the public schools. The cost to society of the failure to provide occupational education cannot be measured, whether viewed in terms of national security, economic growth, or political and social stability. There is no way to measure the cost to the individual in terms of his loss of a societal role, his loss of self-dignity, or the loss of his potential participation in our culture.

The importance of education to the individual and his success in occupational preparation, as well as his role as a citizen, cannot be overestimated. However, education alone is not enough for the youth and adults in today's work force. To attempt education without occupational training is to ignore the facts of modern technological life. When occupational training takes place in one's education should be a matter of individual goals and plans, not a matter of age or educational structure.

One of the crises of our age is the inability of young people to participate in the real experiences of society or to contribute to the improvement of society. Technology has made our young people economic liabilities. Their great need is to give, to be worth something, to make a difference. In today's situation, over half our youth have no recognized roles to provide them with a measure of responsibility and independence. In the past, most of these opportunities were provided in the home, the community, or in productive work. Today, these options have disappeared for most youth. "Playing school"— the make-believe involvement in advisory or adult policy-making boards—will not satisfy today's young people. Participation in the recognized activities of daily societal operation must be provided in the school program and in private and public agencies doing the daily work of society.

Our public schools must make fundamental changes immediately or they will become more irrelevant in the lives of large numbers of our people. Up to this time, efforts to change the schools have resulted in minor innovations in curriculum, methodology, and instructional techniques. Such pedagogical tinkering has become so irrelevant that large segments of society question the ability of the schools to respond to the times. The alternatives being considered today are contracts with private industry, a new public school system financed by the federal government, and a competitive private system financed with public funds. The less than one-half of 1 percent of the education dollars spent on research and experimentation has had little, if any, effect on the purely operational activities.

The development of a comprehensive national manpower program must include incentive funding which rewards co-

operation among public agencies at the federal, state, and local levels. All the pleading, all the pledges, and all the administrative admonitions will do little unless there are direct benefits to the individual agencies for coordinating their efforts. No one federal agency, single state agency, or lonely local agency can do the manpower job alone. Competition may have its merits, but it is unlikely to serve the diversity of need and the variety of people of this nation in the development of a workable manpower policy.

Work in a technological age has become the basis for the individual's adult role and status. That there is a difference between general education and vocational education is a long-held theory which technology has exploded. The changed nature of work is so great in this country that the person without a work role finds himself isolated from contact with the majority of people. This condition is true for our youth, our older generation, our married women, and our disadvantaged. This continuing separation of education and a work role in the educational system is the major reason for the rejection of education.

We must establish a permanent operational relationship between education and employers in business, industry, and public agencies as a basis for both education and manpower training. The present crisis efforts at temporary employment of disadvantaged youth and adults by employers is destructive of permanent solutions to the basic problem. Much more than temporary income for "make do" work is necessary. The concept of work experience as learning only for the poor, the uneducated, and the unemployed is denigrating to those involved as well as supportive of a philosophy that work experience is not part of quality education. On-the-job training unconnected to self-improvement through learning and broad skill development is a palliative rather than a cure. Work experience as a methodology in education and training is a fundamental need for all.

Expansion of postsecondary education below the baccalaureate level is necessary to reduce technological manpower shortages and to provide optional career patterns for youth and adults. Openings in technician occupations doubled during the 1950's, while openings in other occupations requiring special training increased by only one-half. By 1975, there will be a needed increase of 77 percent. Unless more youth and adults move upward into these shortage areas, openings below this level are closed to those with less education and skills.

Continuing education has become necessary for everyone. The nation's educational system must develop new ways so any individual may obtain additional education and new occupational skills regardless of previous education level or job competence. Eliminating adult illiteracy must become a first priority for schools and employers.

Discrimination in today's society has become more a matter of education and skills than color or race. Since a higher percentage of minority groups lack education and occupational skills, they experience the highest levels of poverty and welfare. For this reason, as well as for the sake of justice and equality, discrimination in education must be eliminated.

A comprehensive manpower policy must provide a basis for long-range planning and stability of funding patterns to states and local agencies. The absence of any basic policy has prevented state and local units from planning any effective approach to the flow or the pool of unemployed. Late appropriations, administrative changes, and uncertain funds have combined to make efforts sporadic, expensive, and confusing to both the individual needing help and the employers who hire the trainees.

Sound career choice is made in direct proportion to the information, exploration, guidance, and opportunity available to the individual to prepare and assistance given him for entry placement in a job matched to the individual. The freedom to choose a career does not assure anyone of making a good choice unless there is a sound basis for judgment and opportunities to try out preliminary decisions, as well as the opportunity for education and skill development and an entry placement which will provide additional learning opportunities. A recent survey showed only 19 percent of high school seniors felt they knew as much about jobs as they would like to know.[2] For too long, choice of occupation and preparation for career development has been left primarily to chance. This is a tragic waste of manpower.

[2] Purdue University Opinion Poll No. 78, November 1966.

American public education will be able to serve all youth and adults only when it can provide the related services necessary to allow learning to happen. Many young people are unable to obtain the health care, special counseling, and tutoring needed to learn, or the clothing, food, and money necessary to stay in school. In nearly all cases these funds are available in special education programs operated by agencies other than the school. If education is the fundamental link between the individual and society, why are related services unavailable until the child has failed? This fundamental question must be answered soon if our schools are to do more than continue the flow of uneducated into the pool of unemployed.

Some form of residential education is necessary for those who need more specialized help than the day school can provide. Such an educational approach is necessary for those who need custodial care for a period of time; for those who cannot get certain kinds of instruction because of sparse population or because they have special talents; and for those who need special kinds of occupational training not available near home. This residential school should be part of the regular system and in no case should be confined to those who have failed. Failure to provide these services early enough demands a very expensive remedial program which becomes stigmatized as totally second-class.

Schools must provide transition to a next step for every individual who enters school. This responsibility provides an assessment of the school's success with every student; it promises the student a reward in relation to effort; it makes learning other than academic achievement valued in the school; it forces cooperation with other agencies in society besides colleges; and it provides a new basis for excellence in education.

Independent citizen advisory councils can become the basis for a continual objective review of both education and manpower programs. Most advisory councils should be appointed by the chief executive of each government or branch of government. Their role is to advise executive, legislative, and operational units of needed change and improvements. Annual reports to the public from such independent groups could create pressure for creative change pertinent to the times.

239

In the months and years ahead, there will be all sorts of proposals and counterproposals regarding education and manpower development. Education and manpower specialists should consider that education and the development of human resources cannot exist in an ivory tower. Quality programs can only be developed through partnerships between education and federal, state, and local governments, private employers and trade associations, labor unions, and the rest of the community. We have reached a point where the allocation of federal funds must become integrated with the efforts of state and local governments.

Manpower policy must recognize that the attributes that keep a person mobile in the labor force are his ability to absorb new knowledge and skills and the opportunity to obtain them prior to unemployment. We are at a point in time when the question of the allocation of national resources for education is being debated as never before; this debate should not divorce education from manpower development at a time when their cooperation is just becoming understood. There is a clear trend toward separation; the facts of technological progress argue that this is poor theory and unsound practice.

Recommendations

These specific recommendations are directed primarily to the school administrators of the country in elementary, secondary, and postsecondary institutions and to the superintendents and school board members responsible for the education of nearly all our young people as well as the continuing education of thousands of adults. The priority is on the preparation of these persons for transition to a work role in a new and changing technological age. The concern is for the changes necessary in our schools to serve the diversity of persons that need education as well as the emerging manpower needs of the nation. The problems are attitude, program, and money. It is impossible, of course, to cover all aspects of the problem, and this has not been attempted. It is hoped, however, that this book will lead to a reordering of priorities both in our schools and in our legislative and administrative bodies at all levels of government. The recommendations which follow suggest broad courses of action and specific suggestions for their implementation. It is hoped that these proposals will lead to the reduction of jurisdictional debate and an increase in coordination of program operation at all levels of government.

Schools should operate throughout the calendar year with the added time devoted primarily to career planning, occupational preparation, and youth participation in adult roles in society. This does not mean, however, an expansion of programs already existing, but rather an increase in options available to the students, particularly in the junior high, senior high, and postsecondary schools. It suggests the inclusion of many educational efforts, specifically in the field of occupational preparation, and volunteer activities now carried on outside the educational mainstream. It envisages the increased use of facilities, equipment, and staff already available. It suggests the establishment of new alliances with employers and other social agencies providing services necessary for effective learning to the student. It proposes new learnings for educational credit and new criteria for student success. It requires an exchange between educators and people in the rest of the work force on a regular basis. It mandates a change in the organization and structure of the schools as well as in the employment service, health units, and welfare agencies. It proposes to involve the students, the parents, and business and industry personnel as teachers. It requires education to expand its services and reorder its priorities. It necessitates a reversal of the concept of education as primarily the preparation for more education. It includes the activities which used to be a normal part of the child's maturation and experience as part of the educational experiences supervised by the schools. It proposes to increase the participation of young people in the activities of society and the assignment of responsibility to young people at an earlier age, with commensurate rewards and recognition. It proposes that schools be accountable for the success of every student.

The high schools and postsecondary institutions should operate during the present summer period. Students would opt to attend whichever of the three out of four, or two out of three, periods they wish. If they choose they may complete school early or decide to take elective programs during the optional period. In effect, the student may opt for whatever pattern of school completion meets his preference and future plans.

Work experience would be required of all students before graduation. This experience could be gained during the school year as part of the student's normal load or during any period of the school year as a full-time worker while under the supervision of the school. Educational credit should be given for such work experience, and it should be evaluated as any other credit course. Work experience would normally be of three kinds: exploratory in terms of learning about a career area; employability skill training to learn attitudes, responsibility, and cooperation; and skill acquisition in an occupational area. Insofar as possible, the work experience should be related to educational and career goals. Responsibility and level of competence would vary with each student, and the work experience should be at the level of student achievement. All work-study, Neighborhood Youth Corps, and other income maintenance work programs should be run by the schools as part of a total program.

Work as a viable learning experience would thus become a part of all education for learning and earning. The primary emphasis should be on learning.

Career orientation should begin in the elementary grades and continue through the junior high school for all students. Emphasis should be on broadening student knowledge of career options rather than on early choices. Annual conferences with the career counselor, student, and parents should begin at the junior high school and continue through high school. The Labor Department should earmark a major share of funds for the development of career guidance materials for use in the school, and local employment offices should hold regular seminars with the teachers in the school to inform them of opportunities in the work force and the emerging patterns for new careers. Senior high school students might well be used as teacher aides in working with elementary and junior high students. This could be carried on during the off-period in the school year and on weekends and evenings.

Related services necessary for student participation in such programs should be provided through the schools. These include health care, transportation, food, clothing, and money necessary to continue in school. In the age group sixteen and above, and in some cases below, much of this money could be earned through cooperative education programs and by including present income-maintenance work-study programs for poor students as part of the education program. This plan would operate through the local schools, the present National Alliance for Business Programs, and similar efforts now scattered through a variety of agencies. The aim would be to make the school the best social agency to meet the needs of young people and to make education the best vehicle through which to achieve individual success.

All federal, state, and local government agencies should be encouraged to provide work experience related to educational and career goals for all youth in school beginning at the junior high school level and continuing through college and professional schools. Part of their budgets should be devoted to youth work experience in cooperation with local educational institutions which would supervise the programs and give educational credit. Priorities for these programs should go to the most needy youths in terms of finances and this type of educational experience.

Whenever possible, work experience of this kind should be on a one-to-one basis with an interested adult employee. Where this is not possible, small groups assigned to an adult should be the goal. Large mass employment of youth should not be carried on as a normal procedure. It is likely that the one-to-one relationship between adolescent and adult may be one of the better outcomes of the program. Young people in today's society have little opportunity for a responsible role in cooperation with an adult. The opportunity for learning and guidance would reverse the isolation of the young from the activities of society.

Optional courses should be available to the student who could choose on the basis of interest or need. Opportunity for catching up or forging ahead would be possible. Opportunities for individual projects, research, and creative activities in a wide range of options should be available. Higher education should expand the opportunities for advanced placement for students who go on to college.

243

Congress should pass legislation creating a new category of wage scales for students who are earning and learning. So long as we continue a simple dichotomy of employee and student, we cannot move toward a smooth transition from school to work. As long as employment is considered in the traditional sense, as any paid activity regardless of terms, conditions, and purposes, the advance of a true manpower development program is impossible. The present system is tied to a concept of education versus work and to a wage policy that prohibits the use of work experience as a learning process. Today a young person completes his education (some don't), perhaps acquiring some incidental work experience on the side, and then is thrown on the open market. The alternative is gradual introduction, with work experience related to education and career goals during high school, junior college, and college, into full-time work. A properly planned work experience program, a subject very unfashionable in both education and labor fraternities, might be possible. The Constitution does not require that youth be paid the minimum wage. The fear that such a wage policy revision would undermine wage standards is pervasive. The fact that youth *always make up a percentage* of the labor force and the fact that their proper education and training is the best guarantee of future production to pay higher wages mandates a consideration of this legislation. The alternatives are too costly in terms of money and human failure.

The age at which youth may begin to work as part of their education should be lowered. As long as work experience is supervised by the school and proper safeguards to protect the youth and the adult worker have been set, many younger adolescents need this option.

Wage rate legislation should be changed to allow the employer to pay lower wages to student workers. Such a law may well take a precedent from other countries which have set wage scales as a percentage of the minimum wage in the occupational area. Youth at age thirteen may be paid 30 percent; at age fourteen, 40 percent; at age fifteen, 50 percent; etc. An alternative would be to vary the payment based on the purpose of the student working; exploratory, 30 percent;

employability skill development, 50 percent; occupational skill training, 60 percent and upward, based on level of competence.

Funds and personnel to carry out such a program should be part of the school budget and staff. Overhead costs to employers should be provided where the program and the nature of the work experience make it desirable. Local employment services should be available to the schools to a degree never before considered. Educational credit should be given in all cases, and a related guidance and education program in the schools should be a fundamental part.

All students should be eligible to participate in the program regardless of education or career goals. In other words, this is not a proposal for the noncollege student; in fact, the most easily created program could occur in the professional occupation areas. It is aimed at broadening the educational experience for all and attacking the problem of attitude as well as competence.

We need to build into our society a new concept of the work role as it relates to education. At this same level of urgency, we need to tear down the barrier to youth involvement in adult roles; it has already happened in sex, money, political action, and independence; now it should happen in the area of responsibility and contribution through a work role.

Cooperative education must be expanded as a major learning method in occupational preparation. While this recommendation is based on the work experience premise, it proposes a major shift in the techniques by which the student gains a large amount of specific vocational competence necessary to enter the labor market as a full-time employee. It suggests further that a permanent partnership be formed between education, business, and organized labor. Playing around with crises that force illicit affairs is no way to solve a problem or produce a legitimate child. In addition, it has equal potential at all levels of education and in all kinds of occupations. Specific job skills necessary for employment are changing so fast that it is impossible to replicate the job conditions in shops and laboratories. Thus, the actual place of work must become the educational laboratory in many instances. If the schools operate all year and labor laws are changed, we have a basis for proceeding.

A staff should be assembled in every school district in the nation with a high school, in every two-year college, and in every four-year college. This is actually the easiest and least expensive way to move into a comprehensive occupational preparation program as well as the easiest way to broaden educational options for many youth.

Local agreements between the school and the employer are necessary in all cases; yet the most important step would be a program commitment arrived at cooperatively and published jointly by the educational authorities, organized labor, government employers, and the alliance of business and industry.

A permanent advisory council for cooperative education should be established to recommend policies and standards. The council should include membership from the agencies, students, and citizens. A similar state and federal committee should be established.

The program should be open to all students, but preference should be given to those students planning to enter work directly.

Work experience, work-study, and cooperative education should be administered in the school under one authority.

Occupational guidance, counseling, placement, and follow-up must become major functions of every educational institution. Such a commitment proposes that the emphasis of the schools shift from the 20 percent who will be graduated from college to the 80 percent who do not acquire the baccalaureate degree.

Elementary schools should teach all children about work and work roles in today's society.

Junior high schools should increase the emphasis on career planning, educational options, and occupational preparation available in the high schools and postsecondary schools. The industrial arts and homemaking curriculum should be redirected, with a heavy emphasis on career orientation and exploration.

State and local employment agencies should establish earlier contacts with students and locate personnel in the guidance departments of school systems and postsecondary schools. A specific budget allocation should be set aside for this function.

A placement office should be established in every high school and two-year institution or in combinations of schools where necessary. Local employment agencies should be required by federal regulation to serve such offices. Part-time as well as full-time placement should be carried out, and the student's work experience should become part of his educational record. Contacts through the schools with employers must be made through a single office. Employers should be urged to hire primarily through the school placement office.

Follow-up of students placed full-time should be a cooperative function of the schools and the local employment agency. Results should be made available to the schools, the state and federal agencies, and the public.

A national center for occupational and vocational-technical programs should be established with federal funds through the Department of Labor and the Office of Education. Such a center should have a computer data bank available through a telephone tie-line and printouts to all states and regional centers. Regional centers with data banks containing local and regional information should be established with tie-lines to every high school and two-year postsecondary institution. Guidance and placement personnel would then have specific data for student use during guidance counseling and placement functions in the schools. Such programs are already in use, and a national effort in this direction would make the cost of individual terminals entirely feasible.

Programs to retain professionals and technicians as guidance workers, counselors, placement officials, and occupational information specialists should be given highest priority by HEW and the Department of Labor. Each state education agency should set aside a share of its state allotment of federal dollars for this purpose. The programs should mandate a period of actual experience with public schools, employment agencies, and personnel departments of business firms. Guidance and counselor certification for public schools and state employment agencies, regardless of present requirements, should be changed to include a period of work experience in occupational guidance counseling and placement offices of schools, employment agencies, and employers.

Manpower training skill centers should become permanent functioning units operated by the public schools for adults.

247

We will continue to have unemployed and underemployed adults in the future. Many of them will need basic education, occupational skill training, related theory, and counseling and related services. In the case of the unemployed, this will include financial support during the training period. There needs to be one single location where the adult can get all the services he needs. The present manpower program fails to offer such a centralized, self-contained facility except through the skill center. This model is the same kind of operation that many youths need.

Skill centers through the state manpower development plan should be guaranteed permanent planning, administrative, and operational funding. All funds necessary to serve adults enrolled in the center should come directly from the center, and all payments for services from other agencies for the enrollees should be paid by the center or the educational unit operating the center. This would allow the skill centers to be more responsive to individual needs as well as effective in dealing with agencies supplying services.

The prime function of the employment service should be to recommend adults for training and to spend more effort in finding the most needy. Present dual administration is ineffective and confusing to enrollees, as well as costly.

Necessary testing, counseling, and guidance prior to entry into training and provisions for legal, medical, and welfare needs should be administered by the skill center.

Specific grants to each center based on a local plan should be the basis for operating the unit. The present project-by-project approval should be abandoned. Those who argue the danger of creating rigidity of operation should be more concerned with the present confusion.

Funding of special training projects based on manpower needs or crisis unemployment should go to outside contractors only after skill centers have been fully utilized.

Adult basic education programs in the school organization should be tied directly to the skill centers and adult vocational programs of the school. In every case, those in basic education courses should become thoroughly acquainted with the options in the local skill centers and adult vocational programs. In many cases, the adult basic education needed by skill center enrollees can be provided by this program.

The fundamental principal is the establishment of permanent responsibility, authority, and capability at the local level. Continual federal financing at the 90 percent level with 10 percent at the local or state level is sound. Under such a plan, every skill center would have to take persons from any area as enrollees. Until manpower development, especially for the unemployed, is related permanently and directly to local agencies, the first solution will be to go to the federal level. The record does not imply great success. Proper safeguards—the protection of individuals from unfair treatment and discrimination—must be the basis for any funding of state or local agencies.

Adult continuing education should be available in every public school system, two-year college, and four-year college in the United States. The opportunity for everyone to learn throughout his life is not only desirable but necessary. We have not provided a plan, a structure, or a method to do this in our country. Where the need has been great, as in the professional and managerial fields, business and higher education have shared the cost with little or no expense to the individual. Yet today some states still prevent expenditures for adult education at less than the college level.

Every state which still prevents state expenditures for adult basic education should be urged to change its laws.

Federal funds should be made available to provide 90 percent of the cost of the services of an adult education coordinator in every school unit with a population of more than 35,000 and in any combination of educational units that has at least that number of people. The opportunity to develop joint school and private efforts in this area has never been considered.

Federal funds allocated to states for adult basic education shall be allowed for high-school-level education only after the adult population with less than an eighth-grade education is reduced to the national average of ten years prior to the year of allocation.

A special federal tax allowance should be developed for employers who provide personnel, time, or direct cash support

249

to local education agencies for adult continuing education below the baccalaureate level. Such a plan might give a 10 percent advantage for each dollar given for the elimination of adult illiteracy and for programs to earn a high school equivalency certificate for adults over twenty-five years of age, and an advantage of 5 percent for gifts of time or money for programs below the baccalaureate level.

Congress should appropriate a special 2 million dollar fund to develop basic reading materials for teaching adult illiterates. Two things should form the basis for content: consumer education and occupational information and training. Such an effort should include the problem of Spanish-speaking adults and demand the same efforts as the New Mathematics and New Science. Materials for use by employers and unions should be included.

Costs of baby-sitters, glasses, hearing aids, transportation, and medical examinations for all adult basic education enrollees who cannot afford these minor services should be provided as part of the program.

Youth volunteer programs must be made available for every adolescent as part of his secondary and college education. "Actually, if mere volume of conversation shapes an attitude priority, the kids far overshadow any other aspect of adult American tribulation, be it war, inflation, race or crime." [3] Our young people today are too often involved only in the things they know about, or can do, simply because the system does not introduce them to or allow them to participate in essential activities. National concern and national needs provide the motivation and the way by which youth can become involved. Since education is the major means by which youth prepares for adulthood, it must become the major vehicle by which youth gains experiences necessary to mature and learn. One way is early involvement in work; the other is youth participation in activities which are needed by society but are not being carried on by adults.

Every high school and postsecondary two-year college should establish a unit to develop youth volunteer activities as part of the school's service to community programs. Recog-

[3] Knebel, Fletcher. "The Mood of America." *Look* 33: 28; November 18, 1969.

nition of individual service to the community should be given through educational credit and accounted for in the student's educational record.

The year-round school would allow students to spend part of the year either as part-time or full-time volunteers in necessary special services. Since many high school and college youth would be available while elementary and junior high school students were in school, one of the major volunteer services could be as teacher aides and tutors to children needing special help to succeed in school.

This type of youth volunteer activity could become fundamental to the recently announced Right To Read goal established by the U.S. Commissioner of Education as a target for the 1970's. Every elementary school has a high school or community college nearby. Every high school student can either walk to school or has transportation provided. Only two elements need to be added: time for the adolescent to work with the child and organized instruction on how to tutor the child. Both of these elements are available in every school and college in this country.

Volunteer services are needed in health care, welfare work, conservation, beautification, public building and park maintenance, recreation, geriatric care, traffic control, pollution control, wildlife conservation, research and laboratory assistance. Youth can provide assistance in these and many other areas of service to the community, the state, and the nation.

Youth volunteer activities should begin as early as the elementary school years with groups of pupils allowed to care for parts of the school site through shrub and flower planting and care, parts of city parks, a city block, or other areas needing care and maintenance that is not now provided. Summer or off-quarter periods should be used for outdoor camping, nature study, and conservation activities. Plans should be developed by the U.S. Forest Service, Bureau of Land Management, Wildlife Service, Interior Department, and Park Service for projects to be done by school youth. Local school officials, in connection with related state agencies, should develop programs in which all youngsters, particularly those who do not get such opportunities, have a chance to volunteer for this kind of service. Funds should be set aside in federal and state budgets for outdoor programs of recreation, conservation, and beautification for use in this effort. A policy should be established whereby school groups can use all local, state, and federal land that can be improved by school pupils and students.

High schools and two-year postsecondary institutions must assume responsibility for the transition to a next step for every student. The fact that those who need help the most get no assistance in finding suitable options when they leave school has become one of the anomalies of our time. Few efforts are made by any social institutions, including the state employment services, to help. The difficulty of finding an entry job which leads to better career options and continual learning is exceedingly great. All the prior efforts of the school and other agencies are to no avail if this transition is not made with a degree of forward planning. Parents can seldom be helpful, and few youths believe the school is concerned unless it is willing to take the risk of being assessed on the basis of its success or failure in job placement.

Entry job placement is much more than earning. The time has passed when the school can avoid this function. Specific legislation should direct the federal, state, and local employment services to make information, personnel, and other assistance available to the schools.

Congress should appropriate special funds to the Office of Education for administration by the Department of Labor to carry out special teacher institutes to inform every teacher of the facts about labor market changes and future patterns, information on economic development, emerging work opportunities, and educational needs. The Department of Labor, with the approval of the Office of Education, should develop a handbook on the work force and job information for classroom teachers at the elementary, secondary, postsecondary, and adult teaching levels. These manuals should be distributed free to every teacher through orders placed by the school administrator. The manuals should be in the form of binder notebooks with separate sections which can be updated as needed. In addition, necessary labor market information should be sent automatically to every school district and postsecondary institution in the country. It should be designed to be easily reproduced and contain special inserts for use by students.

An annual public report should be made by every school on the pattern of student entry job placement and educational choice both for graduates and dropouts. This annual report should be required by the local educational agency as a condition of receipt of state and federal vocational education funds.

Incentive funds should be distributed by the Department of Labor and the Office of Education to states which reduce school dropout levels. Such funds should be given to both the local employment service agency and local school units on the basis of improvement in dropout reduction through a joint school-employment-service plan. Where a school achieves such a record without help from the employment service, all the incentive money should go to the school.

An independent Comprehensive Manpower Development Council should be established by Congress. The concept of a single agency responsible for manpower development is not consistent with the nature of the problem, the levels of government involved, and the variety of inputs needed to carry out a comprehensive manpower policy. The solution is to bring together those resources already available in the nation, provide a system to deliver services to the youth and adults when needed, and develop a multiple attack on the problem. This requires a comprehensive manpower policy to set goals which are definitive and not jurisdictional in derivation or operation. It must involve the private sector in the development of manpower as well as in its use.

The National Council would be appointed by the President and would consist of fifteen outstanding citizens in areas of competence defined by law with overlapping terms of five years. It would also include six nonvoting members of federal agencies which directly administer manpower development and prevention programs.

The Council would review federal manpower programs and make recommendations to the Congress and the agencies administering the programs.

It would make annual reports of its findings and recommendations to the President and to the public. In addition, special reports could be prepared when necessary.

253

In addition, it would have incentive funds to allocate to federal operational agencies for innovative programs, joint agency approaches, and for purposes of creating change at the federal level. This money would be made available from a fund consisting of 1 percent of the appropriations of each agency represented on the Council. The necessary money to operate the Council would come from the same source prior to incentive allocations to federal agencies.

The National Council would not appear before the Bureau of the Budget, the appropriation committees of Congress, or any Congressional or executive agency concerned with funding. Its funds would be entirely dependent on agency appropriations. The Council might appear before legislation committees in explanation of its own positions, but not in defense of or in criticism of any agency operation.

The Council could ask for information and assistance from any government agency, but the agency would be free to take whatever action it wished.

The National Council would receive annual reports from each of the State Comprehensive Manpower Councils and would hold only one annual convention of State Council representatives.

The National Council would concentrate on improvements and new approaches to manpower development rather than act as an overseer, evaluating the day-to-day performance of federal agencies.

Each state should establish a State Comprehensive Manpower Development Council independent of any operating agency or branch of state government. A manpower development program in each state is necessary to serve all individuals as well as all employers of the state. If education is to play the necessary role, then a State Council must be established which proposes ways to utilize education most effectively. This is not likely to be done at the federal level because of the minor federal fiscal investment and the education authority vested with the state. Eventually the emphasis on correctional manpower programs should be eliminated if developmental plans are well made.

The State Manpower Council would serve as the policy-making board for the remedial manpower programs in the

254

state. This would shift the emphasis to reducing the flow of people into the pool of disadvantaged and slow down the growth of remedial manpower programs as permanent new social institutions.

The State Comprehensive Manpower Development Council would be appointed by the governor with overlapping terms of office so it cannot become the tool of any one administration.

The State Manpower Council would have representatives who are nonvoting members from each of the state agencies having manpower operational programs plus fifteen outstanding citizens knowledgeable in the areas of manpower policy concern.

The Council would review all state plans relating to manpower administration and develop a total state plan which would become both a short-term and long-term guide to manpower development, job development, and economic growth in the state. It would also include the plan for matching supply and demand tied in with a national job bank of the U.S. Department of Labor.

Annual and special reports would be made to the legislature, the governor, and the general public.

Money to operate and staff the Council would come from a set-aside of all federal money for vocational education, vocational rehabilitation, welfare, Economic Opportunity Act, and the Manpower Development and Training Act as made available to the state. This should be not less than 3 percent, of which between $100,000 and $300,000 would be available to the Council.

A state incentive fund which the Council administers would be available from these set-aside funds for purposes of allocation to state agencies for new or cooperative approaches to manpower development and coordination.

The State Manpower Council would serve as the policy board for the staff administering the Manpower Development and Training Act funds allotted to the state.

The State Council would receive no direct appropriations or any outside funds, so its deliberations and planning would be as free as possible from political or private control. The major purpose of the Council would be development of improved state planning and agency coordination rather than overseeing state administrative units.

Long-range objectives and short-range efforts would be to reduce the flow of persons into the pool of unemployed and poor.

Congress should appropriate and the administration should expend as much money in reducing the flow of untrained youth as in reducing the pool of unemployed adults. These investments should gradually reverse as the pool is reduced.

Money for necessary services, including health care, maintenance money, special guidance, and necessary support for work experience on the job or in volunteer activities in needed public activities should be made available through the agency that administers the educational and skill development of youth.

Special categorical funds should be appropriated to establish entry job placement operations in all secondary and post-secondary institutions where youth enter directly into work. These educational placement functions should be coordinated with state and local employment units so necessary liaison between school and employers can be broadened.

Special earmarked funds should be appropriated to the U.S. Department of Labor and a portion allotted to every state for the purpose of servicing the educational institutions responsible for placement.

Annual follow-up reports on youth at one-, three-, and five-year periods should be made by the federal and state employment units on the success of placement operations. These reports should go to all concerned agencies, Congress, state legislatures, and the National and State Councils.

Special funds for postsecondary institutional support at the subbaccalaureate level should go to programs for technical and subprofessional career training. These separately authorized funds should be allocated to states through the established state administrative units concerned with vocational and technical occupational preparation and should become part of the annual state plan which is reviewed by the State Manpower Councils.

Postsecondary institutions such as community colleges, technical institutes, and area vocational-technical schools should operate all year and greatly expand their programs for adult retraining and career upgrading.

The possibility that the education and technical training needed by all volunteers and draftees of the armed forces should be done in postsecondary institutions and considered part of their enlistment period should be explored. Specific military and technical skills could be provided by the military. This would reduce the cost of military training, provide career transition when servicemen complete training, and allow the military to concentrate on the military aspects. The present expenditures for technical and theoretical education should provide the necessary tuition, room and board, and educational costs for these young people if they choose to elect this pattern of military service. It would, in addition, provide one to two years of educational credits for many of the nation's youth at less personal expense and lower government cost. It would tend to equalize educational opportunity for those with less family income who now fail to try postsecondary education.

Preferential student loan provisions should be established for career technical education since many leading institutions fail to give loans to other than degree-seeking high school graduates.

Part of the placement operations of all schools should be related to the securing of student loans and opportunity grants or scholarships for postsecondary technical careers.

Present student assistance programs, such as Neighborhood Youth Corps, should be administered by educational institutions. Present emphasis in these programs on student financial aid should be shifted to include a heavy emphasis on the related education necessary for these youths.

Planned educational components related directly to the work experience component should be required which would include orientation and guidance for the job supervisors.

There are few such programs now located in rural areas, and these youths form a large part of the flow to urban areas.

The present inability of the schools to offer necessary earning while the student is learning causes youths to leave school for more narrow programs and greater earnings offered by out-of-school programs.

Such a plan would prepare youths who are the least edu-

257

cated and the least skilled to move up into the cooperative work experience programs and to stay in school.

The component of manpower supply as a part of a comprehensive manpower program should become the prime responsibility of the educational sector of our society. In a technological society, education is the bridge over which every individual must travel to a career or adult role.

A reduction of this magnitude would allow the Department of Labor, in cooperation with other federal agencies, to concentrate on job development and the provision of necessary economic and labor market information so badly needed. In addition it would allow the Labor Department to focus on placement and follow-up in cooperation with the educational community—matters which now have little priority.

It would provide a continuum of preparation of human resources at all levels and in all areas of career options. It would focus responsibility and involve all levels of government.

The nation must have a cabinet-level Department of Education and Manpower Development. The nation will never reduce its pool of unemployed until the federal government gives equal interest and investment to reducing the flow of untrained youth and makes education for careers below the professional level as important as education at the college level.

The present plethora of federal, state, and local agencies concerned with manpower supply must be focused at the federal level in an agency which has a chance to bring this part of a total manpower policy and program into the highest level of policy making.

This action would finally put emphasis on the prevention of human failure and the development of human resources as a top national priority.

The present pattern of concern after people have become failures is too late, too costly, and too prone to continue both education and manpower development as they are now.

Education is now the link between the individual and his role as a citizen, a worker, and a dignified person. The federal government can no longer stand aside and be concerned only with "picking up the pieces"; it must become involved in seeing that there are fewer pieces to pick up.

The present trend toward a dual school system, one for the poor and one for the middle class, would be reversed.

The present practice of returning to the eighteenth-century concept that all people need are work skills would be revised.

The inability of the states and local educational agencies to be heard in the deliberations of national policy would be overcome.

Other federal agencies could focus on the other aspects of manpower policy and program, now neglected.

Appendix

Manpower Conversion Model [1]

It is herewith proposed that the theoretical starting point of vocational education be the manpower conversion equation illustrated in Figure 1. The principle value of this model is that it generates a set of basic objectives for vocational education against which *effectiveness progress* can be measured, and it does so within a realistic framework that relates vocational education to the national good.[2]

The manpower conversion model indicates that public occupational education is one part of a three channel total system for the conversion of undeveloped (unskilled) potential manpower to developed (skilled) actual manpower.

The basic idea is simple. The model states that the *primary objective* of public and private systems for occupational education and training, taken as a collective whole, is to *induct and convert undeveloped potential manpower resources into skilled manpower resources of sufficient kinds and numbers so that the output will meet the skilled manpower requirements of the expanding national economy.*

A serious imbalance between the collective system's output of skilled manpower and the requirements of the growth economy implies both an unemployment problem for undeveloped manpower (or unneeded skilled manpower) and an economy hampered by unfulfilled manpower needs.

Ideally, a balance in the equation implies that for every newly developed skilled manpower resource there would be an available job, and for every such job opening, there would be

---

[1] Enninger, M. U. "How Should the Schools Fulfill Responsibility for Student's Transition from School to Work?" Paper prepared for the Department of Health, Education, and Welfare, Vocational Education Task Force, 1969.

[2] The concept of a theoretical model to generate basic objectives is a minor innovation for vocational education. Generally, in this field, objectives are not derived. They are stated because of claimed self-evident truth.

an available and qualified person. Thus, the model ties the objectives of public systems of vocational education to the national full-employment policy and to the manpower needs of the expanding national economy.

The basic challenge to public systems of occupational education, particularly the major city systems, is to increase their roles as significant suppliers of manpower skilled at the occupation entry-level.

Some General Implications

In the interest of brevity, these are stated without the benefit of supporting rationale.

1. *Public vocational education should adopt the self-concept of a major manpower conversion system.* The educators in this field should think of themselves as managers of manpower conversion systems ready to adopt the principles, concepts and tools of modern management.

2. *Public vocational education must base its curriculum planning in such a way that it takes into account the characteristics of those to be served,* i.e., the non-college bound undeveloped manpower resource, *as well as the manpower requirements forecast for the region served.* It has not attempted to harmonize the two end elements of the Figure 1 equation in the past with any impressive energy.

3. *Public vocational education must function as an integral part of a total system.* Planning must incorporate an awareness of what is going on locally with respect to the other two manpower conversion channels, i.e., private occupational education or training systems and training programs and opportunities in business and industry. It can't function at maximum effectiveness in isolation.

4. *Public vocational education must grow.* Growth in enrollments and outputs is implied by the equation. The population growth means a growth in the point-in-time number of undeveloped manpower resources. The skilled manpower requirement growth, coupled with the decline of unskilled manpower requirements means a growing demand for occupationally skilled manpower. Not to grow means to diminish as a major source of manpower conversion.

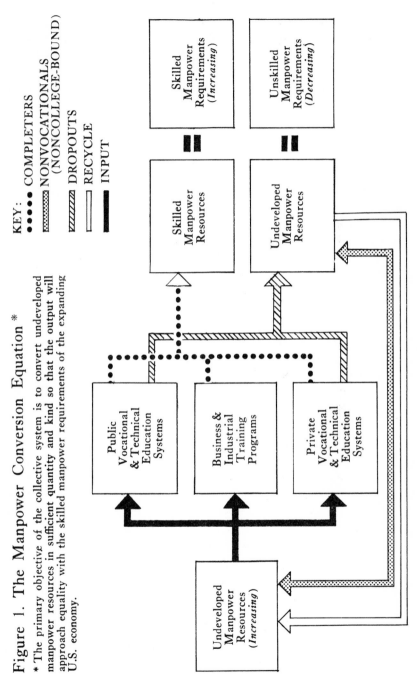

Figure 1. The Manpower Conversion Equation *

* The primary objective of the collective system is to convert undeveloped manpower resources in sufficient quantity and kind so that the output will approach equality with the skilled manpower requirements of the expanding U.S. economy.

KEY:
●●●●● COMPLETERS
▨▨▨ NONVOCATIONALS (NONCOLLEGE-BOUND)
▧▧▧ DROPOUTS
▭▭▭ RECYCLE
▬▬▬ INPUT

263

5. *Public vocational education must compete in terms of effectiveness.* The pressures created by the high costs of education will put a premium on effectiveness and efficiency. If the public systems of occupational education trail the private systems in effectiveness, the resources will gravitate toward the latter. The concept of competition should be introduced into the total system.

Some Basic Objectives

Without going into the logic of the deductive process at this time, several basic objectives can be derived from the model. These are some, not necessarily all, of the *measurable* objectives for which school system administrative heads should be held responsible and accountable for *improvement* toward the ideal. It is recommended that these objectives, as a collective whole, with others yet to come, be used to *evaluate the effectiveness of public vocational education systems as suppliers of trained manpower.*

1. *Enrollment growth.* To show a continuing increase in the percentage of non-college bound youth enrolled in occupational programs at the secondary and postsecondary school level.

2. *Offerings growth.* To show continuing increase in the range and diversity of vocational curriculum offerings until such offerings adequately reflect both manpower requirements and the range of talents in the school-age population served.

3. *Holding power.* To show continuing improvement in student holding power so as to increase the percentage of students who complete the vocational curriculum of their choice.

4. *Knowledge and skill.* To show continuing improvement in the percentage of completers who have attained at least minimum standards of adequacy in both general and occupational entry-level skills.

5. *Occupation motivation.* To show continuing improvement in the percent of completers motivated to enter the field for which trained or a field of equivalent or higher skill involvement.

6. *Placement performance.* To show continuing improvement in the percent of qualified program completers placed in the occupations for which trained or in related occupations.

It can show that failure to achieve these objectives prevents or contradicts the primary objective of the manpower conversion model, namely to balance the output of skilled manpower with the requirements for skilled manpower.

Bibliography

Booklets

American Association of State Colleges and Universities. *Leadership and Responsibility on the Changing Campus: Whose in Charge Here?* Washington, D.C.: the Association, 1968.

American Vocational Association. *Definitions of Terms in Vocational, Technical, and Practical Arts Education.* Washington, D.C.: American Technical Association, 1964.

Becker, Joseph M.; Haber, William; and Levitan, Sar A. *The Programs To Aid the Unemployed in the 1960's.* Kalamazoo, Mich.: W. E. Upjohn Institute for Employment Research, 1965.

Board of Vocational Education and Rehabilitation, Division of Vocational and Technical Education. *Annual Report for Vocational Education in Illinois, July 1, 1967, Through June 30, 1968.* Bulletin No. 215. Springfield, Ill.: the Board, 1969.

Brown, Ralph, editor. *Manpower and Active Employment Programs for Developing Countries.* Proceedings of the Eighth International Manpower Seminar, June 1–August 12, 1967 and Ninth International Manpower Seminar, September 21–December 2, 1967. Washington, D.C.: U.S. Department of Labor, Manpower Administration, International Manpower Institute.

Burt, Samuel. *Industry and Community Leaders in Education.* Kalamazoo, Mich.: W. E. Upjohn Institute for Employment Research, October 1969.

Burt, Samuel M., and Striner, Herbert E. *Toward Greater Industry and Government Involvement in Manpower Development.* Kalamazoo, Mich.: W. E. Upjohn Institute for Employment Research, 1968.

Bush, Donald O., and others. *Between Education and the World of Work.* Rocky Mountain Educational Laboratory, June 1968.

Coleman, James S., and others. *Equality of Educational Opportunity.* U.S. Department of Health, Education, and Welfare, Office of Education. Washington, D.C.: Government Printing Office, 1966.

Council of Chief State School Officers. *State and Local Responsibilities for Education, A Position Statement.* Washington, D.C.: the Council, 1968.

Davidson, Roger H., and Levitan, Sar A. *Antipoverty Housekeeping: The Administration of the Economic Opportunity Act.* Ann Arbor–Detroit, Mich.: Institute of Labor and Industrial Relations, University of Michigan and Wayne State University, 1968.

Dickenson, William E., editor. *New Dimensions in School Board Leadership: A Seminar Report and Workbook.* Evanston, Ill.: National School Boards Association, 1969.

Education Commission of the States. *Analysis of State Programs in Community Centered Post High School Education.* Denver, Colo.: the Commission, 1968.

————. *Occupational Education: Changing Contexts.* Report No. 1. Denver, Colo.: the Commission, 1967.

Emerson, Lynn A. "Technical Training in the United States." *Education for a Changing World of Work.* Report of a Panel of Consultants on Vocational Education. Washington, D.C.: Government Printing Office, 1963.

Enninger, Max U. *The Process and Product of T and I High School Level Vocational Education in the United States.* Pittsburgh, Pa.: Institute for Performance Technology, American Institutes for Research, September 1965.

Evans, Rupert N. *School for Schooling's Sake: The Current Role of the Secondary School in Occupational Preparation, The Transition from School to Work.* Report based on the Princeton Manpower Symposium, May 9-10, 1968, Princeton, New Jersey.

Fine, Sidney A. *Guidelines for the Design of New Careers.* Kalamazoo, Mich.: W. E. Upjohn Institute for Employment Research, 1967.

Focus on the Seventies. Chicago, Ill.: Field Enterprises Educational Corporation, 1968.

Greenleigh, Arthur. *Opening the Doors: Job Training Programs.* A Report to the Committee on the Administration of Training Programs. New York: Greenleigh Associates, 1968. Part I, 163 pp.; Part II, 292 pp.

Hansen, Gary B. *Britain's Industrial Training Act: Its History, Development, and Implication for America.* Washington, D.C.: National Manpower Policy Task Force, 1967.

Hu, Th-Wei; Maw, Lin Lee; and Storfer, Ernest W. *The Cost Effectiveness Study of Vocational Education: A Comparison of Vocational and Non-Vocational Education in Secondary Schools.* University Park: Institute for Research on Human Resources, Pennsylvania State University, 1969.

Hull, William L.; Frazier, William D.; and Stevenson, William W. *Research Handbook for Vocational-Technical Education.* Stillwater: Research Coordinating Unit, Oklahoma State University, 1969.

Job Corps Study, A. Report of the Commissioner of Education required by Public Law 90-576, September 1968.

Kaufman, Jacob J., and others. *An Analysis of the Comparative Costs and Benefits of Vocational vs. Academic Education in Secondary Schools.* Pittsburgh: Institute for Research on Human Resources, Pennsylvania State University, October 1967.

―――. *The Role of the Secondary Schools in the Preparation of Youth for Employment: A Comparative Study of Vocational, Academic, and General Curricula.* University Park: Institute for Research on Human Resources, Pennsylvania State University, 1967.

Keyserling, Leon H. *Achieving Nationwide Educational Excellence: A Ten-Year Plan, 1967-1977, To Save the Schools.* Washington, D.C.: Conference on Economic Progress, 1968.

Lessinger, Leon M. "Accountability for Results: A Basic Challenge for America's Schools." *American Education,* June-July 1969.

Levitan, Sar A. *Antipoverty Work and Training Efforts: Goals and Reality.* Policy Papers in Human Resources and Industrial Relations No. 3. Washington, D.C.: Institute of Labor and Industrial Relations, University of Michigan and Wayne State University, with the National Manpower Policy Task Force, August 1967.

―――. *Youth Employment Act.* Kalamazoo, Mich.: W. E. Upjohn Institute for Employment Research, 1963.

Mangum, Garth L. *Contributions and Costs of Manpower Development and Training.* Policy Papers in Human Resources and Industrial Relations No. 5. Washington, D.C.: Institute of Labor and Industrial Relations, University of Michigan and Wayne State University, with the National Manpower Policy Task Force, 1967.

―――. *Reorienting Vocational Education.* Policy Papers in Human Resources and Industrial Relations No. 7. Washington D.C.: Institute of Labor and Industrial Relations, University of Michigan and Wayne State University, with the National Manpower Policy Task Force, 1968.

Menefee, Selden, and Cornejo, Esperanza. *Occupational Education in the Junior College.* Selected Proceedings from Two Workshops on Occupational Education sponsored by the Program with Developing Institutions in the Occupational Education Project. Monograph No. 3. Washington, D.C.: American Association of Junior Colleges, 1969.

Michael, Donald. *Cybernation: Silent Conquest.* Santa Barbara, Calif.: Center for the Study of Democratic Institutions, 1962.

National Advisory Committee on Adult Basic Education. *Adult Basic Education, Strengthening the Foundation of Our Democratic Society.* Second Annual Report, August 1969.

National Advisory Council on Vocational Education. *First Annual Report, July 1969.* U.S. Department of Health, Education, and Welfare, Office of Education. Washington, D.C.: Government Printing Office, 1969.

National Manpower Policy Task Force. *The Nation's Manpower Programs.* Washington, D.C.: Government Printing Office, 1969.

Oettinger, Anthony G. *A Vision of Technology and Education.* Reprint No. 1. Cambridge: Program on Technology and Science, Harvard University, 1966.

Piel, Gerard. *Consumers of Abundance.* Santa Barbara, Calif.: Center for the Study of Democratic Institutions, 1961.

President's Commission on Law Enforcement and the Administration of Justice, Task Force on Juvenile Delinquency. *Task Force Report: Juvenile Delinquency and Youth Crime.* Report on Juvenile Justice and Consultants' Papers. Washington, D.C.: Government Printing Office, 1967.

President's Committee on Youth Unemployment. *The Challenge of Jobless Youth.* Washington, D.C.: Government Printing Office, 1963.

President's National Advisory Commission on Rural Poverty. *The People Left Behind.* Washington, D.C.: Government Printing Office, 1967.

Proceedings of National Conference on Research. 1968 Vocational Education Amendments. Stillwater: Coordinating Unit for Research in Vocational Education, Oklahoma State University, 1969.

Rhine, Sidney H., and Creamer, Daniel. *The Technical Manpower Shortage: How Acute?* New York: National Industrial Conference Board, 1969.

Sheppard, Harold L., and Belitsky, Harvey A. *Promoting Job Finding Success for the Unemployed.* Kalamazoo, Mich.: W. E. Upjohn Institute for Employment Research, 1968.

Smith, Harold T. *Education and Training for the World of Work.* A Vocational Education Program for the State of Michigan. Kalamazoo, Mich.: W. E. Upjohn Institute for Employment Research, 1963.

Striner, Herbert E. *1984 and Beyond, The World of Work.* Kalamazoo, Mich.: W. E. Upjohn Institute for Employment Research, 1967.

Theodores, James L., and others. *Crisis in Planning: An Analysis of Some Factors That Influence the Kinds of Schools We Have, How They Got That Way, and What We Must Do About Changing Them.* Columbus, Ohio: Council of Educational Facility Planners, 1968.

U.S. 89th Congress, 2nd Session, House Committee on Education and Labor, Select Subcommittee on Labor. *Manpower Development and*

Training Act Amendments of 1966. Hearings on H.R. 14690 and other bills. Washington, D.C.: Government Printing Office, 1966. 211 pp.

U.S. 89th Congress, 2nd Session, House Committee on Education and Labor, General Subcommittee on Education. *Vocational Education Amendments of 1966.* Hearings on H.R. 15444 and H.R. 15445, bills to amend the Vocational Education Act of 1963. Two parts. Washington, D.C.: Government Printing Office, 1967. 912 pp.

U.S. 89th Congress, 2nd Session, Senate Committee on Labor and Public Welfare, Subcommittee on Employment and Manpower. *Manpower Services Act of 1966 and Employment Act of 1966.* Joint Hearings on S. 2974/H.R. 13037 and S. 2032/H.R. 13362. Washington, D.C.: Government Printing Office, 1966. 640 pp.

U.S. 90th Congress, 2nd Session, Senate Committee on Labor and Public Welfare. *To Amend the Vocational Education Act of 1963, and for Other Purposes.* Report on S. 3770. Washington, D.C.: Government Printing Office, July 1968.

U.S. 90th Congress, 2nd Session, Senate Committee on Labor and Public Welfare, Subcommittee on Education. *Hearings on S. 3099, To Amend the Vocational Educational Act of 1963.* April 3, 4, and 5, 1968.

U.S. Department of Health, Education, and Welfare, Office of Education. *Administration of Vocational Education, Rules and Regulations.* Vocational Education Bulletin No. 1. Revised 1966. Washington, D.C.: Government Printing Office, 1967.

————. *Criteria for Technician Education, A Suggested Guide.* OE-80056. Washington, D.C.: Government Printing Office, 1968.

————. *Digest of Educational Statistics, 1968 Edition.* Washington, D.C.: Government Printing Office, 1968.

————. *Education for a Changing World of Work.* Report of Panel of Consultants on Vocational Education, prepared at the request of the President of the United States. Washington, D.C.: Government Printing Office, 1963.

————. *Education and Training, The Bridge Between Man and His Work.* Third Annual Report of the Secretary of Health, Education, and Welfare to the Congress on Training Activities under the Manpower Development and Training Act. Washington, D.C.: Government Printing Office, 1965.

————. *Education and Training, Key to Development of Human Resources.* Second Annual Report of the Secretary of Health, Education, and Welfare to the Congress on Training Activities under the Manpower Development and Training Act. Washington, D.C.: Government Printing Office, 1964.

————. *Education and Training, Learning for Jobs.* 1968 Report of the Secretary of Health, Education, and Welfare to the Congress on the Manpower Development and Training Act. Washington, D.C.: Government Printing Office, 1968.

———. *Education and Training, Passport to Opportunity.* Fourth Annual Report of the Secretary of Health, Education, and Welfare to the Congress on Training Activities under the Manpower Development and Training Act. Washington, D.C.: Government Printing Office, 1966.

———. *Expanding the Choices, Education and Training.* 1967 Report of the Secretary of Health, Education, and Welfare to the Congress on the Manpower Development and Training Act. Washington, D.C.: Government Printing Office, 1967.

———. *1963 Report of the Secretary of Health, Education, and Welfare to the Congress on the Manpower Development and Training Act.* Washington, D.C.: Government Printing Office, 1963.

———. *Projections of Educational Statistics, 1975-76.* Washington, D.C.: Government Printing Office, 1966.

———. *Vocational and Technical Education, Annual Report, Fiscal Year 1965.* Washington, D.C.: Government Printing Office, 1968.

———. *Vocational and Technical Education, Annual Report, Fiscal Year 1967.* Washington, D.C.: Government Printing Office, 1969.

———. *Vocational Education—The Bridge Between Man and His Work.* General Report of the Advisory Council on Vocational Education. Washington, D.C.: Government Printing Office, 1968.

U.S. Department of Labor. *Manpower Report of the President and a Report on Manpower Requirements, Resources, Utilization, and Training.* Washington, D.C.: Government Printing Office, 1969.

———. *Manpower Report of the President and a Report on Manpower Requirements, Resources, Utilization, and Training.* Washington, D.C.: Government Printing Office, 1968.

———. *Manpower Report of the President and a Report on Manpower Requirements, Resources, Utilization, and Training.* Washington, D.C.: Government Printing Office, 1967.

———. *Manpower Report of the President and a Report on Manpower Requirements, Resources, Utilization, and Training.* Washington, D.C.: Government Printing Office, 1966.

———. *Manpower Report of the President and a Report on Manpower Requirements, Resources, Utilization, and Training.* Washington, D.C.: Government Printing Office, 1965.

———. *Manpower Report of the President and a Report on Manpower Requirements, Resources, Utilization, and Training.* Washington, D.C.: Government Printing Office, 1964.

U.S. Department of Labor, Bureau of Labor Statistics. *From School to Work: The Early Employment Experiences in Seven Communities, 1952-57.* Washington, D.C.: Government Printing Office, 1961.

————. *Educational Attainment of Workers.* Special Labor Force Report No. 30. Washington, D.C.: Government Printing Office, 1962.

————. *The Long-Range Demand for Scientific and Technical Personnel.* Prepared for the National Science Foundation. Washington, D.C.: Government Printing Office, 1961.

————. *Technician Manpower: Requirements, Resources, and Training Needs.* Bulletin No. 1512. Washington, D.C.: Government Printing Office.

U.S. Department of Labor, Manpower Administration, Bureau of Apprenticeship and Training. *The National Apprenticeship Program.* Washington, D.C.: Government Printing Office, 1965.

Wickenden, William E. *A Comparative Study of Engineering Education in the United States and in Europe.* Society for the Promotion of Engineering, 1929.

Wolfbein, Seymour. *Manpower Problems of the 1970's.* Washington, D.C.: U.S. Chamber of Commerce, 1969.

Young, Earl B., and others. *Vocational Education for Handicapped Persons, Handbook for Program Implementation.* Publication pursuant to a grant from the U.S. Department of Health, Education, and Welfare, Office of Education, 1969.

Articles and Speeches

Allen, James E., Jr. "The Right To Read—Target for the 1970's." Speech before the annual convention of the National Association of State Boards of Education, Los Angeles, California, September 23, 1969.

American Association of School Administrators, a department of the National Education Association. "Education and National Manpower." *Hot Line,* Vol. 2, July 1969.

Barnett, David. "Industry's Role in Poverty War." *New York World Journal Tribune,* September 27, 1966.

Bell, Daniel. "The Post Industrial Society." Boston: Liberty Mutual Insurance Co., 1962. (Multilithed.)

Bowen, Charles R. "The Need for National Manpower Policy." Paper prepared for the Bureau of Adult, Vocational, and Library Programs, Office of Education, U.S. Department of Health, Education, and Welfare, Washington, D.C.

Bowles, Samuel. "The Efficient Allocation of Resources in Education." *Quarterly Journal of Economics* 81: 189-219; May 1967.

Brademas, J. "View from Capitol Hill." *Grade Teacher* 85: 12+; November 1967.

Carmichael, Oliver C. "A Hundred Years of the Land Grant Movement." *Saturday Review,* April 21, 1962.

Chase, Edward. "Learning To Be Employable." *Harper's Magazine,* April 1963.

———. "Politics and Technology." *Yale Review,* March 1963.

"Children of Change, The." *Kaiser Aluminum News,* Vol. 27, May 1969. (Kaiser Center 866, Oakland, Calif.)

Cohen, Wilbur J. "The Learning and Earning Force." Speech before the annual conference of the National Council for the Social Studies, Washington, D.C., November 29, 1968.

Corazzini, Arthur J. "The Decision To Invest in Vocational Education: Analysis of Costs and Benefits." *Journal of Human Resources,* Vol. 3, Supplement, 1968. pp. 88-120.

Dennard, Cleveland L. "Vocational Education for the Disadvantaged: Planning, Organizing, and Operating Through a Systems Approach." Paper presented to the National Workshop on Vocational Education for the Disadvantaged, Atlantic City, New Jersey, March 14, 1969.

Diebold, John. *Governor's Conference on Automation.* State of New York, June 1-3, 1960.

Djilas, Milovan. "New Left Pouts Worn Out Creed." *Washington Post,* October 19, 1969.

DuBridge, Lee A. Address before the Symposium on *Challenges Facing Technology of Tomorrow,* Newark State College, Union, New Jersey, September 4, 1969.

Enninger, M. U. "How Should the Schools Fulfill Responsibility for Student's Transition from School to Work?" Paper prepared for U.S. Department of Health, Education, and Welfare, Vocational Education Task Force, 1969.

Evans, Rupert N. "The Secondary School and Occupational Preparation." *Bulletin of the National Association of Secondary-School Principals* 53: 23-40; February 1969.

Feldman, M. J. "Why Manpower Training Should Be a Public School Mission." *American Vocational Journal* 42: 26-28; November 1967.

Gans, Herbert J. "The Equality Revolution." *New York Times,* November 3, 1968.

Gardner, John W. "Creative Leadership in Our Cities." Address before the seventy-third Congress of the American Industry, sponsored by the National Association of Manufacturers, New York, New York, December 4, 1968.

———. "Redesigning Society To Build the Individual." *Washington Post,* September 1, 1968.

———. "What Kind of Society Do We Want?" *Reader's Digest,* September 1969.

Goldberg, Herman R. Speech at the New York Board of Regents Symposium on Occupational Education, Albany, New York, November 14, 1968.

Grote, C. N. "Toward Fulfilling a Total Obligation." *Industrial Arts and Vocational Education* 58: 28-29; May 1969.

Harris, Norman C. "Meeting the Post High School's Educational Needs of the Vast Middle Group of High School Graduates." Speech before the North Central Association of Colleges and Secondary Schools, Committee on Articulation in Schools and Colleges, Chicago, Illinois, March 19, 1963.

Heller, Walter W. "Men, Money, and Materials." *Educational Record,* January 1963.

Howe, Harold, II. "Education and Social Reconstruction." *Educational Leadership* 25: 321-23; January 1968.

Irwin, Constance, and others. "Year Round School Program." (Symposium) *NEA Journal* 45: 82-84; February 1956.

Kaufman, Jacob J. "Occupational Training Needs for Youth." *Journal of Human Resources,* Vol. 3, Supplement, 1968. pp. 121-40.

Lynch, Gerald J. "Education, Its Relevancy to Society's Vocational Requirements." Speech before the Burbank, California, Chamber of Commerce, honoring award-winning students in industrial education and work experience programs of the Burbank Unified School District, May 28, 1969.

Mangum, Garth L. "Vocational Education for the Disadvantaged: Lessons from Government-Funded Programs." Paper presented at the National Workshop on Vocational Education for the Disadvantaged, Atlantic City, New Jersey, March 13, 1969.

Matthews, Howard A. "Education for Urban Disadvantaged." Paper prepared for the Committee for Economic Development, September 1969.

———. "Tomorrow Is Now." *American Education.* U.S. Department of Health, Education, and Welfare, Office of Education, June 1967.

Melby, Ernest O. "The Community School: A Social Imperative." *The Community School and Its Administration.* Board of Education, Flint, Michigan, Vol. 7, No. 2, October 1968.

Miller, W. W. "Oklahoma's Twenty-One-Year Experiment in Residential Vocational Education." *American Vocational Journal* 43: 18-20; October 1968.

"Money in the Classroom: Corporations Sponsor Vocational Education." *Forbes Magazine* 103: 70+; April 15, 1969.

Morse, Wayne. "Education for Jobs in a Technological Society." Speech before the American Vocational Association's annual meeting, Dallas, Texas, December 10, 1968.

Nowlis, Helen H. "Role of Young Adults Must Be Made Clear." *Boston Evening Globe,* September 12, 1969.

"Occupational Information." Report No. 4 to the Appalachian Education and Economic Development Commission, by the Educational Advisory Committee to the Appalachian Regional Commission, 1969.

Parsons, Cynthia. "Schooling for Skills." *Christian Science Monitor,* 1967.

Pragan, Otto. "Bridging the Vocational Gap." *American Federationist,* Vol. 76, July 1969.

Pucinski, Roman C. "Education in a Trillion Dollar Economy." *American Vocational Journal* 43: 10-12; February 1968.

Ray, E. M. "Social and Philosophical Framework." *Review of Educational Research* 38: 309-25; October 1968.

Reagan, Ronald. "Technical Education: The Pathway to Social and Economic Stability." Adopted from a speech before the fortieth annual convention of the California Industrial Education Association, Fresno, California, March 15, 1969.

Reed, J. J. "Educational Change for Manpower Development." *Vocational Guidance Quarterly* 17: 82-86; December 1968.

Rogers, Carl R. "On Education." *Kaiser Aluminum News,* No. 1, 1967.

Rosen, Howard. "Vocational Guidance: Room for Improvement." *Manpower,* Vol. 1, August 1969.

Russo, M. "Fourteen Million Vocational Students by 1975." *American Education* 5: 10-11; March 1969.

Ruttenberg, Stanley H. "Manpower Training—The Seeds of a Dilemma." *Manpower,* January 1969.

Schultz, Theodore W. "Investment in Human Capital." *American Economic Review,* Vol. 51, March 1961.

Switzer, Mary E. "Rehabilitation: A Decade Hence." *Rehabilitation Record,* Vol. 5, July-August 1964.

Tennyson, W. Wesley. "Career Development." *Review of Educational Research* 38: 346-66; October 1968.

Thompson, Scott D. "Activism, A Game for Unloving Critics." Speech before the annual convention of the National Association of Secondary-School Principals, San Francisco, California, March 1969.

"Training and Technology, Summary Report, Phase I Activities, June 1966–September 1969," conducted at the U.S. Atomic Energy Commission's Oak Ridge Y-12 Plant, January 1969.

Venn, Grant. "Adult Education: A Nation's Concern." Speech before the Minnesota Adult Education Association's annual meeting, University of Minnesota, Minneapolis, April 19, 1968.

276

————. "The Challenge of the Seventies." (Editorial) *School Administrator,* January 1969.

————. "A Challenge of Vocational Education for Schools, States, and the Nation." Speech before members of State Boards for Vocational Education at the American Vocational Association's convention, Cleveland, Ohio, December 6, 1967.

————. "Eye on Tomorrow's Jobs." *American Education* 5: 12-15; March 1969.

————. "Hot Cities, Jobs, and Adult Education." Speech at the Forum on Priorities for the 1970's, Second National Leadership Conference on Adult Basic Education, San Antonio, Texas, April 16, 1968.

————. "Junior College Participation in the Vocational Education Act." Speech before the Workshop on Federal Programs and Junior Colleges, Washington, D.C., December 7, 1967.

————. "Learning Beyond the Classroom." *American Vocational Journal* 42: 14-16; September 1967.

————. "Learning Outside the Classroom." *American Vocational Journal,* September 1967.

————. "New Directions in Vocational Education." Speech before the National Association of Manufacturers' seventy-sixth Congress to American Industry, New York, New York, December 8, 1967. (Published by the National Association of Manufacturers, 277 Park Avenue, New York, New York.)

————. "New Horizons in Vocational Education." Speech before the fifth annual convention of the Canadian Vocational Education Association, Toronto, Canada, May 27, 1968.

————. "New Schools for a New Society." *Hot Line,* Vol. 2, February 1969.

————. "Objectives and Goals of Occupational Education." Paper prepared for the Stanford Research Institute Conference on Vocational-Technical Education, Airlie House, Virginia, April 10, 1967.

————. "Occupational Education for Everyone." *Bulletin of the National Association of Secondary-School Principals,* No. 332, December 1968, pp. 112-22.

————. "Occupational Education: Work Experience Programs." *The 1967 Selected Papers.* Washington, D.C.: American Association of Junior Colleges.

————. "One Million Dropouts." *Canadian Vocational Journal,* Vol. 4, Fall 1968.

————. "The Role of Schools in Manpower Development." Paper presented at the National Manpower Advisory Committee meeting, Washington, D.C., September 29, 1967.

———. "Vocational Education and Rural Youth." Speech before the National Outlook Conference on Rural Youth, Washington, D.C., October 25, 1967.

———. "Vocational Education: From the World of Stability to a World of Change." Speech before the National Conference on Program Planning and Budgeting for Vocational Education Personnel, Washington, D.C., March 1968.

———. "Vocational Education in a Dynamic Labor Market." *Manpower,* Vol. 1, October 1969.

———. "Vocational Education in Transition." Speech before the National Association of Secondary-School Principals' annual meeting, San Francisco, California, March 1, 1969.

———. "Where Else Can They Go?" Speech before the Milwaukee Technical College, Milwaukee, Wisconsin, June 6, 1968.

———. "Womanpower, U.S.A." Speech before the annual national meeting of the Future Homemakers of America, Los Angeles, California, July 12, 1967.

"Vocational Education: The New Approach." *Nation's Schools* 80: 36-37; August 1967.

Walters, Robert. "De Facto Segregation Feared in Job Corps." *Washington Star,* December 29, 1966.

Weber, Robert. "Man and His Environment—1980." Background paper prepared for the annual meeting of the Board of Trustees of the Educational Testing Service, May 7-8, 1963.

West, E. H. "Education and Jobs." *Journal of Negro Education* 37: 359-63; Fall 1968.

Books

Belitsky, Harvey A. *Private Vocational Schools and Their Students: Limited Objectives, Unlimited Opportunities.* Cambridge, Mass.: Schenkman Publishing Co., 1969.

Bolino, August C. *Manpower and the City.* Cambridge, Mass.: Schenkman Publishing Co., 1969.

Bowman, Gardaw, and Klopf, Gordon J. *New Careers and Roles in the American School.* New York: Bank Street College of Education (for the Office of Economic Opportunity), 1968.

Cervantes, Lucius F. *The Dropout: Causes and Cures.* Ann Arbor: University of Michigan Press, 1965.

Chamber of Commerce of the United States. *The Concept of Poverty, Task Force on Economic Growth and Opportunity.* Washington, D.C.: the Chamber, 1965.

Darcy, Robert L., and Powell, Philip E., editors. *Manpower Education in a Growing Economy*. Athens: Center for Economic Education, College of Business Administration, Ohio University, 1968.

DuBridge, Lee. "Educational and Social Consequences," in *Automation and Technological Change*. (Edited by John T. Dunlop.) Englewood Cliffs, N.J.: Prentice-Hall, 1962.

Dunlop, John T., editor. *Automation and Technological Change*. Englewood Cliffs, N.J.: Prentice-Hall, 1962.

Economic Report of the President, together with the *Annual Report of the Council of Economic Advisors*. Transmitted to Congress, January 1969. Washington, D.C.: Government Printing Office, 1969.

Fortas, Abe. *Concerning Dissent and Civil Disobedience*. New York: New American Library, 1968.

Freedman, Marcia. *The Process of Work Establishment*. New York: Columbia University Press, 1969.

Gardner, John W. *No Easy Victories*. (Edited by Helen Rowan.) New York: Harper and Row, 1968.

Gleazer, Edmund J., Jr. *This Is the Community College*. Boston, Mass.: Houghton Mifflin Co., 1968.

Gordon, Kermit, editor. *Agenda for the Nation*. Garden City, N.Y.: Doubleday and Co., 1969.

Greenfield, Harry I. *Allied Health Manpower: Trends and Prospects*. New York: Columbia University Press, 1969.

Harbison, Frederick, and Myers, Charles A. *Education, Manpower, and Economic Growth*. A Joint Project of the Industrial Relations Section, Princeton University, and the Industrial Relations Section, Massachusetts Institute of Technology. New York: McGraw-Hill Book Co., 1964.

Harrington, Michael. *The Accidental Century*. Baltimore: Penguin Books, 1967.

Harris, Seymour E. *Education and Public Policy*. Berkeley, Calif.: McCutchan Publishing Corp., 1965.

Heller, Walter W. "Employment and Manpower." *Men Without Work, The Economics of Unemployment*. (Edited by Stanley Lebergott.) Englewood Cliffs, N.J.: Prentice-Hall, 1964.

Hoffer, Eric. *The True Believer*. New York: Harper and Row, 1966.

Jefferson, Thomas. *On Democracy*. (Edited by Saul K. Padover.) New York: New American Library, 1953.

Johnson, Lyndon B. *Public Papers of the Presidents of the United States*. Book I, January 1–May 31, 1965. Washington, D.C.: Government Printing Office, 1966.

Kaufman, Jacob J., and Foran, Terry G. "The Minimum Wage and Poverty." *Toward Freedom from Want.* University Park: Industrial Relations Research Association, Department of Economics, Pennsylvania State University, 1967.

Kaufman, Jacob J., and Lewis, Morgan V. *The Potential of Vocational Education: Observations and Conclusions.* University Park: Institute for Research on Human Resources, Pennsylvania State University, 1968.

Knezevich, Stephen J., editor. *Administrative Technology and the School Executive.* Washington, D.C.: American Association of School Administrators, a department of the National Education Association, 1969.

Landy, Edward, and Kroll, Arthur M., editors. *Current Issues and Suggested Action.* Guidance in American Education II. Cambridge, Mass.: Harvard University Press, 1965.

Lebergott, Stanley, editor. *Men Without Work, The Economics of Unemployment.* Englewood Cliffs, N.J.: Prentice-Hall, 1964.

Levitan, Sar A., and Mangum, Garth L. *Federal Training and Work Programs in the Sixties.* Ann Arbor: Institute of Labor and Industrial Relations, University of Michigan and Wayne State University, 1969.

Levitan, Sar A., and Siegel, Irving H. *Dimensions of Manpower Policy: Programs and Research.* Baltimore: Johns Hopkins Press, 1966.

Mangum, Garth L. *The Manpower Revolution: Its Policy Consequences.* Garden City, N.Y.: Doubleday and Co., 1965.

Mayer, Frederick. *A History of Educational Thought.* Columbus, Ohio: Charles E. Merrill Books, 1960.

Mayhew, Lewis B. *Contemporary College Students and the Curriculum.* Southern Regional Education Board Research Monograph No. 14. Atlanta, Ga.: Southern Regional Education Board, 1969.

Morphett, Edgar L., and Jesser, David L., editors. *Preparing Educators To Meet Emerging Needs.* Reports prepared for the Governors' Conference on Education for the Future, Denver, Colorado, 1969.

National Association of Secondary-School Principals. *Looking Ahead.* Bulletin No. 332. Washington, D.C.: the Association, a department of the National Education Association, December 1968.

Obermann, C. Esco. *The History of Vocational Rehabilitation in America.* Minneapolis, Minn.: T. S. Denison and Co., 1965.

Okun, Arthur M., editor. *The Battle Against Unemployment, Problems of the Modern Economy.* (General Editor, Edmund S. Phelps.) New York: W. W. Norton and Co., 1965.

Report of the National Advisory Commission on Civil Disorders. New York: New York Times Co., 1968.

Sanford, Terry. *What About the People?* New York: Harper and Row, 1966.

Schaefer, Carl J., and Kaufman, Jacob J. *Occupational Education for Massachusetts.* A Report Prepared for the Massachusetts Advisory Council on Education. Springfield, June 1968.

Schreiber, Daniel, editor. *Profile of the School Dropout.* New York: Random House, 1967.

Sheppard, Harold L., and Belitsky, Harvey A. *The Job Hunt: Job Seeking Behavior of Unemployed Workers in a Local Economy.* Baltimore: Johns Hopkins Press, 1966.

Siegel, Irving H., editor. *Manpower Tomorrow: Prospects and Priorities.* New York: Augustus M. Kelley, Publishers, 1967.

Smith, Adam. *An Inquiry into the Nature and Causes of the Wealth of Nations.* (Edited by Cannan.) Book 2. New York: Random House, 1937. (Reissued by Modern Library.)

Theobald, Robert. *The Challenge of Abundance.* New York: Clarkson N. Potter, Publisher, 1961.

Transition from School to Work, The. A Report Based on the Princeton Manpower Symposium, May 9-10, 1968. Research Report Series No. III. Princeton, N.J.: Industrial Relations Section, Princeton University, 1968.

Venn, Grant. *Man, Education, and Work.* Washington, D.C.: American Council on Education, 1964.

Whitehead, Alfred North. *The Aims of Education.* New York: New American Library of World Literature, 1949.

Whittemore, Robert C. *Makers of the American Mind.* New York: William Morrow and Co., 1964.

Zytowski, Donald G. *Vocational Behavior: Readings in Theory and Research.* New York: Holt, Rinehart and Winston, 1968.